Living Proof
There's Another Way to Heal Your Body and Restore Your Life

By Mary Rust

Health, Healing and Life Transformation Specialist
www.MaryRust.com

Medical disclaimer

The author of this book does not distribute medical or other professional advice. The concepts and content of this book are not to be construed as medical advice, diagnosis, treatment or cure for any emotional, mental, physical or medical condition. The intent of the author is to share her personal experience and offer information that may be a part of your own healing and spiritual well-being process. In the event that you or others utilize the concepts or practices in this book, the author assumes no responsibility for the effectiveness or direct/indirect consequences. The reader should consult his or her medical, health or other professional advisors before applying the information and suggestions in this book. This book is not a substitute for medical advice.

Copyright © 2020 by Mary Rust

All right reserved

ISBN: 978-1-64184-270-9 (Paperback)

ISBN: 978-1-64184-271-6 (Ebook)

TABLE OF CONTENTS

My Love Letter to You.................. ix

Introduction xi

1 Getting Real with My Self and My Reality: Recognizing that My Life Wasn't Working....................... 1

    Falling from the Top of the World............... 1

    My Fairy-Tale Dream Did Not End "Happily Ever After"...................... 7

    Falling Deeper and Moving Further Away from Home.......................... 15

    Starting Over and Barely Surviving............. 18

2 When Crisis Calls. The Call That Killed Me to Save Me 21

    Answering the Call......................... 21

    Choosing to Accept or Reject the Gift of Cancer... 25

    My Human Mind Goes into Panic Mode 30

    Battle of the Minds........................ 33

3 Don't Know What to Do ... Mom Always Knows Best 35

Losing My Mother and My Unconditional Source
  of Love 35
Mom's Message for Me 38
Mom's Transition Home 41
Mom is Still with Me, Loving
  and Guiding Me Home 44
Should I Follow my Head or Heart? 47

4 Gathering More Information and Choosing My Healing Path 50

Finding My Practitioner and Opening Up to More... 50
Meeting My Other Medical Team ...
  Do Doctors Really Know Best? 54
Divine Inspiration over Dirty Dishes ...
  Surrendering to Life and Death 59
Round Two with My Medical Team ...
  The Boxing Match Continues 63
Choosing Peace and Love as My Treatment Plan ... 66
Connecting to "Another Way" to Heal 69

5 There is Another Way to Heal Your Body 71

Who Are You? 71
Perfect Source Energy and the Veil of Illusion 77
The Thinking-Feeling Circuit 82

Are You Creating from Your Human Mind
or Your Divine Mind?......................84
Connecting to the Stillness Within.............86

6 Creating an Energetic Expression and Healing with Inspired Action... 91

Divine as My Guide 91
Healing through Energetic Expression
and Inspired Action 96
Creating Your Own Energetic Expression.........99
My Personal "Why" with Cancer 107
Healing Through Inspired Action 110

7 Working with Your Mind to Heal... 117

Stages of the Mind Through Your Healing Process ..117
Meeting Your Mind Where It Is At 122
Resistance Will Happen ... Do Not Let Resistance
or Fear Sabotage Your Healing..............125
EFT - Moving Your Mind through Resistance
and Fear 129

8 Working with Your Body to Heal... 136

Love and Acceptance 136
Intimate Relationship with My Body 138
Trust Your Body........................141
Connecting and Integrating Your Inner Body
to Your Outer World 142

9 Working with Your Spirit and Soul to Heal 145

Perfect Health: The Way Life was Meant to Be ... 145
Living What You Are Not to Discover
   What You Are. 146
Loving and Accepting All of Life. All of Life Serves
   Your Soul. 148
Life with the Divine Mind 150
Life with the Human Mind. 152
Be-ing Who You Are. 154

10 Woo-Hoo! I'm Cancer Free ... Now What? My Healing Journey Continues 156

My Physical Healing. 156
Living Cancer-Free 159
The Power of Your Mind. 162
Redefining the Spiritual You 167
The World Begins to Communicate with Me. 173
When Life Repeats Itself ... Messages Through
   Patterns 180

11 Coming Home -- Deep Inner Healing of my Soul. 185

A Call to Come Home to the Land of Love ...
   Moving Back to Colorado. 185
Heart as Home and Soul. 191
Problems in My Own Home 193

Uncovering My Shadow, Meeting My Shadow,
   Healing My Inner Home 198
Heart-Center Meditation, Dreams that Heal,
   Life as Teacher and Healer 203
Make No Judgments, Make No Comparisons,
   and Eliminate the Need to Understand 208
Looking for Love in All the Wrong Places 211
Crisis Came to Heal ... Messages of the Body 218
Answering the Call to Come Home ...
   Fully Healing my Body and Restoring my Life ... 223

Final Reflections -- A Call to Come Home 227

My Final Reflection 228
Your Next Steps: A Call for Inspired Action 232

EFT Exercise: Using EFT for Your Own Personal Practice 235

Definitions 239

Afterword ... So What Happened to My Relationship with Ed? 241

About the Author 245

My love letter to you - Beautiful Brave Soul,

Sometimes life shows up in ways you least expect. Situations happen that you never see coming. As challenges surface, they stir up emotion, pain, fear and confusion. By meeting these challenges, you come face-to-face with the "uncomfortable unknown." The unknown is a portal to help you grow in ways you never expected. You are called to dig deeper than you have ever dug, surrender more than you thought possible, and tap into a strength that is far greater than you have ever known.

This book is dedicated to you, beautiful Soul. You are on an incredible journey of self-discovery and self-love which offers powerful healing potential. You are being christened by your Soul to become more than you ever believed you could be.

By choosing this healing path, your journey will uncover the truth of who you are and allow you to become a warrior of Love; a pillar of divine strength initiated from life's fires as you transform into the glorious Phoenix. You have the opportunity to rise in your innate power, strength, and wisdom as you tap into this unlimited potential.

I applaud, commend, and walk with you on your courageous journey. You are a warrior, my friend. You are a divine being with gifts and strengths beyond your human understanding. I am honored to walk with you. I am honored to explore with you. I am honored to uncover all that life has for you. Thank you for allowing me to be a part of your exquisite journey.

I love you more than you know ... until you Know,

Mary Rust

INTRODUCTION

On December 16, 2008, I received a call no one wants to hear. It was a call that changed my entire life and reason for being and living. It was a call that made me question everything I thought I knew about life and death as well as health and healing. It was a call that changed everything, both within me and outside of me.

I didn't want to answer the call that day, but life gave me no other choice or option. Life forced me to answer. Thank God I did. If I hadn't answered, I don't know if I would be here today.

Life calls when you least expect it, at least it did for me. I had no idea I needed a wake-up call, but someone, something, knew I did. The truth was, I was slowly dying from the inside out, and I didn't know it. Or maybe I did know it, but simply refused to face it.

Maybe I chose to ignore the signs and symptoms coming into my life as I turned a blind eye to my misery, pain, and path of destruction. I thought it was easier, safer, and much more comfortable, to avoid my pain rather than face it. I didn't want to face my pain and admit failure, especially when the source of failure was rooted within me.

I had become an expert of survival. I had mastered the tools to manage and deal with my pain rather than uproot and heal it. I dealt with my pain by ignoring it, stuffing it, and covering it up with an exterior mask of perfection. Every day, I skillfully put on my mask of illusion through a painted-on smile, a perfect body, and an outer persona that exclaimed "I'm the master of my world," but on the inside, I felt like a liar, a fake, and a fraud. On the inside, I felt empty and broken. I knew something was missing. I knew something was wrong. I was slowly dying and decaying on the inside, but didn't know how to escape the prison of my own making. My prison was the only way I knew how to survive this world, my life, and my feelings. I didn't know how to escape. My Soul needed and wanted me to escape. My Soul tried multiple times to get my attention, but I was not able to hear my Soul's pleading messages. I was too busy trying to survive.

In brief moments, however, I heard and acknowledged the quiet pleadings of my Soul, by questioning how I could feel so incomplete inside when I had mastered everything on the outside. It didn't make sense, I had everything I had ever wanted, but I still felt empty, broken, and lost. Every time I began to get in touch with these feelings, I felt uncomfortable and scared. I didn't like these feelings, so I ignored them and continued to play the survival game.

How long was I going to play this game of self-denial and delusion? How long could I tolerate my own misery? The answer was … as long as it took to break me … all of me, so I could finally find and connect to the real me … the complete me.

As a young child, I had been taught to fight for what you want. Be strong, be tough, and you can get through anything in this world. When the going gets tough, I needed to get tougher. Life is hard, and the only way to survive is through hard work, struggle, and pushing through the pain. My rewards will come when accomplishments are achieved. Until then, pain, suffering, and misery are an essential means to an end. I lived by the notion that once I reached my goal, all my pain and suffering would end and it would all be worth it. But with each goal I accomplished, I still felt empty and my pain stayed with me. Instead of attending to my emptiness, I quickly retreated and created another goal. This kept me stuck in a pattern of fight and struggle, thinking the next goal would solve my problems with pain. But it never did.

This fight and struggle became my life. This is how I thought life worked. This was my truth, and my truth became my reality. Pain, misery, and suffering became my reality. When my life got tough, I got tougher. I kept telling myself to be strong. I can get through this. I can get through anything. I've been through hard things before, I can and will do it again. The only way to get through the hard knocks of life is to push through, press through, stay positive ... go, fight, win!

So, my entire life became a fight. The more I fought with life, the more life fought with me. Life was a battlefield and I was in the middle of it. I chose to fight the battle, the war of life. Fighting, struggling, and surviving. The fight was all I knew. I had grown comfortable with the fight. In fact, I was not only comfortable with the fight, I owned it, I relished it, and needed it like an addict needs his addiction. The fight consumed me and became me. The fight was me and my life depended on the fight.

I had trained myself to survive in my self-created misery, just as a soldier trains and prepares himself for the battlefield. I was that soldier; highly trained, skillfully attuned, and fully prepared to fight my own life. I had been fighting this battle for years, collecting battle scars and deep wounds along the way. I fought with ease and grace, putting on an armor of fake happiness, joy, strength, and courage each morning to offset the raging anger, resentment, torment, and blistering wounds festering within me. I didn't want to face or acknowledge my pain, suffering, and weakness. As any great soldier knows, there is no time on the battlefield to be weak, wounded, or distracted from the fight. So I kept living my lie and battling my life, telling myself I was fine, that life was good. But life wasn't good.

I did everything I could, including creating a life and a body that looked perfect and amazing from the outside, as a way to avoid addressing how empty and broken I was on the inside. I tried to fill my interior self-worth, self-love bucket through outside accomplishments, achievements, and praise. I thought outside things could heal my inside wounds and make me feel better. Reaching and achieving my goals was supposed to make everything better, right? But the more I tried, the less it worked. Why wasn't it working anymore?

This strategy seemed to work when I was a little girl. I loved the praise I received from my parents when I got an "A" on a paper, or finished first in a race. I felt good when my teachers, coaches, or classmates cheered me on and said, "Great job, Mary. Well done. You're amazing. I'm so proud of you." While the praise I received felt uplifting at the time, it also taught me that in order to be great, to feel great, I must do great things. If I accomplish great things, I am great. On the other hand, if I'm not the best, if I'm not perfect in every way, if I don't win, I am nothing. I am empty and I am worthless. I spent a lifetime trying to fill my self-worth bucket by striving and struggling to be the best.

I knew no other way to live. I desperately wanted to be loved and acknowledged, so I continued to live my life within my own illusion. I fought and struggled with my life in an effort to prove my worth through outside sources, all while denying the inside truth that I was already perfect, whole, and complete. I thought it was easier and safer to live in denial, but nothing was further from the truth. The truth was, my life sucked, and I needed help, but I wasn't able to admit it, see it or know how to get out of it.

It wasn't until life forced me to look within myself that I was finally able to heal, transform, and fully live again. I was forced to face my pain, meet my fears, honor my feelings, heal my internal wounds and question everything I thought I knew about life, so that I could rediscover the real truth buried deep inside.

I began to ask soul-searching questions. Why is my life not working? What is the *real* problem with my life? *Who* is the real problem? OMG … What if the real problem is *me*? I don't know if I can handle that. It's much easier to blame outside people and situations for my pain. I don't want to admit that *I* am the cause of my pain. Pain and suffering comes from the outside world, right? How can *I* be the source of my own pain and suffering? I began to second-guess myself.

What if I am the source of my pain? What if the world is not my problem? What if *I* am the problem? What if the only thing and person I'm fighting is ME? What if the war, pain, and suffering I'm fighting and experiencing is actually a war within myself? What if I chose to stop fighting? What if the pain and suffering in my life was not something I was supposed to fight, but something I was supposed to embrace and love instead?

Facing and asking these questions was the beginning and an end of a deep healing cycle that radically transformed my health and my life. I wouldn't have believed it myself had I not fully lived and embraced this experience.

Life is constantly calling and urging us to move forward to the truth of who we really are and the unlimited power, potential, and wisdom we carry, but few are able to connect to it. Continuing to fight with our outside world distracts us from connecting with the beauty, peace, and Divine Wisdom our inner world offers us.

I was one of those people. I lived my life struggling each day to survive. I told myself my life was fine. I thought I was alright, but I really wasn't. I was living a lie. For years, I pretended my life was great, and I got really good at playing the part. I lived my life as a lead actress, scripting and acting out my perfect lie. By playing the part, I didn't have to look at my internal truth. I lived in struggle and denial each day, telling myself that life would get better. I just needed to get through this rough stage, then things would surely turn around. But they never did.

I continued to play the victim to life by telling myself I wasn't a victim. I told myself that I just needed to suck up and deal with it. I needed to put on my big-girl panties and push through. Life would eventually get better, right? Wrong!

Life did not get better, it got worse. As one stage passed it led to another more difficult stage; and the cycle of stages continued until I finally woke up and began to see what life was trying to tell me. Life did not get better until I chose to get better myself. I wasn't able to make this choice until life brought me to my knees and stripped me of everything I thought I needed. Life sent me small whispers, louder calls, then multiple full-blown crises to finally break my addiction to my suffering so that I could finally see what I was doing to myself.

Life had to break me in order to save me. It stripped everything away so that I could find my foundation of truth to rebuild all the broken pieces within me. Life called me to heal and I had to answer the call, or I was slowly going to die. I needed to find a way to heal and restore my life because I was a sick and broken woman on the inside and didn't know it. I needed a wake-up call.

That's what life does. Life sends pain, suffering, and crisis to your life as a wake-up call. Life loves you enough to break you in order to save you, but only if you stop long enough to hear and answer the call. The question is, "Is life calling you?" Are you ready and willing to answer the call? Do you even know that you need a call? I had no idea I needed a wake-up call, but there was someone, something that did. Thank God, my Soul knew exactly what I needed, because I didn't have a clue.

The truth is, most of us are suffering and operating in some form of crisis, but we are too busy surviving and controlling the situation to fully recognize it. We have become a society of habitual survivors and don't even know it. Not only do we not know it, we have no idea how to get out of it. Most of us will never break this self-induced survival pattern.

We continue to push through our personal suffering because that is what we think we should do, that is what we need to do, that is the only way to do it, right? Really? Come on, seriously? Does that really sound right to you? Do you really think life was created because you needed to learn how to suffer through it? Is that all life is for? Is life really designed to help you master pain and suffering by fighting for your life? No, of course not.

While you may choose to continue to live your life in pain and suffering, I can tell you from personal experience that life is so much more than pain, suffering and survival. That is not your *true* purpose in life. Life was not designed for you to stay stuck in pain and suffering, or simply "deal with it." Life is designed to help you move through pain and suffering and live in freedom, vibrant health, love, peace, and abundance, but the only way to transcend your suffering is to choose to heal yourself from the inside out. You hold the key to healing and you are the only one who can save yourself.

Most people never truly heal, so they end up staying stuck in their survival patterns. They look to their outside world to save them and try to fix their inner pain with Band-Aid solutions that cover up symptoms. By trying to fix problems through outside solutions, they never see or get to the root of the problem, the real cause of the inner pain. They don't know how to truly heal and they consciously or unconsciously stay stuck in pain and suffering. They stay stuck far too long and they don't even realize it. Pain and suffering becomes their life, it IS their life, like a sick addiction. And as with all addictions, people eventually become numb to their reality and continue to survive rather than thrive. Take a close look at the world around you and within you. How many people do you know that are stuck in pain and suffering? Are you one of them?

The good news is, pain and suffering does not need to become your reality. There is a way out. There is a way to move through pain and suffering by healing and restoring your life to its original fullness and glory, but you must wake up and choose to thrive, rather than just survive. Luckily, you don't need to experience a full-blown crisis to begin this deep healing process. You can begin right here and right now by taking an honest internal inventory of yourself. Here are some questions designed to open you heart and mind to a new level of healing.

Where are you in your own life? Are you fully living or are you slowly dying? Love and honor yourself by going deeper and taking an objective look at your inner world. Are you truly happy, healthy, and living your purpose? Is life fulfilling? Do you wake up each morning excited to be alive and move through your day with passion and purpose, knowing that each moment is precious and perfect, or do you move through your life knowing something is missing? Are there parts of your life that seem empty or unfulfilled? Has your life lost its meaning and worth? While you may get through every day, have you come to realize that each moment is no different or special from the last? Has your life become methodical? Is your life dull, dry, and lifeless? Have you settled for a life that does not inspire or serve you? Do you live your life through other people's expectations, rather than what you truly want? Do you even know what you want? Does society make your rules by surrounding you with the *have-to's, need-to's, should-do's* and *must-do's*? Who's making the rules? Are you completely free to design your own rules and boundaries, or have you been sacrificing your Soul to follow someone else's rules, needs and/or expectations? Are you truly aware of what's going on in your inner world, or are there areas of your life you are neglecting or refusing to see?

Now let's look at your outer or physical world. Do you experience physical, emotional, or mental pain on a regular basis? Are you stressed out and overworked? Are your relationships totally fulfilling or are your relationships depleting you? Are you in toxic relationships? Do you feel lonely, depressed, or isolated? Have you become numb to your feelings and have withdrawn in an effort to survive your outer world? Have you done the opposite of withdrawing and have become a master of the fight, seeking and maintaining control over every aspect of your life? Do you live with physical aches, pains, and frequent illness? Have you sunk even further down the rabbit hole and your life is in a full-blown crisis or multiple crises? Do you suffer with chronic disease or depression and have a struggle simply getting out of bed each morning? Your answers to these questions will reveal much to you and are opportunities to open new doors to deep healing. Is life calling you to open the door to healing?

I wrote this book as an act of love for anyone called on his or her own healing journey. My hope is that you will be able to connect to the raw and intimate details from my life and be able to weave them into your own life circumstances. Use this book as a tool to connect to your own thoughts, feelings, emotions, and life experiences. While the specific details of our journeys and experiences differ, the lessons, pain, trials, and errors are much the same. Use my pain for your own healing purpose. Connect to me and be with me as I share the pitfalls, failures, and self-sabotage that led to the final crisis that broke me and saved me at the same time. Hold my hand and I'll hold yours as we walk together through the pain that holds the power to transform into miracles, messages, revelations, redemption, restoration, and healing. Let's get raw and vulnerable with each other, leaving no stone unturned.

Open your heart and mind to experience this journey for yourself. Open yourself to share my pain as your pain, my struggle in your struggle, my loss with your loss, my defeat and your defeat, my fall with your fall, my misery as a reflection of your misery, my confusion with your confusion -- and my total recovery as your total recovery to full and complete redemption and restoration. It is only by acknowledging, loving, and accepting all of life's experiences that we can finally heal and live life in its fullest expression.

As you read this book, you may find aspects, concepts, and ideas that are new to you and that you may not fully understand. Do not dismiss them right away. Instead, take them in, process them, feel them, and allow them to be with you. There is a Divine intelligence, a source within you, which has the ability to completely and fully integrate these aspects, concepts, and ideas. Your inner source will be able to translate the truth to you in a way that will help you understand, learn and grow.

Be open to new possibilities and new understandings of the healing potential within you. Unless you are willing to open yourself to new possibilities, you will never be able to access them. As you read the intimate details and connect to the emotions in my healing journey and life story, take time to connect to the details and emotions of your own healing journey and life story. The details in your life -- and how you perceive them -- have important messages to share with you. Open your heart and mind to them. Let them speak to you. Let them heal you. Allow yourself to feel and experience them with new eyes, new ears, new thoughts, new feelings, and new perspectives. Opening and experiencing your life through new perspectives has the power to heal and restore your life in ways you don't even know yet. There is another way to heal and restore your life in new and miraculous ways, if you open and allow them to work within you.

So, let's begin. Grab a beverage and nuzzle down into a comfy chair. If there is a chill in the air, wrap and nourish your body with a snuggly blanket or sit by a warm fire. Have a tissue box on hand (spoiler alert: you may need them) and open your heart and mind to an intimate journey of life and healing.

Read and feel these words as if I am sitting with you, sharing and bearing my heart and soul to you. Allow my pain, fear, trials, and experience to touch in ways you never saw coming … for that's what life does. It hits you when you least expect, when you never see it coming, and then it gives you your most important lessons for life transformation.

Be open to the lessons and messages that surface for you in this book. Allow the words to transform and transcend you to new levels of awareness and inspire you to new heights of love, compassion, purpose, healing, and growth. It is no coincidence that this book is resting in your hands at this very moment. Be with me and be with this book. We have much to share and communicate with you.

1
GETTING REAL WITH MY SELF AND MY REALITY: RECOGNIZING THAT MY LIFE WASN'T WORKING

Falling from the Top of the World

It was a calm, cool evening on the 22nd Day of October, 1999. The vast Las Vegas desert was radiating with energy as 18 of the world's greatest fitness competitors lined the stage of the Mandalay Bay Resort awaiting their fate. It all boiled down to this moment. I stood tense and tight under the brilliant lights of the Mandalay stage. My heart was pounding out of my chest like a revved-up engine with nowhere to go.

Every muscle and fiber of my being had been meticulously carved and created. I stood perfectly poised, statuesque, and eloquent like Michelangelo's *David* magnificently displayed in the Galleria dell'Accademia. I felt a bead of sweat roll down my brow and was reminded of all the hours, months, and years of intense training and dieting. I gazed out to the crowd in gratitude and then looked at the judges with pleading eyes as if to say, "Do you see me? Will you choose me? Did I do enough, train hard enough, diet down enough, to win the title ... Am I enough this time?"

I stood motionless, still and composed, awaiting my fate. The time had come to announce the winner. The final countdown began: in 10th place, in ninth place ... *My heart began to beat faster and stronger as the placement numbers got smaller ...* in fifth place, in fourth place. *OMG, I feel as if I'm going to pass out ...* in third place ... *my heart began skipping beats, I can't breathe, this is getting real ... I knew this was it ... I knew my fate was going to be determined in one moment, one instant, one second ...* in second place ... *a numbing silence came over me, everything went blank and the next thing I heard was ...* Mary Yockey!

What?! What just happened? I was dazed and confused. I started to look around me as the girls next to me hugged and congratulated me, urging me to step forward. I was in disbelief. I was just crowned the new Ms. Fitness Olympia and all I could do was stand there dazed and confused. I methodically stepped forward to claim my title. I had finally made it. I was "enough" this time. The new 1999 Fitness Olympia Champion is Mary Yockey!

October 22, 1999, was my night, my moment. I was finally enough. I had finally reached my goal, my top prize. The war and battle was finally over. I did it and I was on top of the world. This is my moment ... or so I thought. As I was standing on that stage, being crowned as the *fittest women in the world* in front of an auditorium of raving fans, clapping and cheering in recognition and support, something inside still didn't feel right. Something within me felt off. Something inside me still said, "You are not enough. You will never be enough."

Suddenly I heard the roar of the crowd and I snapped back to the venue. People were still on their feet, clapping and applauding in recognition. I smiled and waved back in appreciation. I stood tall, forced a pretty perfect smile, and showed my pretty perfect body in an attempt to fill the role that everyone came to see, a newly crowned Fitness Olympia Champion!

A gruff voice inside me said, "Good luck filling those shoes, you're going to need it!"

"What?" I thought. "I just got crowned Fitness Olympia. I have the medal around my neck to prove it. I did it. I'm the new Fitness Olympia Champion. What are you talking about?"

"You know exactly what I am talking about. A metal means nothing, when you are nothing," said the voice.

"Well," I responded internally, "Obviously, you don't know what you are talking about. I refuse to listen to your nonsense. Don't bother me. I am enough this time!"

"Yeah, we'll see," said the voice.

I woke up the next morning in pure exhaustion and jubilation, wrapping my mind around the fact that I had won the Fitness Olympia. I had achieved the title of the "Fittest Women in the World." It was a dream come true. All the blood, sweat, and tears I had poured into my training had finally paid off and I was going to be the best Fitness Olympia Champion ever. I wasn't going to allow that conceited, condescending voice in my head win. I would prove it wrong with my new mission. My next goal was to become the most inspirational role model for women to accomplish their dreams, improve their lives, and become their own superstars. I was going to become the best living inspiration of health and fitness, and nothing was going to stop me.

With the Fitness Olympia title in hand, I felt as if my entire life purpose was finally unfolding. I thought nothing could go wrong. Everything would work simply for me. I didn't need to struggle with life and life didn't need to struggle with me. Things will manifest easily. Everything I focused my attention on will seamlessly come to fruition. I will accomplish everything I set my mind to accomplish. The world will be a magical place just for me, and I will be the magician. Now that I have the title, everything will be different.

I loved being a role model for women in the health-and-fitness industry. I felt like I had connected to my passion and purpose. I longed to inspire people. It made me feel alive and empowered. I wanted to make a big impact and inspire as many people as possible to live their life to the fullest. I genuinely thought winning the Fitness Olympia was my next big break and I was looking forward to opening new doors of opportunity.

Within weeks of winning the Fitness Olympia, I signed a large endorsement contract with one of the world's top nutritional companies. I was the first female fitness competitor to represent this company and I was honored to hold this position. I was thrilled to have the chance to work with them and expand my impact. My life, my dreams, and my goals were all coming true.

Not only were my career dreams coming true, I also had an exciting romantic relationship unfolding. My romantic life was blossoming, too! I had met Ed four years earlier, working as a real estate agent. Ed was a general contractor and built homes for a living. He built them, I sold them. We were a perfect match. Not only was Ed a successful business partner, he was also a spontaneous, vibrant, charming man who balanced out the conservative, safe side of me. Our life together was fun and spontaneous. He brought out the child in me and we laughed and played like two kids in an amusement park, eating cotton candy and running on an all-the-time sugar high. I loved my life with him. Ed had proposed to me over the summer, and we were planning on getting married and starting a family in the near future. I was actually living my fairy-tale life like a fairy-tale dream. Life was finally working for me. Or so I thought.

Within two months, my fairy-tale dream took an unexpected turn. My extended family arrived sooner than I expected or anticipated. Within a few weeks after signing my dream endorsement contract, I found out that I was pregnant. I was over-the-top excited about the news of my pregnancy. I always wanted to be a mother. It was a childhood dream to have a family. Becoming a mother was now a clear reality and it was going to happen!

With the recent news of my pregnancy, my career mind was brewing with creativity. My mind exploded with ideas on how to integrate fitness and pregnancy together in inventive ways. I immediately visualized a "fit pregnancy" feature with my nutritional company and Weider (one of the top muscle-magazine distributors at the time). What a perfect opportunity to combine pregnancy and fitness. Women would love it! I imagined how cool it would be to follow my entire pregnancy and feature how to stay fit and healthy through pregnancy in real time. I was also dreaming about doing an after-pregnancy feature to help women get back in shape after the baby. Then I imagined multiple fit-with-baby classes. The possibilities were endless, and I was so excited to move forward with these new ideas.

Unfortunately, my nutritional-endorsement company had a substantially different opinion regarding my pregnancy. They didn't share my thoughts or excitement. My pregnancy was not received with open arms. When they heard the news, I was immediately fired. My new endorsement contract was considered void and it was shredded right before my eyes. I was stunned, shocked, and heart-broken. My dreams of becoming the most inspirational fitness celebrity was instantly ripped out of my hands and literally shredded into a thousand pieces. My heart ached, withered, and died. It too, bled and broke into a thousand pieces along with my endorsement contract, my life and my dreams. All of the hard work, sweat, pain, diet, tears, and glory were all for naught, swept away in one mighty blow from the top-level nutrition executives. I was useless to them. They wanted nothing to do with me or my pregnancy and sent me packing like a dog thrown out on the streets having to fend for himself.

My pregnancy was the end of my health-and-fitness career and the end of my dreams of becoming a fitness role-model. I was left on the street with a bitter resentment, feeling like an orphan girl nobody wanted or appreciated. What did I do to deserve this? Did I really have no value? Am I that detestable? Do my dreams and desires count for nothing?!!! Apparently none of that mattered … I simply just didn't matter.

"See, I told you so," said the gruff voice within me (this was the same voice I heard after winning the Fitness Olympia). "You were never able to fill those shoes. You just weren't good enough."

The defeated part within me began to agree, "Maybe you're right, maybe I'm not good enough."

The end of my fitness career was the beginning of a dark, lonely, and painful fall. It marked the beginning of the end of life working easily for me and the beginning of everything dismantling and crumbling apart. It was the first event in a series of events that changed everything. I did not choose this fall and heartbreak. It chose me, and it was the first of many crushing events to come.

While I never saw this fall coming, nor would I ever have chosen it, it was exactly what I needed to move forward with my real life and real dreams. Life doesn't always give you what you want, but it always gives you what you need. I certainly didn't know I needed to crash and burn, fall and crumble, but my Soul knew. My Soul knew that if I really wanted to be a role model and become "living proof" that there is another way to heal and restore your life, there was something more I needed to learn and discover. My current dreams needed to be broken and dismantled in order for my authentic self to be discovered and revealed.

This was the first of many life lessons and circumstances that needed to happen so I could learn, grow, and evolve into the person I wanted to be. All of my falls, crises, and hardships played an important role in healing and transforming myself and my life forever. It's amazing how blind and disconnected I was to myself and my Soul until situations and circumstances came into my life and forced me to see.

My Fairy-Tale Dream Did Not End "Happily Ever After"

After losing my endorsement contract and being shunned by the fitness industry, I was left with bitter resentment and sorrow. The resentment was so strong, so painful, I simply could not bear to face it. So, the strategical soldier in me thought it was best to stuff and suppress my feelings and boldly move on. I told myself, "To hell with the fitness industry. I don't need them!" But secretly, a part of me did need them. By rejecting them, I chose to close the door on one of my heart's desires, which was to become a living, breathing inspiration of health and wellness. By rejecting them, I was rejecting a precious part of me.

In an effort to survive my internal pain, I quickly shifted gears and focused on my new family and new life. Surely this new life will save me from the pain I had just experienced. After all, having a family was another dream of mine. If I can't be a superstar in the fitness industry, I will be a superstar mom! So I switched gears and focused all of my thoughts and energy on becoming the best mother in the world.

I thought that becoming a mother would make me happy, fill my love bucket, and deliver the *happily ever after* dream I so desperately wanted. Underneath it all, I was hoping that it could also heal the pain and resentment that I stuffed from losing my fitness contract and career. Boy, was I wrong! I soon found out that trying to fill my inner love bucket and heal my inner pain by having a child is a recipe for disaster. It just doesn't work that way. I learned that you can never replace inner pain by trying to fill it through outer resources. Children need love and nourishment toward their own purpose; they are not designed to be an antidote to heal our inner pain and disconnection from our own purpose.

As most mothers find out, there is nothing in your past life experience that can prepare you for becoming a mom. I was heading into motherhood dumb, naïve, and blind. I thought becoming a mother would restore my life and heal my pain.

I thought a child would bring me the love I always wanted and craved but my vision of motherhood was quite different from the raw reality of motherhood.

I thought that becoming a mother would provide me the perfect-picture fantasy with a house full of love, smiles, and happy blissful times. That's what magazines, marketing ads, TV shows, and movies portray it to be. Why would my experience be any different? Why couldn't I experience the *happily ever after* like I saw in the media? That's what motherhood should be, right? Unfortunately, that was not my experience. Motherhood did not deliver my perfect-picture fantasy. Motherhood was not what I expected. If I really knew what motherhood was going to be like, I never would have gotten pregnant!

Needless to say, whether I was ready or not, motherhood was coming. I gave birth to my first child, Logan, on September 17, 2000, less than one year following the Fitness Olympia. Logan was an active and busy boy which kept me on my toes. (OMG, I never knew how much work a baby would be!)

I was left exhausted and depleted each day. I was up all hours of the night, nursing, rocking, and caring for this new life. I was completely and utterly sleep deprived, not knowing if it was day or night or which day of the week it was. I went from signing autographs, photoshoots on the beach, and a life of freedom and luxury to sleepless nights, unending diaper patrol and a living, breathing, 24/7 milk factory. I missed my old life! I am not designed to be a mother. I didn't want to do this anymore, but I knew I had to. I was at the point of no return. I had to figure out a way to get through this, not only for me, but for this precious life I was holding in my arms. Would I ever be happy being a mother? Would I ever become the mother this child deserves? I had no idea.

Unfortunately, I had little to no help from Ed, my husband. He was too busy and engrained in his work to have time to take care of a baby. I felt like my son's care was all up to me. No one was going to step in to relieve me from this responsibility. I thought I had to do this on my own. That's what a "good" mother does and I was determined to be a "good" mother. My son deserves a "good" mother. There was no Fairy Godmother who was going to swoop down and rescue me (though I secretly wished and prayed that there was). Motherhood was my choice and my job. I was bound and determined to make my family just like the ones in the magazines and on TV. There was still a part of me struggling for the title of "good enough" by being a good mother.

Once again, when I make a commitment to something, the soldier in me steps in. I lock my personal needs in a closet and dive in head-first. I put all of my energy, time, and life into my new baby. I felt it was my sole duty to love and care for him. His needs became my needs, his wants became my wants. I sacrificed all of me for him. I thought that was what I had to do to become the perfect mother. And once again, I found out I was wrong.

Have you ever sacrificed yourself and or given yourself away for the needs of another at the expense of your own Soul? While giving of yourself to another can be a beautiful gift, continually giving yourself away at the expense of your Soul in not in anyone's best interest. There is a huge difference between giving yourself as a gift and sacrificing your Soul.

I did not understand the difference between the two. I gave too much of me as a mother and continually sacrificed my Soul. While I thought my sacrifice was in Logan's best interest, it ultimately wasn't. I didn't know this at the time, but I would soon find out that giving all of myself away doesn't work.

Giving all of yourself away is like being in a life-threatening auto accident where everyone is injured and you try to help everyone else despite the fact that you are internally bleeding from your own wounds. Eventually you end up dying trying to take care of others instead of taking care of yourself first. When you die from your own wounds, you are no help to yourself or others. Instead, it is better to tend and mend your own wounds first, then you will be able to help others.

Instead of taking care of my internal needs, I gave away all of my energy, love, and support to others without taking care of myself first. Eventually my love and energy bucket ran dry and I had nothing left to give. I had no idea what I was doing to myself. I was draining my life force and I didn't know it. I would discover this later, but for now, I just kept on giving and sacrificing myself, trying to find and create my *happily ever after* perfect family.

Even though motherhood was hard, I did find a way to manage and survive. Through trial-and-error, I figured it out and discovered new life systems that seemed to work. These new systems got me through and I learned how to survive motherhood. Just as life was settling in, I considered having another baby. That would make life twice as fun, right? Wrong. Life got twice as hard.

I thought it would be best to have another baby soon because I wanted my children to be close in age with each other. I wanted my kids close in age, not because I was ready for another child, but because I wanted them to have a close relationship with each other, which is something I longed for with my own siblings.

I did not feel close to my own brothers because they were six and seven years older than I was. Because of our age difference, I felt separate from them, like they lived and grew up in an entirely different generation than I did. They were big boys doing big-boy things and I was the annoying little sister no one wanted to play with. I felt like a burden when my mom asked my brothers to take care of me. I felt lonely, insignificant, and unwanted, just like I felt when the nutritional company fired me.

I didn't want my children to experience the isolation I felt as a child, so I opted to have another child right away to potentially avoid that situation. I also (unconsciously) made that choice in an effort to heal my own pain. Again, trying to heal my pain through others does not and did not work.

Despite my brilliant thinking that having kids close in age would solve the problem of sibling separation and isolation, it really didn't work. My kids are entirely different personalities and despite being close in age, they are not close in their relationship. Their personalities are very different and often conflict with each other. As I look back, a greater age gap might have eased their relationship conflicts. Go figure. That plan totally backfired!

Have you ever made a decision for someone else that is connected to your own past hurts and life circumstances? Many times, we unconsciously make decisions and decide what is best for another person based on *our* personal hurts and wounds. I made the decision to have another baby in an effort to outsource my own healing process. I wanted to heal a past wound in myself by having another baby. I was trying to heal my own wounds by creating a different situation for my kids. Not only did it not work to heal my pain, these decisions had no influence on my children's relationship either. What I really needed to do was recognize my old wounds and heal them, but I wasn't able to connect the dots to my internal pain at the time. So they continued to stay buried within me.

I also wasn't connecting to my personal needs as a mother. I needed help raising my kids, but I refused to ask for help. I was slowly losing myself by trying to do and be everything for them. I was not well mentally, emotionally, or physically raising one child; now I was bringing another child into this mix. I thought this was the right choice, but in reality, it sent me deeper into the rabbit hole of my unconscious suffering.

Despite my own pain, I chose to have another baby -- and she was on her way. Two and a half years after Logan was born, I delivered my baby girl, Hannah. While having two children (one boy and one girl) did fulfill my image of the perfect family, having two kids didn't make my life any easier or happier. My life just got twice as demanding and exhausting. I was desperately wanting and trying to be "good enough" by being a good mother, but in reality, I was denying my internal needs and slowing killing myself.

Ultimately, I needed help, but I was too proud to ask for it. I wanted someone to save me and I wanted that someone to be Ed. Ed was my husband, he should save me. Why didn't Ed jump in and rescue me? Couldn't he see I was tired, exhausted, worn out, and needed his support with his kids? Couldn't he see I was drowning trying to do everything and be everything? Of course not. How could he see it when I couldn't see it myself? How could he see it when I did such a good job hiding it behind the mask of perfection and the illusion that everything was under control? There was a part of me that desperately wanted him to see me dying and save me, and another part of me that never wanted him to see me struggle because that would mean I was a failure and a bad mother.

Therefore, I never asked for help. I couldn't ask for help because that would mean I was a failure. I couldn't face being a failure so I stayed strong because that's who I am. That's what being a good mother all is about. Come hell or high water, I was going to be a good mother. I thought I could do everything on my own ... and I was wrong. What I really needed to do was be my own savior and ask for help, but I was too proud and afraid of failure to ask for help. I continued to battle my own war, within myself, by myself.

Meanwhile, Ed was in his own battle, striving, climbing, and clawing to make it to the top of his profession. Ed had his own love bucket to fill and he was attempting to fill it through his business. Ed dedicated his life to his career. The strong work ethic I had once admired in him now became a crutch and curse in our relationship. Ed's work consumed him and he became a "work-o-holic." His work became his life and his identity. If he wasn't successful in his job, he wasn't successful in life. He worked long and late hours which left very little if any time for his family.

Our lives became separate and we became separate from each other. Long gone were the days of spontaneity and fun. Life was all business now. He was consumed by his job and I was consumed with household chores and kids. Work, kids, repeat. That was our life, there was nothing left for us. There was no time for ourselves or each other. I was married, but felt utterly and totally alone. I was living the life of a married, single mother on the inside and projecting a happily married woman on the outside. The days were long and hard, and the nights were even lonelier.

After giving all of myself away during the day, I would crawl into bed by myself at night. Ed was missing. He was nowhere to be found. He was missing because he was either so focused on his work or he was out drinking and socializing in the bar with friends. I felt abandoned and alone. Where was my partner, my friend, my companion? He was nowhere to be found. I had lost him in work and alcohol and we had lost each other.

As I sat alone in my empty bed, I often thought, "Is this what I signed up for? Is this what a happy marriage and family looks like and feels like? Does everyone feel so abandoned and alone or is it just me? What's wrong with me? Why am I so unhappy? Why do I feel so alone? From the outside we look like the perfect family, with the perfect house, the perfect kids, the perfect relationship, but on the inside I feel broken, empty, and alone. What happened to my *happily ever after*? Does *happily ever after* even exist, or does it just not exist for me?"

Life was not the happily-ever-after I had expected. I was lonely and isolated. I was tired and depleted. There was no love or support coming back to me, only sleepless nights, dirty diapers, nursing, feedings, messes, and chores. I had no idea what I signed up for when I agreed to motherhood, but I pressed on, putting a smile on my face every morning and crashing on my bed every evening, exhausted and alone.

I lived a double life. I tried to present the world with a picture-perfect family and life, but inside deeply resented

-- even hated -- my life. My inner world was consumed with loneliness and broken dreams. I hated and resented my life; I hated and resented motherhood. I then hated myself for hating my life. How could I hate being a mom? What kind of person could feel this way? I couldn't understand how I could love my kids so much but hate being a mom. Why did my dreams of motherhood fail so miserably? Why am I failing so miserably? I couldn't face myself or my pain. I didn't want anyone to know how unhappy and miserable I had become. I wanted people to know how perfect my life was, so I stuffed the pain and I pressed on.

To avoid my pain and convince myself that my life was still perfect, I would tell myself, "At least I live in a nice home and don't have to struggle for money. At least I didn't have to work and take care of the kids, too. Being a stay-at-home mom was something I always wanted, right? Buck up and deal with it, Mary. Stop your pity party and look at all the blessings you have."

The reality was, I probably would have been better off working, even part time, to give myself a break and get some adult interaction during the day. My Soul was trying to tell me that I craved and needed a break from being a full-time mom, but I didn't listen. I couldn't hear my Soul because I was so wrapped up in avoiding my pain and trying to be a "good" mother. I thought being a stay-at-home mom was the best thing for my kids and family. My Soul was trying to get my attention, but I was so consumed in my thought of what a perfect mother should be that I couldn't hear the whispers of my Soul.

This was just one of many Soul whispers and signs that I didn't pay attention to that led to my own misery, unhappiness, and further fall. As life has it, when you don't pay attention to the "whispers" in your life, the whispers turn into a call, then a shout, then a scream. If you don't stop and start paying attention, life gives you full-blown, multiple crises that force you to listen, as I was soon to discover.

Falling Deeper and Moving Further Away from Home

My cushy financial situation and security was about to crumble and fall. The storm was building and brewing, yet I didn't have a clue. Five years after my son was born, the real estate market crashed, and my husband's business crashed with it. Ed and I had put everything on the line by investing in a large housing development and building several spec homes. This investment seemed logical at the time because the market was strong. Ed's company was thriving and future growth and expansion was inevitable. Everything was selling … until it wasn't.

The real estate crash of 2006 happened fast and furious. All of our money, savings, and investments were tied into the tumbling real estate market and we came down with it. It was the perfect storm no one saw coming and it was the beginning of the end for us and many others. There was nothing we could do but sit and watch our livelihood diminish into a stockpile of debt. It was a living nightmare.

We tried to salvage as much as we could through fire sales and consolidation, but selling homes, furniture, and tools 20 cents on the dollar doesn't come close to salvaging much at all. We lost our investments, our home, our friends, and our family. We also lost our dignity, our sense of identity, and our pride. It became very clear that many of the people who called us friends were only friends because we provided a source of income for them. Those people had nothing to do with us when we ran out of money. I was devastated. I was broke, alone, and left with nothing. Again … I was nothing. When was this cycle ever going to end?

Ed and I knew we had to leave our home because there was nothing left for us. There was no way we could make a living in these conditions. Due to the nation-wide crash, there were very few options to relocate as a builder. We did, however, find a small corner in Wyoming that had a decent real estate market and economy due to coal and natural gas.

MARY RUST

    I never thought I would leave my home town of Loveland, Colorado, but now being out of luck, out of money and out of any other option, Gillette, Wyoming, looked like a promising possibility to recover. Gillette was a little town in the northeast corner of Wyoming that was still booming despite the market crash. We knew we had to move if we were going to feed our family and make ends meet. We packed what little we had and headed to Wyoming for a chance to start again and recover.

    Both of us were beaten and broken. We left Loveland with a U-Haul and a caravan of trailers. We headed north to start our lives over. Ed led the way and I followed. I had no idea how we would make things work, but I knew we had to try. I packed the final box in the back of my car, closed the door and rolled out of my driveway saying good-bye to everything I had ever known.

    As I crossed the Colorado border, I began to cry. Each tear embodied loss, failure, dreams, turmoil, and grief. Leaving Colorado and saying good-bye to everything I had ever known was like ripping off a full body Band-Aid and exposing the raw and real reality I had to face, hoping, but not knowing, what was yet to come. Every dream I had ever envisioned had been crushed into the cold hard asphalt on which I was driving. I prayed this move would lead to answers because I knew I had none myself. I was done and numb from loss and defeat.

    I happened to glance in my rear-view mirror and saw a car full of miscellaneous items. They meant nothing to me anymore. There were representations of my meaningless life and all of my failures. I then saw two precious, innocent, beautiful children looking back at me. Their eyes caught my attention and whispered back to me a sense of hope. Hope for a new future. Hope for redemption. Hope I could make peace with myself and finally be the mother they both deserved. There was an ancient wisdom flowing to me through their innocent eyes and for the moment, I was reminded of hope, peace, and love. In that moment, I felt something that I haven't felt in a very long time. In that moment, I felt calm, quiet, and safe. In that moment, I felt peace, love, and hope. Tears of gratitude rolled down my checks and I gently smiled at the two beautiful Souls reaching out to me with hope and love.

Then another voice inside my head interrupted and said, "There is no time for these tears. You need to be strong, there is no time for that nonsense. Buck up and be strong!"

I instinctively snapped myself out of my peace, wiped my tears, put on my big-girl panties and pressed forward because that's what I was supposed to do. I need to be strong. I need to survive. Fighting and staying strong is what I do. It is all I knew how to do. My mind told me to stuff the pain and put a smile on my face. Do not let anyone know what is really going on inside. Tears are a sign of weakness and this is no time to be weak. Your kids need you to be strong. Staying strong meant I had to stuff my pain and continue to paint the perfect picture on the outside. If I stayed strong enough, life would change. Hope would happen, right?

So that's how I arrived in Gillette, WY. I arrived with a strong confident perfect, painted, pretty package on the outside of a raw, broken, women on the inside. This was my life. This is the only way I knew to deal with my life. If anyone saw the pain within me, I thought I would not be liked or loved, so I continued to live a perfect version of a broken reality. I had to learn how to survive because survival is all I knew and survival was all I had at the time.

"My God," I cried, "is this what I signed up for!?" "NO! This is not what I signed up for!" I yelled.

Part of me sobbed with sadness and the other part raged with anger. I was angry that life was not working out the way I anticipated and at the same time I was suffocating in guilt that I felt this way. The sobbing and screaming raged within me, always contained and compressed under a perfect little smile on a pretty, picture-perfect, packaged face.

Starting Over and Barely Surviving

We arrived in Gillette and Ed began to work. That is what Ed does, he works to survive. He is a fighter and a survivor. He would do anything and everything to put food on the table. Ed is also a risk taker. He gambles and takes risks I wouldn't even dream of taking, but I'm forced to take them because I married him. His risks are way out of my comfort zone. Within a month of our arrival, Ed started construction on two new homes without obtaining a construction loan on either of them.

Ed applied for loans on both homes prior to starting construction, but the local banks would not lend us money because we were new to town and we had just lost everything we owned. Our financial portfolio was "less than acceptable," in the eyes of a bank. Approving a loan to construct homes without a purchaser was far too risky for the banks. Until we secured a buyer to purchase the homes, they would not lend us the money we needed for construction.

Ed, being the risk taker that he is, started the homes anyway. He hoped and trusted that we would find a buyer before the first payments to our subcontractors were due. He figured it would all work out, and somehow it did, though the stress during this time was physically tormenting me.

I am not comfortable taking risks. My stomach was constantly tied in knots, which was affecting my health. I was terrified we would not be able to pay our subcontractors and finish the homes. We were already living off credit cards for personal expenses and we were almost a half-million dollars in debt from the collapse in Colorado.

Now, Ed was starting construction on two homes we had no way to fund, which added more debt. We were in over our heads, figuratively buried in a mound of debt and it was overwhelming me. I had no idea how long we could play this risky game, knowing any day the game could turn and we could be left homeless and alone.

Each month the debt increased, and I was worried for myself, my kids, and my sanity. We were all living in survival mode, trying to keep our heads above the water, not knowing when and where the next influx of money would come from.

When we did have money come in, most of it went back to pay debt in Colorado. Every dollar coming in was going out just as fast. Life was a battle and we were still in the middle of it. As usual, I stuffed the pain and misery, put on a smile, and painted a pretty-perfect picture on the outside.

Every so often, I gave myself pep talks to shift to positive-thinking mode. That always works, right? Wrong! Pep talks were the only thing I knew how to do at the time. They really didn't address my pain at all, they just helped me stuff and hide the pain so I didn't have to deal with it. I remember the last pep talk I told myself before my final crash and fall. Yes, my Soul was getting ready to give me a full-blown crisis to get my attention.

Remember earlier when I told you to listen, pay attention, and respond to the whispers in your life? Here's why. If you don't pay attention to the whispers in your life, life will give you a nudge, a shout, a scream -- and then a full-blown crisis. Life will break you to the point where you are finally ready to listen and pay attention. Life does this because it loves you and wants more for you. Life will not stop until you pay attention.

I wasn't paying attentions to the whispers, nudges, shouts and screams from my Soul. I didn't listen to my hurt and resentment when I lost my endorsement contract. Instead of listening, I chose to abandon my passion and purpose and hid that part of me in a closet. I didn't listen to the exhaustion and emptiness I felt raising my kids. Instead of listening, I refused to ask for help with chores and raising my family. I refused to take care of my mental, emotional, and social needs by hiding at home and not getting together with friends. I didn't listen to the loneliness and abandonment I felt from my husband. Instead of listening, I chose to stay silent and just deal with it, letting our relationship grow silent and distant as well.

Ed's work was consuming him, our marriage, and both of us in ways we didn't even recognize, so Life gave us a financial collapse. Life was trying to reach us through events, feelings, and emotions, but we were both too busy to stop and listen. Just when I thought I couldn't take any more, my Soul rescued me by giving me more crisis. I had no idea it was coming. Like most Soul callings, they call when you least except them but when you need them the most.

It was a regular day. I had just sent the kids off to school and I was standing next to my bed, folding laundry. I was still trying to survive my life by maintaining a positive attitude, doing daily chores, and avoiding addressing my problems through positive thinking. I kept telling myself I had so much to be grateful for. I thought, "I have a roof over my head. I have two beautiful, heathy children. I have a husband who was doing everything he could to pull things together. Though it was a struggle, he still has hope and a strong will to get through this. He is a hard worker and I know he would keep trying until it killed him," which it was slowly doing. "Last, but not least, I had my health" …. Or so I thought.

Two weeks later, I received a call that no human being ever wants to hear. It was the call that broke me, inside and out. It was the call that finally "killed" me in order to save me. It was a call that was born out of the denial and delusion I had been living in. It was a call to reality, a call that forced me to reflect from the inside out rather than cover up and deny myself from the outside in. Thank God for the call. This final call and crisis was the only thing that would save me from my own misery, save me from the pain I kept stuffing and storing, and save me from the life that was killing me from the inside out. This crisis was calling to save me from me.

2

WHEN CRISIS CALLS. THE CALL THAT KILLED ME TO SAVE ME

Answering the Call

December 16, 2008, two days after my 36th birthday, would be a day I would never forget. It was the day I received the call that changed my entire life and reason for being and living. It was the day that shifted me and my life forever. I will be eternally grateful for this day.

It was a mild winter afternoon in Gillette, WY. The sun's rays glistened in the frosty air and a light blanket of snow dusted the streets. Our neighborhood was winding down from the boisterous energy as grade-school children made their way home from their busy day and afterschool activities. I, too, was making my way home. I had just started working as a real estate agent and was driving home from a long day's work. I pulled my car in our driveway and walked onto the porch and through the front door.

Once inside, I dropped my work bag, took a deep breath and released the day's anxiety through a heavy sigh. All I wanted to do was crash on the couch and put my feet up. I was dog-tired and ready to relax. But before I could retire, my stomach started to groan and growl. I remembered that I skipped lunch because I was tied up showing properties to new clients. I debated which was more important, crashing on the couch or attending my belly. My stomach responded with persistence and won out. I dragged myself into the kitchen for a bite to eat.

As I entered the kitchen I immediately froze as I sensed my husband's drawn and weary face staring back at me. I knew immediately that something was wrong, very wrong. He never looked like that. He was as pale as a ghost and literally looked as if he was about to faint. I stood across the kitchen from him and asked what the matter was.

He said, "I just received a call from your oncologist … you have cancer." Tears welled up in his eyes and I could feel his fear, anxiety, and desperation from across the room. His life force was draining out of him. He was terrified of losing me and having to live life without me.

I was blank. I was simply still and silent. Then his words finally hit me, "What did he just say?" I thought. I was so worried about him I wasn't able to connect what he just said. "You have breast cancer," he said.

It was surreal and unreal. I felt like I was in a dream knowing full well that this was reality, I think? I couldn't process his words at first. They were just words and then finally they started to resonate. My whole body became numb with disbelief and couldn't feel anything. It was like the whole world sped up and slowed down at the same time. I repeated the words to myself trying to make sense of them, but it was if I were speaking a different language. Nothing was processing.

I repeated the words to myself, "I have cancer. I have cancer?? I have cancer!" I was trying to process the words through different dialects and expressions but nothing seemed to work.

Then my analytical mind tried to rationalize my situation, "What? No, that's impossible. I can't have cancer. I feel just fine. I'm healthy and strong. I don't have any of the traditional signs associated with cancer. It doesn't make sense. I can't have cancer. Surely this is a mistake ... or is this really true? Do I really have cancer? Do I even know what 'true' is right now?" I was so confused and shocked I couldn't process anything, then tears began to flow, and I stood, totally disillusioned. "Now what?" I thought, "What the fuck am I going to do now?"

Ed came over and held me. We embraced in silence. We both knew neither of us had a clue what we were going to do. It was in this stillness, being held in the quivering arms of my husband, that I realized all of my worry, stress, uncertainty, fear, anxiety, and failures I had been holding on to and battling, didn't matter. None of them mattered anymore. The only thing that really mattered was this moment. That's it.

The only thing that mattered now was life itself, because for the first time in my life, I didn't know how long I had to live. I was facing the possibility of death. It was as if cancer had called and was giving me this moment to make a choice. Cancer was calling me.

Cancer was asking me, "This is your moment. Are you ready to start fully living, or do you want to continue to slowly die? What do you really want? You can either start fully living or continue living a slow death until death becomes you. Here's your chance. Here's your choice. Do you want to *live* or do you want to *die*? What do you really want?"

In that moment, a switch instantly flipped within me, and I realized I wanted to live. I wanted to stop surviving and struggling and I wanted to start thriving and fully living. I finally recognized that I had so much to live for, and I realized that I wasn't really living up to this point.

For the first time, I had to get very real with the reality I was presenting to myself and the exterior world, verses the reality that was buried within me. My reality of painting a picture-perfect smile on top of a decaying rotten interior wasn't really working. Instead, it was slowing killing me from the inside out. There is nothing worse than living a slow death while still being in a physical body. The truth of the matter was that I was not living at all. For the first time, I had to drop the smile and the false facade and get very real with why cancer called and came into my life.

For the first time, I wanted to live. I wanted to live more than anything in the world. I knew I had to find a way to live, but I had no idea how. I knew I needed to answer the call, but, I had no idea how to respond to it. What the fuck was I going to do?

Luckily, there was someone, something, that did know how to respond. It was this something, someone that made the call of cancer and knew if I could only connect and trust this guidance, it would not only teach me how to heal physically, it would teach me how to restore my life and fully live again.

Cancer was a call from my Soul that knew exactly what I needed, even when I didn't. My Soul had all the answers I had been looking for but I was not able to fully connect to them. My Soul had the love I so desired but was never able to receive. My Soul had the wisdom to know exactly what I needed to do to heal and restore my life. My Soul had the answers to heal my internal pain and suffering, when I had no clue. My Soul had the answers to everything I needed to know.

Up until this point I relied on my own wisdom, understanding, and delusion of positive thinking and emotional stuffing. All of my positive thinking and stuffing had failed. My own choices, decisions, patterns, and programs had brought me to the exact place and situation I was facing now. My view on life and the way I was handling it, brought me disillusionment, lack of love, an empty and lonely marriage, financial collapse and finally a health crisis called cancer. There was no amount of positive thinking, stuffing, and surviving that could save me now. I needed to reconnect with my Soul. I needed to reconnect with my higher wisdom and trust Its guidance. My own guidance had failed me. My Soul was calling to save me.

Even in shock and disbelief over my diagnosis, I nevertheless experienced a wave of stillness and peace cover me. In this stillness, which stemmed from the shock, I heard a faint whisper from within. A soft and silent voice said, "Ah, now

I have your attention. Now you can hear me. Now you can connect with me. Now I can help you. I couldn't help you before because you continued to ignore me. You continued to set me aside. Now you are ready, able, and willing to hear me, follow me, and trust me. But first you must let go of your old ways of thinking and doing. They no longer serve you. You must unwind and let go of your old ways and open the door to new ways. Choose to connect, trust, and follow Me instead. I have all the answers you are looking for. I have everything you need to heal and restore your life, but I cannot help you unless you open the door and let me in. I have this. I have you. I was the One who called you. I am the One who has been trying to get your attention all along, but you just didn't recognize and hear my voice until now. Trust me. Are you willing to trust me now?"

This voice seemed familiar, yet it also felt distant. I asked myself, "Is this a voice I could trust?" Part of me wanted to trust it and another part of me screamed, "Hell no! Do not trust this voice!"

Thus began an inner dialogue between two voices I would hear moving forward. I had two distinct and separate voices within me and I knew I needed to choose which I would follow and trust moving forward. I still had no idea what I would do.

I decided it would be in my best interests not to think anymore. I was done for the day. Maybe this was just a bad dream. I went to bed, hoping the morning would bring a new day and the bad dream would be over. Well, I guess we can all dream.

Choosing to Accept or Reject the Gift of Cancer

I woke up the next morning, rolled over, and peered into my husband's eyes. My heart ached and I longed to seek comfort from somewhere, someone. I was scared and confused. I had no idea how I was going to get through this and I didn't know what to do. The "unknown" terrified me and I was not comfortable being in my own discomfort.

My eyes reached out to Ed, "Help me!" they pleaded. Yet I knew there was nothing my husband could do or say that could save me from my own fear and pain. The raw reality was that he, too, was struggling with his own discomfort and we both knew it.

Ed graciously looked back at me and said, "I love you, honey. We will get through this."

His eyes mirrored the pain we shared and confirmed the reality that my bad dream was real. I was going to face this new reality, my discomfort, and the fear of the unknown whether I wanted to or not. Fear and pain was staring me in the face and I had to face it. Stuffing, ignoring it, and storing it were no longer an option.

I still had so many voices and stories in my head all competing for attention. The only thing I knew was that I desperately wanted to find a way to heal. Cancer woke me up and I knew I wanted to live because I had so much to live for. Until this point, I had been taking life for granted and wallowing in my own self-misery.

This recognition stirred new questions within me. I internally began to question everything, "Why me? Why cancer? Why now? How can the fittest women in the world get cancer?" This just didn't make sense. None of it made sense. Cancer didn't make sense.

I had none of the typical risk factors for cancer. In fact, I was the picture-perfect reality of health ... on the outside.

What I didn't realize was that I was sick and suffering on the inside. I hid my inner sickness so well with a perfect smile and fit physique, no one, including myself, would ever know any different. It was this inner illness my Soul wanted to uncover and it was the inner illness that I was going to unfold and discover through my healing journey.

I had no idea I was sick on the inside at the time of my diagnosis. I had no idea of the destruction and dis-ease I was carrying on the inside. This destruction and dis-ease was causing a physical manifestation on the outside. I had no idea, but my Soul knew perfectly well that my false persona and hidden secrets were killing me from the inside out.

Thus, I received cancer as a wake-up call to uncover the sickness within me. My Soul gave me an emergency wake-up call through cancer two days after my 36th birthday, not as a curse, but as a gift. A gift of love from above. The question now was, "Am I going to accept this gift, or would I reject it and continue to fight and struggle with life?"

Who thought cancer could be a gift? I certainly didn't see it that way. I always thought it was a curse, but now, I'm beginning to question everything, even cancer. Could cancer be a gift? I later discovered that cancer was my greatest gift.

My greatest gift was delivered in a perfect pretty little package called cancer, but it still needed to be received by me. I still had to receive and accept this gift in order to heal from it. This would be one of the hardest parts of my healing journey. Would I receive, accept, and trust this gift and healing journey? Or would I reject it and try to fight cancer and continue to barely survive each day?

The choice wasn't easy, but it was entirely necessary. I was being called to accept cancer into my life and to learn all the lessons and blessings it came to serve and teach me. Would I accept or reject this gift? I still wasn't sure.

"Why me!?" I cried, "This isn't fair!" My human mind wanted to rebel, fight, and reject my current reality. My human mind wanted to get this process over and move on with life. It was fully prepared to become a cancer survivor but it had no idea how to become a cancer thriver. My mind wanted to maintain and take control just as it had done all of my life, but my Soul wanted more.

My Soul wanted to save me, heal me, and teach me how to live. I needed to choose which path and which mind I was going to follow. One mind would lead me on the path to survive; the other would teach me how to thrive. The battle in my mind was just beginning and was the first of many challenges along the way.

My human mind constantly played tricks on me during this process and I had to become very aware of what game it was playing and who was doing the talking. I had no experience "consciously" playing this game but plenty of experience "unconsciously" playing it. As it turns out, my human mind had been running the show for many years.

I was living my life from years of programmed thoughts and concepts formed from society, world, and religious and educational views that did not resonate with the truth of my internal essence. My Soul got locked in a cage and couldn't live and express freely in my life because my internal programs kept it locked and bound. It is these concepts that get imbedded in our neurological systems and can become unconscious programs that ultimately run, ruin, and rein over our lives.

Science tells us that 95% of our lives are run by these unconscious programs and only 5% of what we think and do are directed by conscious choice. I had been running my life from the 95% unconscious human mind and it had led me into the exact time and space in which I found myself.

By the time I was diagnosed with cancer, I was unconscious, exhausted, diseased and barely surviving life. I really wasn't living at all. Cancer came into my life to wake me up from the patterns and programs that were running my life. Cancer came as a call to open my heart and mind to something else, something more. I needed to open myself to new ways of knowing, seeing, perceiving, believing, and living life itself. My Soul was calling me to take my life back and learn to master it, rather than being victim of it.

We all have unconscious operating patterns formed from our past experiences, family upbringing, and society programming that hijacks us and keeps us in a state of fear and survival. Don't get me wrong, some of the unconscious programming is very useful in your physical life, but when the majority of the unconscious programs are being run by fear, suffering, anxiety, stress, and the unconscious mind, they will eventually fail, and life begins to fail with it. Many times our Souls create a big event, such as a crisis, to pull us out of our unconscious programming.

The beauty within crisis is that it can help you let go of what you think you know as "truth" and finally discover the real "Truth." This is how crisis can serve you, but only if you are willing to look at it this way and be willing to question your "truth." If you are unable to open yourself up to new ways of thinking, being, perceiving, believing, and living, you will find yourself in the same life lesson over and over again.

This is why life repeats patterns. Your life will repeat certain patterns to try to teach you a lesson. These repeating patterns are a call from your Soul. The pattern will repeat itself until the message is acknowledged and learned. The pattern must be recognized, accepted, and learned or it will continue to come into your life. Each time the event or life circumstance will get larger and more intense until it becomes a full-blown crisis, as it was with me.

Patterns start as whispers and then get louder and larger until they get your attention. I had to lose everything before my stubborn mind was willing to let go. Cancer was my final crisis before I was willing to let go of everything I thought was real and true in my life. I had to question everything I thought I knew in order to learn the lessons my Soul knew I needed to learn. If I hadn't answered the call to cancer, God only knows what would have happened next.

Pay attention to the small whispers in your life. They are trying to tell you something very important. They will not stop until you answer the call. The choice to answer will always be yours. This is the beauty and the gift of free will. Answer the call sooner than later.

There are people in this world who refuse to answer the calling of their Soul and have spent a lifetime surviving, rather than thriving and fully living. They continue to experience pain and suffering over and over again as they transition from one crisis to the next. They refuse to answer, accept, and receive the call. They never get to experience the fullness and beauty that life can be, because they are stuck in their own misery.

Life is a gift. You can accept or reject this gift. You also get to choose how you would like to experience this gift of life. You choose whether to just survive -- or actually thrive.

My Human Mind Goes into Panic Mode

After hearing my cancer diagnosis, my human mind reacted and immediately went into high alert. It is a normal and natural for your body and mind to go into panic mode when faced with a crisis. Your human mind is designed to protect itself. High alert is what is supposed to happen when a crisis is set into motion. You unconsciously shift into high alert because your body senses a threat and your human mind jumps into survival mode.

Survival mode is great when you are face-to-face with a tiger or bear. You want your body and mind to instantaneously react and go into high alert. However, when you are faced with a stressful situation where the crisis is not an immediate life-threatening event, a highly stressed body and mind does not serve you well. Survival mode creates an internal crisis that makes you overreact and puts you in a state of emergency. Your body cannot heal and restore itself when there is an internal crisis happening within your mind and body. When you think you are in crisis, your body innately shuts down its healing capacity as a survival skill so you can enter into a fight-or-flight state. Fight or flight is a perfect state of being if you want to out-run a tiger, but it is not a state of being you want to be in if you want to heal. When you go into fight-or-flight mode, your body cannot heal.

It is important to recognize this state of the mind. It is not a healing state and it is imperative to shift this state if you want to heal and restore your life. I immediately went into fight-or-flight the day after my diagnosis. When I did, my fear-based emotions began to rise and I got very worked up. This is what happens when you hear life-threatening news. This is how our human mind is programmed to respond, however, this is not want you want to do. Here is a perfect example of my unconscious mind in fight-or-flight mode:

"Oh my God, what am I going to do? I'm freaking out. I'm too young to die. I don't want to die. OMG, what if I die! What about my kids? What will they do when I'm gone?" (Yes, my mind was already killing me before I even gave myself a chance to live).

Tears welled up and rolled down my cheeks. My thoughts and fears immediately focused on my kids. I loved them more than I loved myself. I knew what it was like to lose a mother and I didn't want that for them. They were too young to lose their mother!

Then my mind shifted to survival mode; "I have to survive! What can I do to stay alive for my kids?" My mind continued to race and rationalize, "What about treatment? What am I going to do about treatment? I have to fight this thing. I don't want to die. I also don't want to get sick from chemo. I don't want to lose my hair, my health, and my life. I don't want cancer. I don't want any of this. I can't believe this is happening to me!"

On and on this voice went, spiraling down in defeat from one fear-based thought to another. It was pure misery. I was engulfed and fully consumed in my own misery and my terrified mind.

Then another voice silently, but firmly whispered, "Stop! Stop! This is not serving you. Breathe and connect with Me. Clear your mind. Let go of the chatter. Let go and connect to Me." This voice paused and allowed me to contain myself. I took several deep breaths and let go of my mind's excessive chatter. I became calm and still.

The voice continued, "Now that you are quiet and still. Stop thinking about what you don't want. Let that go. Begin to *feel* into what you *do* want instead."

"Oh," I said, "that's a great question. What do I want? What *do* I want?"

In the stillness and in my calm mind, I was able to connect to my heart and *feel* into what I wanted instead of what I didn't.

"Well," I said. "I want to heal. I want to heal my body so that I can live more of my life." I sat for a moment longer and came to a deeper realization and said, "What I really want is to live. I want to live more than anything in the world."

The soft voice then asked, "Why do you want to live? Why is that important to you? Why is it so important that you live?"

I sat for a moment and let the question sink in. I then replied, "I want to experience more life with my children and family. I want to experience more life itself. I want to experience more sunsets, more sunrises, more traveling, more relationships. I want to appreciate every single moment in life no matter how small it is, no matter if I only had one more moment, one day, one week, one year, or a hundred years. I want to fully live again. I want to heal my body, so I can live my life. I want to touch, see, feel, love, hold and experience more life with a functional whole healthy body."

"Yes," my Soul whispered. "That is what you really want. Stay in touch with what you really want, why you want it, and you will heal your body and restore your life. Where your mind goes, your body will follow. Stay in the energetic expression of what you want, not what you don't want, and you will heal and restore your life."

Tears began to fill my eyes, not because of terror and anxiety, but through the love and peace and tender care I felt from my Soul. I closed my eyes and allowed my Soul to love and hold me. It was perfect, peaceful, and calm. I did not feel fear, I felt only love, and it was healing for a while … until my human mind started to rattle again.

Battle of the Minds

My human mind was still freaking out. It was scared and wanted to maintain control. Ultimately it felt out of control and the only way it knew how to feel better was to gain control. Controlling my life was one of the ways my mind thinks it is safe, so it fought for control over my Divine Mind. There was a constant battle between human mind and Divine Mind through my entire healing journey. It was my in-house struggle that I needed to recognize and observe so I could retain the power to choose between my two minds.

My Divine Mind continued to ask, "What do I really want to experience? Fear and struggle, or peace and serenity?" I always had a choice in this question, but I had to choose between one mind or the other.

This battle is also at war between your head and your heart. Your head controls your human mind. Your heart controls your Divine Mind. Therefore, this battle is often described as a battle between your head and your heart.

The battle between my heart and my head was so real and so intense. It was like having a full-blown war stuck and running between my head and my heart. My unconscious human mind was loud, demanding, scared, and anxious. However, it did not know what to do. The voice in my heart was silent, calm, sure, and wise. Its strength was held in its silent wisdom, but it could easily be overpowered by my loud, obnoxious human mind.

I was not yet trained in accessing the power of my Divine Mind and so I was often confused by my human mind and its battle tactics. My human mind would overtake me, and I had no idea what to do or how to do it. It would paralyze me in fear and panic. I knew I had to learn how to recognize my human mind's fear, pause it in its tracks, and make it feel safe so I could move into a healing state and connect to my Divine Mind. I knew if I was going to heal, I needed to become very good at this process. My human mind needed to come with me, work with me, and support me instead of paralyzing me.

My human mind was, indeed, an important part of my healing process. I needed my human mind to be on alert and protect me from immediate danger or physical harm from my outer world. I also needed my human mind to organize data and carry out my human tasks and responsibilities. But on the flip side, I needed my human mind to let go of its commanding control and trust my Divine Mind to do the guiding and leading from now on. This would be a huge adjustment for me. I have always led my life with my human mind; now I was choosing to lead with my Divine Mind. My human mind needed to become my Divine Mind's servant, carrying out the tasks of my Soul with grace and grounded awareness.

Both minds needed to come to terms with each other, operate in their created roles and work together if I was going to heal. I had no idea how to do this, but I knew it was imperative that I find a way to work with and honor my "minds." We were in this together, whether we liked it or not.

3

DON'T KNOW WHAT TO DO ...
MOM ALWAYS KNOWS BEST

Losing My Mother and My Unconditional Source of Love

I woke up on Day Three after my cancer diagnosis and my human mind began to panic again. I woke up in dread, terrified that I was going to die. My human mind immediately took control of my thoughts and began filling my head with death, fear, and anxiety. I was consumed by my fears. I was not only afraid for myself, I was afraid for my entire family, especially my children. They didn't deserve this. They are innocent. Why would God take away their mother? It's just not fair! This whole cancer thing isn't fair! I begin shaking with rage. The anger, pain, and frustration of my innocent children having to live their lives without their mother pierced me deep into my core. I felt like I was ripping into two pieces. My heart wept and bled for them as I pictured them living the rest of their lives without a mother.

I knew all too well what it is like to lose and live your life without your mother. My past wounds began to bubble and surface, as an overwhelming sense of loss and despair crept over me like a black demonic plague. This plague consumed me, swirling and engulfing me with my own grief, loss, and despair. I was immediately plunged into my past, into the exact moment I lost my own mother to cancer. A part within me pleaded, "Please don't take me into this pain again. I barely survived the first time, please not again." Tears filled my eyes and I could feel the pain cut my cheeks like razors as they dripped from my eyes. Losing my mother to cancer was life-shattering.

I was exceptionally close to my mother. We were best friends. I could talk to her about anything and she loved me unconditionally. She loved me, no words needed. Just being in her presence was enough to know how fully and completely loved I was. She was my unconditional love source, so when I lost her, I lost my only source of love. I emotionally died the day she passed, and love died and vanished within me.

I was 18 years old when my mother was diagnosed with ovarian cancer. I had received a call mid-day while attending cosmetology school. I remember standing at the pay phone while my dad delivered the news over the phone. The doctors had found a tumor the size of a softball surrounding her ovaries. No one, not even the doctors, had expected or anticipated that this routine surgery would lead to a mortal cancer diagnosis. The surgeon was scheduled to remove a few cysts on her ovaries. No one expected cancer. Things didn't look good. At best, her doctors gave her two years to live. I was stunned and numb, almost as numb as when I received a call with my own cancer diagnosis.

I couldn't believe this was happening. My mother had always been healthy and took great care of herself. She was an operating room nurse and had an extensive background in health care, yet she still got cancer. WTF? What did she do to deserve this? What did I do to deserve this? I tried to process the news the best I could. I managed to get through the rest of my day and drove home to see her.

When I arrived, my mother was beaming with optimism. She had been programmed to be a beacon of light in the middle of darkness. That was one of the things I remembered and admired about her. She always had a smile on her face and she could make anyone's day brighter with her smile. She was full of joy ... on the outside. (Does this pattern sound familiar?) Despite her capacity to love others fully and completely, I'm sure there were some deep wounds she carried, but she didn't let anyone know. I certainly wasn't aware of them. I only knew of her love as she gave all of herself to her family. (I repeat: Does this pattern sound familiar?)

My mother was also a fighter. She wanted more than anything to fight and beat this diagnosis. She had a will of steal and wanted to fight like hell ... and fight she did. Her entire journey through cancer was a fight. She fought long and hard, from beginning to end. I was with her through it all. I was there for all of her treatments, her pain, her sorrow, her victories, and her defeats. I hoped and I prayed for a miracle, but a miracle was not meant to be. All the fighting in the world could not and would not save her. Nevertheless, I stood by her side, I held her hand, and I walked with her through the greatest fight of her life.

She went through several treatments, including chemotherapy, surgery, and drugs. The cancer receded, for a while, and then it came back, more aggressive than ever. She fought again, one last time. She never gave up because she wanted to live more than anything. She wanted to see her children get married and have families of their own. She wanted to hug and hold the grandkids and be the love and light of world that she was to her own family. I cry to this day knowing how much she wanted to experience more life, but life had other plans for her.

She fought to the end until she knew it was her time to go. She survived four years. I saw and watched her go from a beautiful, fully vibrant woman, to a sick, weak, and debilitated cancer patient. It was heart-breaking to watch someone you love suffer and wither away. Her body was dying, but there was something within her that was fully alive and well. Her Soul stayed strong amidst the fight.

I felt her Soul through this entire fight. Her Soul never withered or died. If fact, it strengthened with each day, gently loving and holding her as she hoped for a miracle cure. Her Soul never tired. It was strong and bold, guiding and directing her path until one day it was time to go home. My mother knew that her miracle to physically stay in this world was coming to an end. It was time to transition home.

Mom's Message for Me

During the last few months of her life, my mother was kept alive through feeding tubes and colostomy bags. The tubes were the only thing sustaining her fragile existence, but now she needed and wanted to let go. She was ready to let go. My mother realized she wasn't fully living and her Soul was calling her home.

I was with her when she made the decision to remove the tubes and allow her body to die. My entire family knew her clock was winding down and we had only a few more days with her. It was the hardest and most intense period of my life. I was only 22 and I was losing my best friend and my source of unconditional love. I was losing my mother.

I spent as much time as I could with her, and we had many conversations. I never thought I would be intentionally discussing and planning funeral arrangements with someone I loved and cared for so much. Mom and I shuffled through her closet and carefully selected the perfect dress she would wear as she laid in her casket. We chose a brilliant blue satin dress with pink and purple flowers. Blue was her favorite color and she wanted to feel and look pretty for her special day. My mother was beautiful that day and her dress was perfect.

After selecting her dress for her funeral, Mom and I continued our conversations. We talked about who she would meet when she would transition home to Heaven. She was worried no one would be there, as most of her family was still alive, but then she remembered her grandmother. She had a special relationship with her grandmother and I noticed a sense of peace and love fill her as she realized she would not be alone. Her grandmother would be there to welcome her home. I left that evening feeling grateful knowing my mother was at peace and that she would not be alone.

The next day I drove straight to my parent's house after work. I wanted to spend more time with my mother. Her energy was slowing declining, but when I walked in, she gathered enough strength to smile and beam with love, as she always did.

We began our conversations again. She proceeded to tell me a story in great detail about a visitation and conversation she had the night before with her grandmother. The visitation was vividly real to her and I knew she must have been making the transition between here (the physical world) and home (heaven, or the spiritual world) already. She was bouncing back and forth between two realities and she told me she was meeting and conversing with several people from the other side.

She was also experiencing bits and pieces of her past-life review by re-living former moments in her life. She spoke about these occurrences with peace and love. I could feel how real they were to her and I could feel the truth of the experience within her.

In our last conversation, she gave me a piece of Divine Wisdom from the other side. It was one last gift and one last message from her before her final transition home. It was a message and a gift I would not appreciate or fully understand for years to come. In our last conversation, we talked about how much she wished she would have found a way to live. She wanted more than anything to have found a way to beat cancer and stay a while longer, but she knew that was not part of her life plan. Instead, she had a message for me.

It was a message that she received from her travels back and forth from Home. Mom gently looked at me. Her eyes glistened with love and compassion. She spoke softly and said, "Mary, this is not the way to cure cancer, there must be another way. A way that the body can heal and restore itself."

I heard and felt her words deep within my Soul. They were filled with truth, strength, and wisdom. I did not fully know what they meant, but I knew they had great meaning. I looked back at my mother and tears rolled down my cheeks. I wished more than anything that she could have experienced a cure for herself. I wanted her to find and experience a cure and another way to restore her health and life, but I knew it wasn't meant to be.

That message was not meant for her and I wondered why. Why did she receive the message now when it was too late? I was angry, furious, and confused. I wanted *her* to live. She deserves to live. Why did she have to die? Why did this message come through when it was too late for her … but not too late for me?

I suddenly realized that somehow this message was for me. I had no idea what this message meant or why it was meant for me. Why did I need this message? I didn't have cancer. I don't understand. But she did understand and she knew she needed to give me one last gift, one last message before she left.

This message was a gift that couldn't save her life. It was a gift meant to save mine. She died and delivered this message so that I could live. I was the one for whom those words were meant, but I had no idea how or why they came to serve me at the time. I couldn't fully receive or accept this gift, because I was not ready for it yet. So my Soul stored them deep in my heart, until one day I could hear them again.

My Soul kept this pretty little package wrapped in love from above until the day I was able to fully understand, receive and accept its contents. The day I received cancer was the day I needed this gift and this message more than ever. It was the day I was finally ready, able, and willing to receive my mother's gift of love from above. Thank you, Mom. I love you more than words can describe.

Mom's Transition Home

The day of my mother's passing finally arrived. In our previous conversations I had asked if I could be with her when she passed. She honored and respected my request, even though she knew it would be difficult for me.

The morning of her passing, she slipped into a coma-like state and we all knew this was the day. Today would be her day to go home. My immediate family came to visit and say their last good-byes. I rushed over after work and sat with her until everyone else had left. My dad was exhausted from the day's activities, so he kissed me good night, methodically climbed up the stairs, and settled into bed.

It was just me and Mom now. I wanted her to know she was safe and that it was alright to go home. I didn't want her to leave, but I knew it was time for her to go home. My mother loved Christian music and so I began to play *In A Little While,* by Amy Grant. It was one of her favorite songs and one of my favorites, too. I heard the chorus as it played,

> *"In a little while*
> *We'll be with the Father*
> *Can't you see Him smile*
> *In a little while*
> *We'll be home forever*
> *In a while*
> *we're just here*
> *To learn to love Him*
> *We'll be home*
> *In just a little while."*

Listening to the words, with deep sorrow, I knew it was her time to be with the Father ... in just a little while. I sat by her side and remembered all the love she had given me and all the memories we had shared together. I cried, then continued to weep, holding her hand.

I was having a difficult time letting go. I didn't want her to leave this physical world but I knew it was her time to transition home. I wanted her to know I was okay with letting go so she could transition in peace and love, with no attachments to guilt or grief. I tried to verbalize the words but I couldn't get them out. It took every ounce of strength within me to release her and let her go.

With a cracked and broken voice, I finally said, "It's good to go home, now. It's okay to let go and go home."

She opened her eyes for the first time that day and then she looked at me for the last time with peace and love. I saw her Soul physically release her body; she was finally free to go home. She was free of the pain and destruction of cancer. She was free from her body's physical limitations. She was free to go home.

She stayed with me for a while, not in her physical body, but as her Soul. I felt her presence surround and love me. Her Soul hugged and held me in the pain I felt from letting her go. She knew it wasn't easy for me to let her go, but she also knew her passing had a greater purpose for her Soul and mine.

She had to go, so that one day I would live, and I would discover another way to heal. She knew that one day her death would inspire me to heal and fully live. She was willing to die for my Soul. There is no greater love than when you surrender your life for another's. This was part of her life plan and purpose and she knew it.

My mother's journey through cancer and passing was an instrumental part of my plan and purpose as well. Her cancer experience and death would one day inspire me to find another way to heal and fully live. I just didn't know it yet.

Though my mother's physical body left that day, my mother's Soul never left me. She was able to experience all of her heart's desires, not as a body, but as a Soul. She was present with every milestone; every marriage, every grandchild's birth, every laugh, every tear, every failure, and every success. She just wasn't in physical from. She was always present as her beautiful Soul.

A Love Letter to My Beautiful Mother, Barbara

Dear Barbara,

Thank you, Mom. Thank you for your love, your wisdom, and your sacrifice. I know you are always with me, guiding and leading me with love from above. I wouldn't be alive and fully living without you. You are my sweet guardian angel. I am so thankful for the life we were able to share together and the life that we were unable to share together. Both of our lives served as gifts in their own perfect way. Thank you for loving me and sharing your Soul with me. I love you with all of my heart.

Until we meet again, Mary

Mom is Still with Me, Loving and Guiding Me Home

Reconnecting to my mother and remembering her message temporarily eased my pain, but I was still faced with the burden of what to do for treatment. The voices in my head continued to devour me. One voice screamed and told me to fight like hell, the other voice gently told me to love, heal, and restore my body and my life. I was spinning in confusion, utterly confused.

I knew I needed to make a decision regarding my treatment plan, but I had no idea which treatment to choose. My human mind stepped in and thought it would be best to do more research. My human mind was programmed to trust and make analytical and logical decisions based on scientific facts and research. Its philosophy was, "When you don't know what to do, ask the experts who do know." So that's what I did. I started researching everything.

My human mind wanted to research science and statistics to find my answer. I grew up in a conservative, practical, and logical family. All truths were determined by science, math, logic, and reason. My father and both brothers were electrical engineers and my mother was an operating room nurse, so our family answers to life were rooted in logic, reason, and medicine. Logic and medicine is where "truth" resided and that's where my human mind wanted to find my answers.

I began to research all conventional treatment options to appease my human mind, but I also had an inner whim to research alternative options as well. Something within me knew there was more for me to learn and discover than what the conventional system had to offer. Something within me knew there was more to the healing puzzle than meets the eye. All I knew was that I needed and wanted to find a way to heal, but I still had no idea how to do it.

After gathering all my research, I thought my answers would become clear. I thought that I would know what to do, but that was not the case. When I compared alternative treatments to conventional treatments, all I found was conflicting information. There were no clear answers. In everything I researched, I found opposing opinions. I found heaps of scientific facts and statistics that supported opposing views. I asked myself, how does this happen? How is this possible? Isn't science supposed to be the "truth?" And yet, I found opposing points of view in everything I researched.

My human mind began to panic again, "How in the hell am I supposed to find the right treatment when everything I research has opposing views? What is the right treatment? What treatment is going to work for me? I need to find the right treatment. I don't want to die!" My human mind continued to rattle in fear, "OMG, what if I choose the wrong treatment? What if I make the wrong decision and die? I don't want to make the wrong choice and die. I have too much riding on this. I'm so fucking scared! I don't want to make the wrong choice."

Yep, there goes my human mind spinning out of control. It began to freak out because the information and answers were not clear. The lack of clarity began to short-circuit my hard-wired mind because my past programming was being questioned and it didn't have the answers it wanted and was looking for.

Another challenge I faced was that there was so much more information regarding conventional treatment and very little information available on alternative treatment. I really had to dig, search, and seek to find any information on alternative cancer treatment. My human mind preferred conventional treatment while my heart was leading me to alternative treatment. My mind, and all of my doctors, were telling me that if I didn't do conventional treatment and act right now, I would die. My heart was asking me to trust that It had the answers I was looking for. If I trust my heart, I would live.

"Shit, what am I going to do? I'm more confused than ever. Fuck, Fuck, Fuck!" (Honestly, it felt really good to curse because I didn't know what else to do).

In my confusion, though, I sensed a soft, subtle voice. I quieted my mind and settled down enough so that I could hear and feel this voice. It said, "Mary, there is another way to heal. A way that the body can heal and restore itself."

"Mom?" I thought, "OMG, is that my Mother?"

No other words came, but I felt her presence holding me, loving me, just as she had held me the moment she passed. I sat still, in her loving presence, and cried. My mother held me and loved me as I tried to process what was happening. I could feel her presence with me and I knew she would be right by my side, just as I was by her side, loving and gently guiding me through my healing journey. I was not alone in this journey. My mother was with me and I needed her more than anything right now. I wish she could have been here physically to hold and love me. I wish I could physically talk to her and have a safe place to land.

A weak and weary voice within me sobbed and said, "I'm scared, Mom."

"I know," she replied. "I'm here for you. I'll always be here for you."

I couldn't believe what I just heard. My mother was right there with me. She was loving and holding me. I could feel her. I could hear her.

"Mom, what should I do?"

"Trust," she said, "Trust in yourself and trust the Divine guidance you are given. You will be perfectly loved, guided, and supported in your decision and your healing journey. Trust."

"Trust?" I (my human mind) questioned, "What does that mean? What does *trust* mean? Which decision do I trust? Which decision is right?"

I wanted her to give me the right answer because I didn't want to make the wrong one. I waited for her reply, but there was no response. I knew I was being asked to make my own decision.

Trusting myself and trusting my Divine guidance was part of my own healing process. I had to learn to trust. I had to learn to trust something my human mind did not know or understand. I had to trust in the unknown.

I thought, "Can and will I trust this voice calling me to find another way to heal? Maybe I could trust it? Even my mother was reaching out to me and whispering in my ear. Maybe I can trust this voice?"

"Maybe not!" exclaimed my human mind. My human mind did not want to trust this advice. My human mind wanted to follow the conventional advice of the doctors, "Doctors know best, they are trained in this kind of thing, trust them!"

There was a part of me that wanted to trust my mind and my doctors, but then there was this other part of me that was drawn to the soft, subtle voice in my heart that said to follow and trust its guidance and love. I then felt my mother's presence, her love, her wisdom, and her guidance.

The soft, subtle voice said, "Mary, there is another way to heal your body and restore your life. Seek and you will find it. Ask and it will be provided to you. Trust and it will be given to you. Follow Its guidance and you will discover more than you have ever wanted, needed or desired."

I rested in my mother's presence and this soft, subtle voice. I was at peace. I knew I was being called to something more, but I didn't know if I was brave enough to follow and trust it. I needed more time to decide.

Should I Follow my Head or Heart?

I continued to research all options for treatment, keeping my heart and my mind a little more open than it had been before. I would take in all the information that I read or heard, and I began to process it through my heart. I began to *feel* into it rather than *over-think* it.

I began to learn the difference between the answers from my heart rather than the answers I received from my thinking, analytical, human mind. The answers from my heart were soft, silent, subtle, and light. I felt a sensation of calm, peace, and grounded wisdom from my heart. My heart replied with a *knowing* response rather than an intellectual *thinking* reaction. The answers from my human mind felt hard, brash, impatient, desperate, and heavy. I would often fall victim to comatose states of over-thinking, over-analyzing, and over-rationalizing when my human mind took control. The answers from my heart and my head felt very different. I was beginning to decipher between my two minds and I was beginning to trust my heart for answers.

This was very different from how I had been living and reacting to life until this point, but there was something very special and intimate about connecting and asking my heart for answers. There was something within me that lovingly and continually guided me to seek and find my answers. I continued to be drawn and attracted to this inner voice and guidance.

My human mind hated this and wanted nothing to do with this inner process. This inner process didn't feel safe, logical, or rational to my human mind. Many times my human mind thought I was crazy; I felt this way, too. Nevertheless, I knew I needed to trust the process of going within for answers, connecting to my heart and trusting the guidance I received. I knew I needed to separate the commanding voice in my head from the gentle, feeling sensation in my heart. I could then understand which voice was speaking and choose which guidance to follow. Following the old familiar voice in my head could lead to death, pain, and suffering and following the soft, subtle voice in my heart could lead to life, healing, and happiness.

The challenge I faced was, would I be able to let one go and follow the other? Would I be able to stand my ground and make my own decisions when my human mind, the world, the medical system, my friends, and my family thought I was crazy to do so? Could I stay strong when the world and everything around me was telling me I was going to die and that I was making a terrible mistake? In the face of massive opposition, would I still be able to trust and follow the guidance, love and wisdom of my heart? I didn't know. I still didn't know. The battle between my head and heart continued.

4

GATHERING MORE INFORMATION AND CHOOSING MY HEALING PATH

Finding My Practitioner and Opening Up to More

At this time, I still did not know what I was doing to do for treatment, how I was going to heal or who I needed to help me with this journey. All I knew was that I was willing to explore all of my options and trust that answers would come to me. Within the first two weeks of my cancer diagnosis, I found my naturopathic doctor (ND). Linda would later become my physical medical angel. She came into my life not through my own doing and researching, but through a friend of a friend who knew a friend who suggested I should call her.

This is how the Universe conspires to help you when you ask and set your intended course into action. Every person, book, idea, treatment, thought, and discovery were supplied to me. There was nothing I personally did to seek any of them out. It was all provided for me, and to me, in the exact moment I needed it. The Universe knew I needed an ND and delivered her to me exactly when I needed her.

Linda was the practitioner and naturopathic doctor I worked with to design a healing protocol to restore my physical health. To this day, I have never met Linda in person. We worked together over the phone, email, and mail-order tests. Most people are astonished that I worked with a doctor I never met, but the fact that we worked together, never met in person and I am still alive gives testimony that YOU are the biggest part of your healing puzzle. No one else can do it for you. There is no doctor, pill, potion, clinic, or treatment protocol that helps your body to heal without you. You are the most important piece in the healing process.

While I never met Linda in person, I could tell over the phone that she was a ball of energy and full of fire. She was, and still is, a no-nonsense kind of practitioner and gets straight to the point. I could feel her energy and passion over the phone. I could also feel her confidence. Linda knew what she was talking about and she could and would challenge the best doctors with their conventional viewpoints and doctorate diplomas. Linda is a storehouse of medical knowledge. She understands conventional medicine as well as alternative medicine. She knew how, why and when to combine and integrate both worlds when necessary. Her specialty was in the alternative field (which she calls science-based medicine).

Linda knew how to heal the body through an integrated approach using diet, supplements, detox protocols, and integrated health care. An integrated health care approach is one that addresses all aspects of you and dives deeper into the physical, emotional, mental and spiritual causes of disease rather than focusing only on treating the symptoms of disease. She studied and researched every new healing modality for safety and effectiveness. She tested and researched every product or protocol before she recommended it to her patients. Everything needed to pass the "Linda" test before it would be advised.

I felt safe and confident with her. I knew I had found someone I could trust (my human mind still wasn't sure and proceeded with caution). By God's grace, I met her right before my appointments with my oncologist and general surgeon. I was grateful I spoke with Linda first regarding her viewpoints on healing. Had I not been informed about alternative treatments prior to my appointments with my conventional doctors, I would have been crushed under their pressure tactics.

My conversations with Linda gave me a new perspective on healing. We visited in depth on her philosophy and treatment protocols for cancer. She shared intimate details regarding her personal experience and success treating and healing cancer. I was inspired by her stories and I felt a new hope growing within me that didn't exist before. Everything she said resonated with me. We would work together to love and support my body to heal itself through diet, supplementation, and detox protocols.

Linda led me through series of tests and diagnostic tools that would assist her to get in touch with the deeper biochemical malfunctions of the body that would then point to the possible causes of cancer. We would then create a protocol to support the body to heal itself.

"What?" my human mind interjected, "Did she just say that she was going to support my body to heal itself?" I paused and reflected, "Yes, that's what she just said. We are going to create a protocol to support the body to heal itself." My human mind listened closer as it knew it had heard this before in soft, subtle whispers and message from my Soul and my mother.

Linda said we needed to address the cause of the cancer rather than just the symptom, meaning the tumor itself. We needed to address the cause, so the cancer would not manifest or come back. When you address the cause of a disease, the symptoms go away because there is nothing to cause them anymore.

For the first time, this sounded really good. This made a lot of sense. Address the cause and the symptoms go away. I liked this approach, but I still questioned if it would work. It was a very different approach than the conventional system that uses surgery, chemotherapy, radiation, drugs, and then more surgery. The conventional system is a cut, poison, and burn system that focuses on symptoms rather than causes. My human mind became curious and wanted to know more, so I continued to question Linda regarding the conventional system.

Linda replied, "Mary you can't cut cancer out. Cancer happens at a cellular level and it's impossible to cut out all the cancerous cells. Also, you can't poison all the cancerous cells with chemotherapy. If you tried, you would end up killing yourself before you were able to kill every cancerous cell. When you use chemotherapy to destroy cancer cells, you destroy healthy cells as well. Chemotherapy is incredibly toxic to your immune system. You need a healthy immune system to fight cancer. Your immune system is your body's innate tool to ward off disease and illness. You need your immune system to keep you healthy and strong. Chemotherapy will severely damage your immune system and your ability to heal."

"OK," I thought, "she was making some good points. My human mind was beginning to resonate with these points."

My attention tuned in a bit more, then she asked me, "If you were healthy and strong, would you voluntarily choose to poison and burn your body with chemotherapy and radiation?"

I immediately responded, "NO, of course not! No one would do that!"

Then she said, "So, why then, if you are sick with cancer, would you voluntarily poison your body with chemo and radiation?"

This question stunned me and tried to process what she just asked. I began to question the conventional system with more intensity. My human mind was beginning to loosen, and I thought, "Maybe there is another way to heal cancer? Maybe the conventional system does have it all wrong. I would never volunteer to do chemotherapy and radiation if I was healthy, so why would I choose to do this when my body was sick? That would be insane!"

This question-and-answer session was strengthening the same messages I was receiving from my heart. I began to ask myself, "What if Linda's right? What if my mother is right? What if my heart is right? What if there is another way to heal and restore my health and life? What if there is another way to love and support the body to heal itself? What if? What if?"

The possibility of "What if" began to grow in strength and intensity within me. I started to grow in strength and intensity. My human mind began to unwind and integrate and agree with my Divine Mind, my Divine knowing heart.

I thought, "What if there is another way? What if I could find it? What if I *am* the other way? What if my body can heal itself? What if I trusted my heart?"

Hope and possibility were beginning to stir within me. What if? What if? What if?

Meeting My Other Medical Team ... Do Doctors Really Know Best?

A few days after my conversation with Linda, I had an appointment to meet with my general surgeon and oncologist to go over their treatment protocols. The first appointment was with my surgeon. He explained that my original excisional biopsy did not have clean margins. That meant that my biopsy was not successful in removing all of the cancerous tissue and there was still cancer in my left breast. He wanted to do another surgery to remove the cancerous tissue as well as take a few lymph nodes for further testing to see if the cancer had spread. They would also be able to stage the cancer as well. To "stage" cancer means to classify the extent of your cancer, such as how large your tumor is, and if the cancer has spread to other areas of your body. Doctor's stage cancer to help them understand how serious your cancer is, what treatment plans are best for you, and your chances of survival.

My surgeon gave me two options to remove the cancerous tissue. I could either do a lumpectomy or a full mastectomy.

Neither option was particularly appealing to me. He briefly mentioned that additional cancer treatment was necessary. Treatment would most likely include several rounds of chemotherapy and radiation. He did not give me exact details but advised me to discuss treatment options in more depth when I saw my oncologist. I left my surgeon's office feeling depleted and defeated.

"Shit!" my human mind rattled, "he didn't get all the cancer out. If only they could have gotten it all the first time I would feel a little better. This fucking cancer is still in me. Why, why, why? Why is this happening? Is this really happening to me?"

I pinched myself, "Ouch. Damn it!" I exclaimed, reacting to the pinch, "Yep, this is really happening."

My next appointment was with my oncologist. He would access all my biopsy results and plug the results into his computer. Once my results were analyzed, out came my official protocol and treatment plan.

I was trying to stay optimistic, and I was hoping for a minimal treatment plan. I just couldn't believe my cancer diagnosis could be that bad. After all, I felt fine. I was completely heathy except for this stupid cancer diagnosis. I had no pain, no fatigue, and I felt fine except for the stress caused by the cancer diagnosis. All in all, I felt great, as if nothing was wrong. Surely the treatment plan would be easy, right?

I walked into my oncologist's office hoping for the best. I was keeping an open and optimistic mind because that is what I learned to do from childhood. Stay positive and positive things happened, right? Wrong. I grew up with the concept to make it a great day and a great day would happen, right? Wrong again.

Everything I learned from childhood regarding positive thinking was being challenged and by the end of my oncology appointment, I came to the conclusion that "positive thinking" was crap. Here's what my positive thinking and attitude got me that day.

Ed and I walked into the oncologist's office, sat down and held each other's hands. I was grateful he was there. I knew he loved and supported me, but I also knew that my situation was killing him. I could feel it.

The doctor walked in and began to shuffle through my paper work. He flipped through pages of blood tests, biopsy results, protocol assessments, and various other reports I had no clue what they meant.

I thought, "Why do doctors always use words no one can decode or understand without a doctoral degree? Isn't there a patient report that can explain what is going on with you in a simplified version? I wonder if this is done on purpose, to make you feel dumb and uneducated so that you don't question the protocol plan. God forbid if you question anything or challenge a doctor with a doctoral degree! What kind of idiot would do that?" (Apparently, I was going to be that idiot, I just didn't know it yet.) "Surely, doctors know best because they use fancy terms that exceed my understanding."

Even though I had no idea what the words on the pages meant, I sensed that my entire life had been condensed into a computerized report. I felt like my fate, my life, and any hope for a future had been analyzed, assessed and reduced to a four-page assessment of numbers and statistics. I was a number; no longer a human being.

I thought, "Surely my life and my health are worth more than a multi-page medical report? Was anyone going to ask *me* what was happening in my life? Didn't that information matter in the treatment plan? Was anyone going to ask *me* about my thoughts, fears, and opinions regarding other options? Did anyone care about *me* or my *life*?"

Nope, apparently that information is insignificant and irrelevant. No one cared or took the time to discover what was really happening with me or my life. No one asked me how I was. No one took the time to see what was going on in my life. To them, those things were immaterial and really didn't matter when it comes to cancer.

My entire protocol and treatment plan was based solely on physical test results and analytics that the computer generated. Everything was systematic, and nothing was personal. I became a number in the systematic program. This wasn't sitting well with me.

After flipping through my charts, the doctor looked at me with an intense and matter-of-fact approach and said, "Here's what I recommend. You need a lumpectomy or mastectomy plus an additional biopsy and diagnosis of the lymph nodes, sixteen weeks of chemotherapy, eight weeks of radiation, one year of Herceptin and then we will need to complete another surgery to remove your ovaries a year from now."

The room went still. I sat motionless, overcome with shock. He lost me at "sixteen weeks of chemotherapy." I don't think I heard or processed anything beyond that.

After a period of dismal silence my body and mind went into a frenzy, "WTF! (I heard inside.) I don't even feel sick and now he is telling me that the next year of my life is going to be nothing but sickness! How could this be? I feel fine. I can't do this. I need to get out of here. Fuck this doctor. Fuck this plan. Get me the hell out of here!" I had no idea if this was my human mind panicking or my Soul being brutally honest. All I knew, is that I needed to leave.

I flashed a cordial smile and thanked the oncologist for the report. I stood up and abruptly left his office. My body went numb again. I was utterly empty. I did not want to think, feel, or be anything at all. I simply couldn't be anything because I was so overwhelmed. I didn't want this, I never wanted this. I never asked for cancer.

Once outside, I took a deep breath and screamed at the top of my lungs, "Auughggghhh!!! How can this be happening!"

I summoned enough energy to make my way home, collapse on my bed and cry and cry and cry until my eyes swelled shut and I finally fell to sleep. Before dozing off, I thought, "Maybe tomorrow I would wake up from this dream. Maybe tomorrow I would be better. God, please wake me up from this dream, this nightmare!"

Little did I know, that was exactly what God was doing, but I had no idea that cancer was my answer and the call to wake up from a hellish nightmare I had been living for a very long time ... but my Soul knew.

I woke up the next morning and began shifting through the paperwork from the oncologist. I tried to process my options from a rational mind. If I started to *feel* into the situation, I couldn't handle it because it was still too raw and painful. I decided I had to take an analytical approach to the situation to avoid insanity. I had to put my feelings aside so I could cope with what was going on. I thought that was the only way I could get through this. Luckily, my heart knew another way.

I spent the next few days analyzing and rationalizing two very different treatment options. One treatment plan was to aggressively fight, attack and kill the remaining cancer in my body. It would take a year to fully complete treatment. I would lose my hair, and possibly my breast. I would be sick during treatment and life would definitely be a struggle. The up side was, the doctors where saying that if I survived this treatment, I would have a chance to live. I wanted more than anything to live.

On the on the hand, Linda, my ND, was offering a treatment option designed to love and support my body back to health through diet, supplementation, and detox. There would be no toxic treatment, so I would not get sick, or lose my hair. I had no idea how long this treatment would take, which I was okay with. My bigger question was ... would it work? I was not able to find a lot of information to support the possibility of success. Would it work? Is it a chance worth taking? Could I treat and heal from cancer by supporting my body to heal? Would I live or would I die? I just didn't know. I want to live. I don't want to die. This conflict was plaguing and torturing me, ripping me in two because I didn't know what to do.

"Please don't make me have to choose between life and death? This decision is too big for me. I can't make this decision. Someone, please make it for me," I pleaded.

Have you ever felt or wanted something to go away in your life? Has there been a circumstance you wish were a dream and all you had to do was wake up and it would go away? Is there something in your life or a choice you need to make and you don't want to face it? What if the one thing you don't want to face or wish would go away is actually the answer and solution to your pain or problem? In order to get through it, you must face it. Take a moment to ponder this thought; it may be the salvation you've been looking for.

Divine Inspiration over Dirty Dishes … Surrendering to Life and Death

Many times, Divine inspiration comes through when I least expect it. I've found it's much easier to connect to my Divine Mind when my human mind is busy and focused on something else. Never underestimate the power in mundane tasks that keep your human mind preoccupied, so your Divine Mind can be heard. Divine Wisdom does not always come in contained moments of conscious mediation or prayer. More often than not, it comes when you least expect it. Be present for those moments so you don't miss them.

One evening, in the middle of scrubbing lasagna off dirty dishes, my Divine Mind started to chat, "Your greatest fear right now is death isn't it?"

Startled, I replied, "Yes, I don't want to die. It scares the shit of out of me."

Divine replied, "What are you afraid of? What would happen if you die?"

I responded, "I'm afraid for my children. I'm afraid they will lose their mother and don't want that for them. There would be no one to take care of them."

"Yes, I know that scares you," Divine replied, "but if you were to die, do you not know that I would watch over them and take care of them?"

"Oh," I said, "yes, of course you would. You would watch out after them."

Divine reminded me, "It is not your responsibility to watch over your children whether you are here in this physical world or beyond. I watch over them and I am with them all the time and I will continue to do so, just as I am with you. You can let that go."

"Ok." I said, "I guess I can let that go. I will trust that you will be with and watch over my family if I die."

I was feeling a little embarrassed that the Divine was calling me out on that topic. I always felt that I had to take care of my kids. I felt that my family was ultimately my responsibility. Divine was reminding me that He had been taking care of them (and me) all along and would continue to do so. In this moment, I could feel the Divine was coming through as a father figure energy, a protector energy, as confirmation that He has me, He has my family and He always will. Divine's energy felt safe and comforting.

Divine then asked, "What else are you afraid of?"

"Oh, I didn't know we were continuing with this conversation," I said, knowing I would have rather stopped talking when we got to the comforting part. I guess there's no running away from this conversation. I continued, "I'm afraid of losing my physical life. I'm afraid to die. My physical life is all I have, it's real to me, it's all I know, and I'm afraid to let go of it."

"Yes, I know," said Divine, "you are afraid of losing your physical body. Your physical existence is all you know. You think you are only a body. If you die, you lose your body and you lose yourself. You have forgotten and have become detached from your true essence, your Soul."

"Yes," I replied, "I think I am my body, that it is all I have. If my body dies I die with it. I conceptually believe I have a Soul, but I don't know what that means, living in a human body. I guess I have been living my life detached and separated from my Soul."

Divine agreed and then asked, "So, what would happen if you died? Would that really be the end of you?"

I thought about this question for a while. I had not thought about death at all because I have never been faced with a situation where death was in my immediate awareness. Now that I was diagnosed with cancer, death was a real possibility for me.

I asked myself, "What would happen if I died?"

The stillness within me knew that I would go to heaven, back to original Source. I sensed there was life after death and I would continue to exist. I believed I would go to heaven, but I didn't fully know what that meant.

I closed my eyes, took a deep breath and went deeper within. I began to connect and feel my eternal essence, my Soul. I began to connect with the spiritual realm and *feel* what heaven is like. I felt beauty, peace, and unconditional love deep within my body. Heaven began to feel real to me. I could feel the eternal truth and existence of the eternal truth within me. I felt eternity and I became eternal. I continued to embody this experience for a while. I knew in my heart heaven was real and I was real in heaven.

I replied to Divine, "If my body died, I experience the freedom of heaven. I exist as an eternal Soul, in a beautiful, loving, and peaceful space because I *am* a beautiful, loving, and peaceful space." I thought, "How bad could that be? … How amazing would that be!?"

I then thought about my treatment plans and possible outcomes. I thought, "If I live, I get to spend more time in this physical reality with the people I love. I will choose to live my life each and every moment in more freedom. I get to spend more time with my kids and watch them grow and learn. I get to experience more life, more love, and more relationships."

"If I physically die, I go to heaven. I get to meet my Mom and all the people who have passed. I get to reconnect with God, eternal Source of all that is, and rest in eternal love. I get to be free, free of physical limits, free as my Soul and spend eternity in love and bliss … Holy shit, maybe I do want to die?!" (Just kidding. I didn't really want to die, but in that moment, I discovered it's a win/win either way).

It was in that moment that I realized I don't need to be afraid to die. I don't need to be afraid to live, either! God and my Soul has me and is with me either way. God has my family and is with them either way. I was finally able to surrender to death. I knew I would be fine if I physically lived or if I physically died.

In that moment, I was able to completely and fully surrender my life to death. By surrendering to death, it gave me full permission to finally and fully live. I felt free and fully alive for the first time in a long time. I was finally free to live because I fully accepted death. I was no longer afraid to die. I knew I would live either way.

The fear of death did not have a strangle-hold on me. I could breathe again, and I felt a heavy burden lifted from my shoulders and my Soul. This is the beauty and the power of full surrender. Surrender is not a giving-up but, a giving-in. It is a giving-in to the love, power, possibility of God and life itself. It is a giving-in to the fact that life is eternal. Life does not end when your physical body dies.

You are and have always been eternal. Living your life from an eternal perspective provides complete freedom and allows you to live from a state of fully living and loving every moment for as many moments as you may have on earth. Death does not exist within the realm of eternal life.

It was also in this moment that I realized no one is promised a physical tomorrow, whether you have cancer or not. No one knows the day, hour, or moment of their physical death. That is why it is so important to live while you are alive in the moment of now. Tomorrow may or may not be there. Life is a cherished gift. As I realized how precious life is, I made the choice to fully live in the moment each and every day. It didn't matter whether I had one moment, one more day, one year or 100 years. I wanted to live and experience this physical world while I still had a physical body to do it.

I no longer needed to live with the fear of death because the fear was released and surrendered. I wanted to live for the love of life, not for the fear of death! I knew from that point on, I would do everything in my power to fully live, whatever that looked like. I still had no idea how I was going to do it, but I knew this was one big step along the way. I knew I was on my way to healing and restoring my health and my life. I could feel it!

Round Two with My Medical Team ... The Boxing Match Continues

I had to go back for another appointment with my surgeon. This appointment was to discuss my treatment plan regarding surgery, chemotherapy, and radiation for the next year and start scheduling these appointments. What my surgeon didn't know was that I was seriously considering moving forward with alternative options with my ND.

My heart was still urging me to go with alternative methods. My heart was calling me to walk the road less traveled and heal and restore through love and grace, supporting the body to heal itself. Now that I wasn't afraid to die, alternative treatment seemed like a real possibility. My human mind was opening up to this possibility as well. It began to think that maybe I can heal. I would rather heal without having to go through toxic treatment. That's what I really want. I want to experience another way to heal. My mind was finally connecting and beginning to trust my heart.

As I was walking into my surgeon's office, a voice whispered to me, "There is another way to heal, trust me. I will lead you, follow me. Trust me, I will lead you home."

These were words of encouragement that my Soul knew I needed to hear as I walked into my surgeon's office. Why was I hearing these words now? They came out of nowhere, but something within me knew I needed to hear them in that exact moment. My Soul knew I was walking into a lion's den, but I had no clue.

The visit with my surgeon was brutal. There was no personal connection, no warmth, no nothing. How about starting with something like, "Hi Mary, how are you doing? How are you handling your diagnosis? Is there anything I can support you with? Do you have any questions? How are you really feeling?"

Instead, I got a man in a white coat, sitting in his chair, opening my file and prepping my treatment plan. By his lack of eye contact, I could tell he really didn't have time or gave a shit about niceties, me, or cancer. To him, cancer happens all the time, cancer is part of his business and the business he wanted to get to was scheduling my treatment plan and moving me out the door. I was stunned and appalled.

He started by asking if I had decided to do a lumpectomy or mastectomy. I said I hadn't decided yet, and that I was considering the possibility of not doing the surgery at all. He immediately stopped typing, pushed his chair back from his computer, looked directly in my eyes and proceeded to send me a death glare. His body and eyes reeked of intimidation in an attempt to belittle me into submission. He proclaimed, "You must do the surgery. The biopsy didn't remove all the cancer and surgery is required. You don't have any other options."

In an attempt to clarify my position, I said I was looking into all options including natural treatment, and that I still wasn't sure what I was going to do. He chuckled under his breath as an act to dismiss the validity of natural treatment. He thought natural treatments were a farce and a joke – a form of quackery.

He continue to justify himself and his inflated ego. "If you don't do these treatments you will die. I can't allow you to do this." He immediately sifted his gaze and glared at my husband, addressing him: "If this were my wife," he said, "I would forbid her to do anything else." Then he looked back at me and said, "I forbid you to do anything else. You are going to die. You are not thinking straight. If you choose alternative treatments what are you going to do about the cancer? The cancer will continue to grow, and it will kill you. I forbid you to do that!"

The room was filled with anger and resentment. He glared at me with contempt, condemning me to even question him. You could cut the negative energy with a scalpel because it was so thick. Ed and I looked at each other in shock, disbelief, and disgust. The room went deathly silent and I had no idea what to say. I knew there was not going to be a cordial ending or compromise with this conversation. It was time to leave.

I took a deep breath, held my composure, and excused myself by saying, "I believe our conversation is over. I need to go, but I will be in touch if I need your services." I shook his hand and sent him a polite-pretty smile on my face that said "Fuck you, I am never coming back!" I was still in shock as I left the office. I didn't know what had just happened or what to think.

Then my human mind chimed in out of fear, "See, I told you so. You will die if you don't do conventional treatment. You don't want to die do you?" Ugh, the last thing I need right now is my human mind to shift back into fear mode and agree with an elevated egotisical doctor!

I chimed back to my human mind, "No , I don't want to die, I want to live. Let's figure a way to do this, shall we? I'm done playing these mind games. I am tired, confused, and exhausted from thinking. Let's go to bed and start fresh again tomorrow morning."

One of the things I internally struggled with in this last chapter was my limiting belief that the only way to heal cancer was through chemotherapy, radiation, and drugs. All of my life, when I was sick or I had a medical problem, my parents took me to the doctor, the doctor wrote a prescription and I got better. Going to the doctor and seeking outside treatment to get well is the process most people are programmed with.

When I was diagnosed with cancer, my human mind thought the only way to get well was to go to the doctor, get chemo, do radiation, have surgery, take drugs, and then I would get well. This is our world-view. I also had a fear that if I did not do treatment, I would die (which was another limiting belief).

These beliefs were neurologically hardwired into my body's system, therefore, they were difficult beliefs to work through and overcome. I was able to work through these beliefs by stepping outside myself, taking another look, and asking if these beliefs were really true. I had to become an outside observer of my beliefs and question them from a new and different vantage point. I began to ask questions. Is the only way to heal from cancer through chemo, radiation, and drugs? The answer I found to this question was, no. There are many people who have healed without chemo, radiation, and drugs. Would I die if I chose a different path? Maybe I would, maybe I wouldn't. Would I live if I chose conventional treatment? Maybe I would, maybe I wouldn't. The truth was there were no guarantees either way, so I needed to choose the path that was best for me.

I had to ask myself what I really wanted and desired. What I really wanted was to heal my body by loving, nourishing, and supporting it back to health. In order to move forward with this new belief, I had to change my limiting belief from, "I can't heal my body through natural protocols" to "I can heal my body through natural protocols." *Whether you think you can, or think you can't – you're right.* -- Henry Ford.

Choosing Peace and Love as My Treatment Plan

After my appointments with my surgeon and oncologist, my mind was spinning out of control and it continued to fight with my heart. Both were strong and convincing. This internal war was beginning to physically wear me down. I was exhausted and tired of fighting the battle. My human mind, and most of the world including family and friends, was telling me I had to fight cancer. I had to be aggressive and fight for my life or I was going to die. My heart, my mother, and God were silently asking me to trust them, surrender and trust Divine Guidance that would teach me another way to heal and another way to live. I was so conflicted between my heart and my mind, my mind and my heart, I didn't know which one to choose.

And then, I received a call. My best friend from elementary school called me in my moment of crisis and confusion (Divine Guidance works through us in many different ways. This call was one of those ways). She was calling to check up on me. She asked me how I was doing. I immediately burst into tears and out poured the internal conflict with which I was struggling. She patiently listened and allowed me to break down and move through my internal emotions. I talked about my inner conflict, dilemma, and mental crisis. I was confused, and I did not know which direction or which treatment plan to follow. I was overwhelmed, over-loaded and paralyzed in the fear of choosing the wrong treatment option. When I was done with my emotional outpour, she simply and lovingly said, "Mary, which option gives you the most peace?"

"Peace?" I said, "I've been so consumed with the war in my head I have never even considered *peace*." I slowly began to calm my mind and *feel* into the word *peace*.

She said, "Follow the *peace*."

Her advice was simple and wise. The word *peace* was simple and wise. I thanked her for her call, hung up the phone, cleared my mind and began to *feel* into the word *peace*. I thought to myself, "What treatment option gives me the most *peace*?"

I made a list and wrote down every treatment option. As I went through each option, I *felt* into it asking my heart how it felt. Depending on the feeling, I would either write the word *peace* or the word *fear* next to each item. When I was done, my treatment option became very clear. The option that gave me the most peace was "the other way."

In that moment I had the clarity I needed to more forward and make a decision. I knew in my heart that I would find another way to heal and restore my life. I chose *peace* over *fear*. Peace and love would be my guiding light through my whole process. In every decision that I would make moving forward, I would ask for answers from my heart, my intuition, and my Higher Guidance, "Does this option feel *peaceful* or *fearful*? Is this treatment based in *love* or *fear*? Does this treatment feel like *restoration* or does it feel like *attack and destruction*?" These questions were my personal-assessment tool for whether I would move forward or decline a treatment option. If the treatment was based in love and peace, I moved forward with it. If the treatment was based in fear and destruction, I would not choose it.

Peace and love guided my whole journey to healing. When I got out of my head and into my heart, when I was able to get out of thinking and into feeling, I found all my answers. I knew I would be Divinely guided through my whole healing process. Up until this point, I was looking and seeking for answers outside of myself and I found nothing. The only thing I found looking for answers outside of myself was confusion and chaos. As soon as I started looking within for my answers, I found them, and I felt them.

All of the answers you seek will be found within you, not outside of you. This was one of the many lessons I learned from cancer. Cancer came to reconnect me to my Divine self and my inner Divine knowing. The self that loves and knows me intimately. The self that is connected to God, the Universe and my Soul. The self that knows all that I have been through and all that I need to go through to fully heal. There is no one or nothing outside me that knows me better than I do, my Divine, eternal I. In this moment, I knew I had everything I needed within me to heal and restore. I knew that if I could trust this internal guidance it would provide everything I needed, both internally and externally, to heal and fully restore me.

My body and my life are designed to heal when they are fully connected and aligned with my Soul, my Divine self. I had simply lost the connection for a little while. I had gone my own way. I, my human I, thought it knew best, but its best was never enough. My "human best" left me sick, broke, lonely, and sad. Now I know, that my human I, by itself and separated from God, didn't know anything at all, but there is an "I Am" (Divine I) inside me that does know all. This "I Am" is the name God gave Itself when Moses asked Its name.

I've always said that the miracle I experienced wasn't that my body healed from cancer. The body is designed to heal. The miracle was that I was able to let go of my human mind, follow my heart and trust this Divine Guidance within. That's the real miracle. The miracle of self-realization and reconnecting to my Divine Self.

You have everything you need to heal, you simply need to reconnect and access it. That's the hardest part. The hardest part of experiencing miracles is surrendering and trusting what you don't know. It is so scary, yet it is the most powerful thing you can do to heal and restore your health and life. Let go and give yourself a chance to fully heal and fully live. Let go and let God love, guide, and support you. Surrender and let go.

Connecting to "Another Way" to Heal

By connecting to my *Divine I* and untangling my *human I*, I was able to connect to a source with a far greater healing capacity than anything the outside world could provide me. This is not a common practice in today's society. We are always looking for outside resources and things to heal us, but outside things are not designed to heal, they are used as tools to assist and support the ultimate healer, which is you. Healing is an internal process, a reconnection and reintegration process of body, mind, and spirit. Outside resources can only support the healing process, they cannot heal our bodies for us ... even if the human mind thinks they can.

Let's investigate this further so you can begin to understand the deeper healing capacity within your body. Stay with me. This concept may blow your mind! In order to get to the cause of any outer physical manifestation, we need to address the heart of the problem. We need to address the original cause of the problem. Using Band-Aid solutions to cover up symptoms never works. A symptom or problem will never go away if the cause of the symptom or problem isn't addressed. That's why I used a "whole-istic" approach. I addressed all aspects of myself, my whole self. To get a better understanding of who or what needs to be addressed, you need to have an understanding of who you are.

5

THERE IS ANOTHER WAY TO HEAL YOUR BODY

Who Are You?

So, who are you? Are you a physical body? Are you spirit? Are you both? If you are a body or spirit, how does the mind or consciousness come into play? Are you all three? How does your body, mind, and spirit really work? Do they work together or are they separate?"

These questions are great to ask because when you have a conscious understanding of who you are and how your body, mind, and spirit are intimately connected, you have a greater capacity to heal your body and your life. You understand how to live from a connected, integrated whole reality that produces harmony, rather than living from a separated, disintegrated broken reality that causes disharmony, sometimes called "dis-ease." When your interior world is integrated with itself, your outer world reflects harmony. When your interior world is separate and disintegrated from itself, your outer world is disintegrated and chaotic. A separate and disintegrated inner world is created when you do not acknowledge or process your inner thoughts, emotions and the true desires of your heart.

Do you recognize this pattern from earlier parts of my story? I had so much internal conflict within me and a deep disconnection from my Soul and my heart's desires, that my body and my life couldn't help but manifest conflict and chaos in my outer world. The same is true for you. Your inner world will be reflected in your outer reality. So let's dive into your inner world and what makes you, you.

I've always believed that I was a spirit having a physical experience, but I didn't know what role my spirit plays in my physical life. I knew they are interconnected, but what does this really mean? To answer these questions, I was led to study quantum physics. In researching quantum physics, I discovered that all matter is created by energy and information. The heart of this energy and information is Source Energy (God).

To simplify this understanding, let's break the body down into the smallest unit of measurement we can find. When we find the smallest unit of measurement of the body, we will find the source of who we really are.

Let's start with the body and break it down into smaller pieces. First, we will break the body down into organs. Next, break the organs down into individual cells, then break the cells down into atoms, break atoms down into atomic particles, break atomic particles down in to quantum particles. Last, but not least, when you break down quantum particles into smaller pieces, scientists have found there is no matter at all. There is only energy and information. This is the quantum field where all possibilities exist.

So, the truth is, you are not really matter at all, you are energy and information. Source Energy (God) is the source of all of creation. This energy is coded with information that informs matter to physically manifest as it does. Matter does not and cannot exist without Source Energy and information. You would not exist without Source Energy and information. Ultimately, you are energy with coded information that is programmed into matter. See **Diagram A.**

Diagram A

Truth of the Matter is...We are not Really Matter at All.

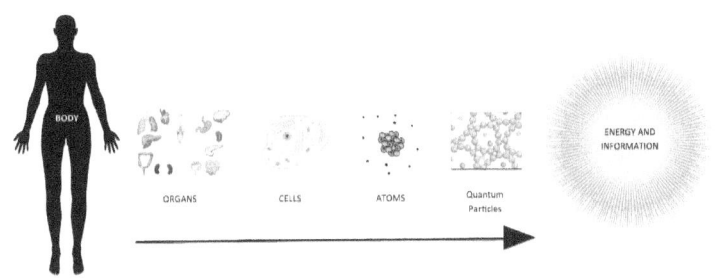

**We are Energy and Information.
Energy and Information is the Source of all Matter.**

Truth of the Matter is, you are not matter at all. At the heart of all matter, you are not a body, you are Spirit and Soul. You are a piece of Source Energy (God). You are Spirit and Soul expressing and experiencing a physical reality in a human form.

I always had a spiritual "knowing" that I was a spirit having a physical experience and not a physical being having a spiritual experience, but I really didn't know what that meant from a scientific perspective. By researching quantum physics and mentally breaking the physical body down into the smallest unit of measurement, I helped my human mind have a deeper understanding of the relationship between energy, matter, and my physical world.

Our entire reality and physical world is created and manifests itself from energy and information. Without Source Energy and information nothing would exist in the physical world. Our physical world is not solid matter. It is flowing fluid energy. This is a difficult concept for the human mind to comprehend and understand. The human mind thinks it is only matter, just as it thinks you are only your physical body, but the truth is your physical reality is an integrated, energetic exchange among your body, mind, and spirit.

This may be a little mind-blowing to think about. Just let this concept rest in your heart and feel the truth within it. Let the truth sink into you so you can work with it later. It is quite fascinating how science and spirituality are merging together as one pointing to the truth of who we are as an integrated energetic whole.

Much of the world's pain and suffering is caused from the concept that thinks the physical world is the only reality. The majority of the world thinks and lives as if they are only a physical body. When the body dies, they die with it. That is why we fight and struggle so hard to preserve the body. We fight for the body's survival because we fear if our body dies, we die. This, of course, is not true either. Energy cannot die, it can only transform. Your essence cannot die, you will simply transform. Your essence and truth of who you are will always exist. It is eternal, as are you.

Let the eternal truth of who you are rest in your heart as well. It will ease the fear of death and allow you to fully live. Come to realize that the truth of who you are does not depend upon your body, exterior conditions, circumstances, appearances, intelligence, or status. You are perfect and precious just as you are. It is your human mind that thinks and judges life as "not perfect", "not worthy," or "not enough." Stop judging your worth or value on your exterior world or circumstance. You are already priceless and you are so much more than your human mind thinks you are. You are so much more than your body.

When you are able to let go of your human mind's concept that you are *only* your body, you expand your awareness to who you truly are as spirit and a Soul. Spirit is perfect source energy and your Soul is an aspect of perfect creation. You have the choice to free your human mind from its limited capacity and choose to live from your Divine Mind with unlimited and eternal capacity.

If you continue to think you are only your body from your human mind's perspective, you will limit your ability to heal and restore your health and life. You will limit life itself. Release your attachment to your body and the world around you and you will break free from your human mind, its judgments and its limited thinking. This is the freedom and gift that is available to all of us when we connect to and integrate who we really are as spirit and Soul. Through this connection, your body will follow your Divine Mind and you will live in the fullness that already exists within you.

So, if you are not your body, why do you have a physical body? Let's look at your body's purpose in this physical world. Your body is an extension of your Soul and it provides a way for your Soul to have experiences in a physical world. Your Soul cannot have a physical experience without your body because your Soul is energy. It needs a physical tool (your body) to experience life in a physical world. You need your body to move, touch, see, feel, hear, and interact with your external world. The body is designed to help you experience the world through your senses. The body can and will deliver important messages to you if you learn to understand, feel, and connect to these messages. It is important to allow your physical body to protect and sustain you. Your body and Soul are intricately connected and they need each other to experience the fullness that this physical life can offer. Your Soul craves and desires this human-life experience. Your human life is precious and valuable to your Soul.

The purpose of your physical experience (human life) is for your Soul's growth and evolution. The physical world is a playground for the Soul to have a physical experience to learn, grow, and evolve. This is your Soul's purpose. This is the purpose of Life itself. Everything in your life is designed to help you reconnect to you, your Soul, and to spirit so that you can live life from the fullest expression of you. This fullest expression of you not only includes the *physical* you, but the *Divine* you as well.

It is important to understand this concept if you are going to use all your capacities to heal. When you tap into the Divine energy, information, knowledge, and wisdom of the Universe (God) you are able to heal and restore your life through a higher and broader capacity than the physical world can offer you. Your Divine energy and information transcend physical laws in life because they are directly responsible for creating your physical body and your physical reality, not the other way around.

This is one of the problems with our current medical system and treatment philosophy. Our current medical system relies on a biochemical and biophysical philosophy when treating physical illness and disease. It tries to use matter to change and heal matter. Our current system does not address the deeper energetic patterns and internal causes of disease within the body.

While using outside resources as tools to assist your body in the healing process may be an important part of your healing process, these resources do not address the underlying internal cause associated with the energy and information systems within the body.

Remember, the heart of all matter is energy and information. If you only use outside resources (physical matter) in an attempt to heal your body, you will be missing the most important piece of the healing puzzle. You must address and heal your inner energetic world if you want to fully heal your body and your life.

Your inner energetic world consists of thoughts, emotions, feelings, perceptions, past programs, consciousness, personality, beliefs, energetic expressions, and Soul "contracts." You cannot fix or shift your inner energetic world through using exterior things and resources. You must go within and begin to heal the energetic distortions within you. You cannot fix, change, or heal your "Inner World" by changing your "Outer World." There is no perfect drug, surgery, treatment, diet, detox program, supplement, job, relationship, car, or home that can heal your inner world. All health and healing starts and stays within you. Once you begin to change your inner world, you will naturally gravitate toward outer-world resources, people, places, and activities that are more aligned with joy, peace, freedom, abundance, and your life's purpose, thus your healthiest self. See **Diagram B.**

Diagram B

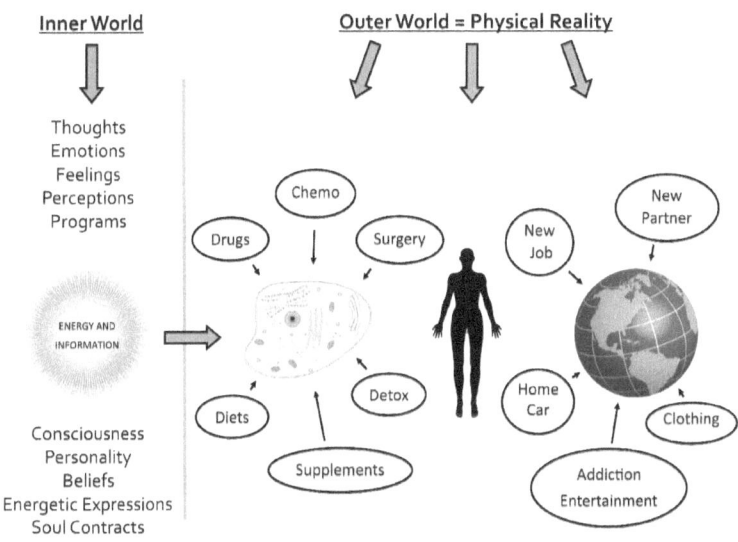

Perfect Source Energy and the Veil of Illusion

Before the Big Bang, all energy and matter was concentrated in the size of a pea. After the explosion and expansion of matter, energetic connections between everything still remained. This connective network that is everything and connects everything, sometimes called Dark Matter, is Source Energy. Source Energy knows all, sees all, and is all. It is eternal and has always been, is now and will forever be. Nothing has existed, exists now, or will exist in the future without Source Energy giving it life.

Source Energy is the "heart" of all matter. Source Energy is your Life Force. Source Energy is within you and all around you. All matter is an energetic expression of Source Energy. Source Energy communicates with everything inside and outside of you. It is universal and connects with all things because it is within all things. Source Energy is all. **See Diagram C.**

Diagram C

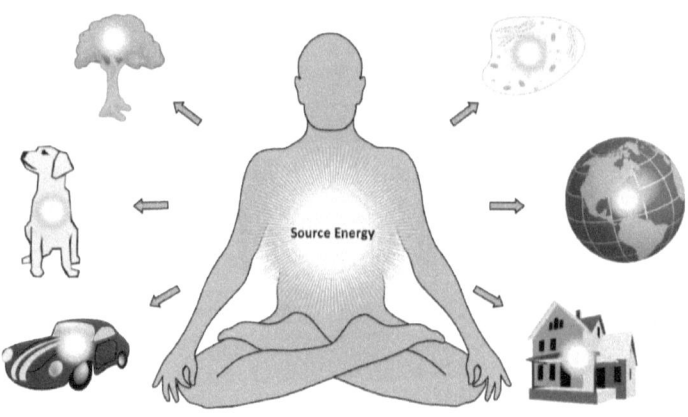

Source Energy is in You and All Around You
Source Energy is the "Heart" of all Matter

Nothing Would Exist in this Reality without Source Energy
All Matter is an Energetic Expression of Source Energy

Source Energy gives life and form to everything in this physical world. Nothing would exist without Source Energy. You are a piece of Source Energy (God). This piece is your Soul. God created your Soul in God's perfect image; because you are a part of God and created in God's image, your Soul has all the attributes of your creator as a piece of this energy source. Source Energy along with your Soul are the parts of you that intimately know you, see you, and understand all that you need to heal and restore your life.

Source Energy is perfect and pure. Source Energy has the capacity to instantly heal your physical body, if you are able to open the door, clear your mind, and accept all that Source Energy can provide you. The only thing that stands between you, Source Energy, and healing is the Veil of Illusion you create within your internal world.

Your human mind creates a Veil of Illusion between your Source Energy and your outer world through its conscious and unconscious thoughts, beliefs, perceptions, past patterns, personalities, and past programming. Your Veil of Illusion distorts the energetic information flowing to you and energetic information flowing out through you. Your Veil of Illusion causes dysfunction and distortion in the energetic information that forms your body and your physical world. See **Diagram D.**

Diagram D

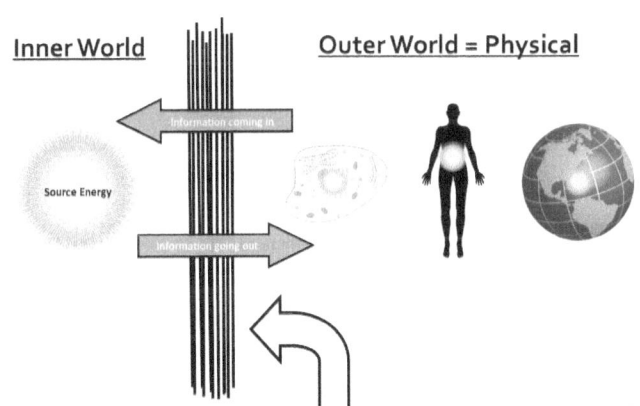

The "Veil of Illusion" your human mind creates is the main cause of your mental, emotional, and physical challenges. This veil can cause illness, disease, pain, suffering, loneliness, guilt, shame, limitation, fear, lack, and a host of other human conditions and experiences. The Veil of Illusion is programmed information. It is mostly created by your human mind's thoughts, perceptions, beliefs, and truths. Each line represents a single aspect of who you think you are, not necessarily who you really are as Source Energy. Your Veil of Illusion can be very thick or thin depending on how many thoughts, perceptions, beliefs, and truths you carry within your energetic field. All information you send to your outer world and any information you receive from your outer world must pass through your Veil of Illusion. The Veil of Illusion acts as a filter and dictates how you create, perceive, and experience your life.

The human mind has a plethora of conscious and unconscious thoughts, concepts, and perceptions, past patterns, and past programming that create a filter of additional information to the flow of perfect Source Energy into your outer world. Your outer world receives this information (combination of Source Energy and your Veil of Illusion) and manifests matter from the information it is provided. If there is distorted information within your Veil of Illusion, your physical body and your physical world will reflect the distorted information. Everything you see, hear, touch, taste, and perceive from your physical world also passes through your Veil of Illusion. How you perceive and experience your world is directly influenced by the information you carry in your Veil of Illusion.

Unwinding and reprogramming the human mind's conscious and unconscious thoughts, concepts, perceptions, past patterns, beliefs, personalities, and past programming is a crucial part of the healing process. When you dissolve and release the patterns imbedded in your human mind and connect and align with your Divine Mind within Source Energy you begin to heal and restore your life. You already have what you need to heal within you. You just need to access it and learn how to use it.

So, how do you access and use Source Energy to heal your outer world? Gaining access and using Source Energy can radically change your health and your life. Source Energy and information is the key to creation. You play a part in this creation process through your inner thoughts and feelings. Your inner thoughts and feelings combine together to form what I call an "energetic expression" that communicates (sends energy and information) to your outer world. Your outer world receives this energetic message and responds accordingly.

Your energetic expressions act as energetic magnets that draw to you what you send out into the world. This is the Universal Law of Attraction. Like attracts Like. The physical world is created and experienced through your thoughts, combined with your feelings, which create an energetic expression. This energetic expression is the creative energy that manifests your physical world and your perceived reality.

Though the physical world seems real and solid to your human mind, it is entirely created by energy and information, which is not solid. It constantly changes and flows with the creative process and your energetic expression that you send out to the world. Your human mind is designed to think that the physical world is real, so you can fully experience life in a physical world. But your physical reality is much more fluid than your human mind can comprehend. Your human mind is not designed to comprehend the complexities of the Universe because it is programmed to help your body survive in a physical world. You will never understand the mysteries of the Universe through your human mind. These mysteries can only be experienced through life itself. That's why your physical life is so valuable to your Soul.

Your conscious and unconscious thoughts and feelings, as well as your Soul's desires, create your physical life experience. You play an important role in creating as well as experiencing everything in your physical world. The physical world is something you may think is real, but in reality, your physical world is a created energetic experience. That's a little mind-blowing isn't it?

The Thinking-Feeling Circuit

As we discovered earlier, when you break your body down into the smallest units, there is only energy and information. The heart of this energy and information is Source Energy. Source Energy is the Source of all creation. Source Energy is within you and all around you. This means you have the ability to communicate with everything within you and all around you.

This is what Christ meant when he said the Kingdom of Heaven is within you. This is why all of your answers are found within you. This is why reconnecting to your Divine Self is so important to heal and restore your life. Everything you have ever needed is within you, but you have been seeking for answers outside of yourself because that is who you think you are from your human mind's perception. You have disconnected from your true essence (Source and Soul) and have put your faith in resources outside of yourself that don't have all the answers.

So, how do you connect to Source Energy and co-create your physical reality? This is where it gets really magical and fun. You co-create your reality from the energetic expression you create from within. It is this energetic expression that sends a signal to the world to manifest your physical reality. Whatever energetic expression you carry within your body will manifest and attract the same expression and experience in your physical world. It is how your inner world creates your outer reality. Your outer reality is your physical body and your physical world.

Your energetic expression is a combination of your thoughts (created in your mind) and your feelings (felt through your body). Thoughts are the language of your mind and feelings are the language of your body. They are intricately connected to each other.

Every thought in your mind sends a signal to your body that creates a feeling associated with your thought. This feeling sends a message back to the mind, which in turn creates a new thought, which creates a new feeling which creates a new thought. This happens over and over, creating a neurological thinking-and-feeling circuit between the mind and body and the body and mind. This thinking-feeling circuit between your mind (thoughts) and your body (feelings) creates an internal energetic expression of thoughts and feelings. This energetic expression is a combination of your inner thoughts and feelings, which eventually becomes your belief systems. See **Diagram E.**

Diagram E

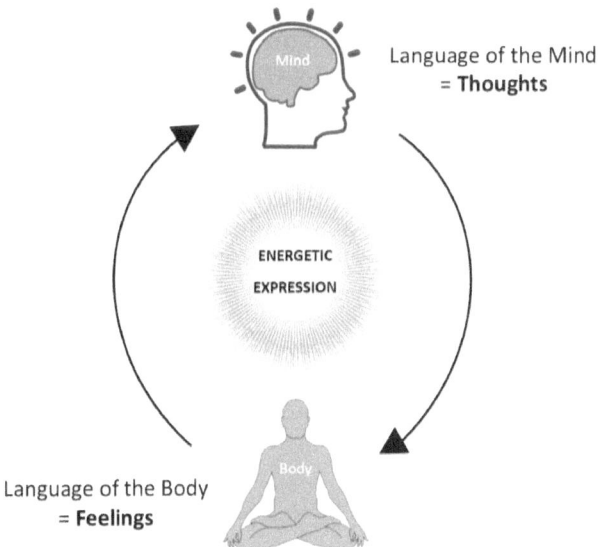

Linking your thoughts and feelings is done through your heart center. Your heart integrates your thoughts and feelings into an "energetic expression." Your heart has the ability to send this energetic expression out to your world and receive/interpret energetic signals coming back to you. You send and receive signals to and from your physical reality through your heart center. Your heart center is also the link between your spiritual and physical worlds.

Your heart sends and receives energetic information. Energetic information is the language of the Universe. It is how you communicate with the Universe. The combination of your thoughts and feelings create an internal energetic expression. This inner energetic expression communicates your message to your outer world -- your physical reality -- and your outer world responds by physically manifesting the message you just sent. Every energetic expression you create and carry on within you is the message you send to the Universe. Whether you know it or not, you are constantly creating and interacting with the world within you and the world around you. Your energetic expression is your prayer (request) to the Universe. You can either consciously create or unconsciously create. Most of us are unconsciously creating and we wonder why things happen in our lives. We become a victim of life rather than a Master of life.

The key is to bring unconscious patterns into conscious awareness and start creating from your conscious Divine Mind, rather than your unconscious human mind. You can create and experience your life through your human mind or your Divine Mind. The choice is entirely yours; however, your experience and what you manifest in your outer world will be entirely different depending on which mind you are creating from.

Are You Creating from Your Human Mind or Your Divine Mind?

Are you creating and perceiving your reality through your human mind or are you creating and perceiving your reality through your Divine Mind? Your physical reality is directly created from one mind or the other mind. Most people are unconsciously creating from their human mind.

Human thinking and feeling circuits can be neurologically programmed into your body by parents, teachers, culture, media, etc. The thoughts and feelings you experience in your past become hard-wired neurological programs within your body. These programs then begin to work unconsciously, and your body begins to run your mind because it is hard-wired to do so. Science has shown that 95% of our lives are running with unconscious patterns and programs formed from past experiences. We live so unconsciously that our past is dictating our present and future and we don't even realize it. It isn't until we can recognize and break this cycle that we can free our mind and choose something else. To break these patterns, you need to unwind the unconscious patterns and programs of the human mind and choose to connect, lead, and live with your Divine Mind.

When you lead with your Divine Mind, you shift from unconscious thinking to conscious Divine knowing and become a co-creator with God and the Universe itself. This is when life becomes magical and unlimited, because you are working with energy and information that transcend physical laws. You are working with God. This is the space of miracles and you become and create as one with God and through God instead of living separate from God.

Imagine how your life could change if you co-created your life with and through the Creator. You could move mountains as a co-creator with God because God is everything. God has access to every atom in the physical reality. But you could only move mountains if you are able to disconnect from the patterns and programs running through your human mind that inhibit your ability to fully connect to God and your Divine Mind. Letting go and surrendering to your Divine Mind is one of the biggest challenges in recreating and healing your body and your life.

Most of us have been so programmed with unconscious patterns that we know only how to operate and live life through the human mind, and do not know how to live with our Divine Mind. We feel safe in our unconscious programs and patterns. However, it's these unconscious patterns and programs that keep us stuck in our own misery, pain, and suffering. We continue to create and experience life in our own misery because we are afraid to let go of our own ideas, thoughts, and perceptions. We continue to perceive and create the world through our own eyes instead of the Divine eyes of wisdom, knowledge, and creation.

The human mind is limited. It struggles, it thinks it knows, but it does not know. It is separate from your true self and God, so it does not have access to the knowledge of the Universe. It does not know how to fully heal and live life. It only knows what it knows through your past experiences and perspectives. It only knows how to create and protect itself from the past and has a difficult time creating a new future because it lives in fear and limitation. Therefore, you create in fear and limitation. You struggle because it struggles.

Your Soul is calling you back to your Divine Mind because it wants to learn, grow, and evolve into more of who you really are. Your Soul is calling you to open your heart and mind to new and expanded ways of being and living. It is calling you home through silent whispers and messages that only your heart and Divine Mind can hear, understand, and answer.

Connecting to the Stillness Within

Unfortunately, we are so busy wrapped up in our own minds and our own understanding that we miss the subtle calls from our Soul and continue to survive instead of thriving in our lives. We live wrapped up in our own truths instead of the eternal truth of who we really are as a spirit and Soul, one connected to and with God.

Your human truths and concepts will limit your life experience and keep you stuck in your past. Your truths, concepts, and perceptions are created by your human mind and are not the whole truth or real truth of who you really are. This concept won't make sense to your human mind, which will fight and argue with you every time you try to expand your truth.

The only way to expand into the whole truth is to lose your mind. You have to let go of everything you thought you knew so that you can grow into everything there is to know. It is not through your own understanding that you understand but through Divine Wisdom that you can understand all and have access to all there is. Your Divine Mind will help you know more, experience more, love more, and be more. This is just one of the many mysteries of life.

It is only through connecting to your Divine Mind that you will find the answers you are looking for. Ask and you shall receive, seek and you will find, give and it will be given unto you. When you only look outside of yourself to find answers, you will ask and never receive, seek and never find, give and nothing will be given in return. If you want answers to any of your problems, you must go within.

The only way to hear the answer is though the inner stillness of your mind and being. You must calm your human mind and access the stillness within your being. It is in the *stillness* that you will find the fullness of life. It is also why the still, calm, soft voice is your guide. *Be still and know that I am God.* (Psalm 46:10)

God (Source Energy) rests in the stillness of your being. God lives with you and is in you. God has and will always be with you, but it is your choice to connect with God or not. Settle your human mind and connect to the stillness of God. Be patient. God will answer. Keep asking in stillness, rest in this stillness and God will answer. Quieting your mind and connecting to your inner stillness is a spiritual practice, and yes, it takes patience, but keep practicing and asking. God will answer.

God answers in many ways. Some of you will hear a voice or a subtle "knowing" within yourself, as I did, in your heart and Soul. Sometimes it is very clear and sometimes it is barely evident. Sometimes it speaks through the deceased, guides, angels, or the Holy Spirit. Sometimes it speaks through animals, other people, signs, or events. Once you ask, God will find the fastest and most relevant way to answer.

Once God answers, trust the message you receive, even if it doesn't make sense to your human mind. The message from the stillness of your heart will always lead you in the right direction for your Soul's growth and inner healing. This stillness is the space of healing presence. It knows you and knows exactly how to heal you.

Listen and trust Its guidance, knowing that your human mind will try to talk you out of it. The human mind does not always like and want what your Soul is calling for. Your human mind is scared and wants to maintain control. Acknowledge your human mind and acknowledge all the fears it tells you, but do not let your fears consume you. Let your mind know it is safe and is in good hands.

Listen to your heart and move forward with inspired (spirit within) action. Inspired action is created from your Divine Mind (thoughts) and your Divine body (feelings) which create a Divine energetic expression (in your heart). This Divine energetic expression inspires you to take Divine action in your world. When your Divine Mind, Heart, and Body (thoughts, actions, and feelings) are in alignment with each other, you create a powerful state of being that attracts your best and most joyful reality.

The only difference in creating what you want rather than what you don't want is your ability to create through your Divine Mind/Feelings rather than your human mind/feelings. You have the choice to create from one or the other. From which thoughts and feelings are you currently creating your reality? As your mind thinks, your body (and outer world) will follow. The following diagrams will give you examples

LIVING PROOF

of Divine Mind (thoughts) and Feelings vs. human mind (thoughts) and feelings. **Diagrams F and G.**

Diagram F

Diagram G

Your thoughts and feelings are powerful tools. It is important to be aware of them and how they play a part in creating and experiencing your world. You have the power to choose your thoughts and feelings once you become aware of them. Choose wisely. You will either live in the prison of your human mind or you can choose to be master over it by living from your Divine Mind. The choice is entirely yours. Choose to be a conscious creator with your Divine Mind and your mind will work for you. Choose to be an unconscious creator and your human mind will rule over you.

6
CREATING AN ENERGETIC EXPRESSION AND HEALING WITH INSPIRED ACTION

Divine as My Guide

I knew I needed to move forward and trust the Divine wisdom and guidance within me. I made the decision to follow my heart and chose to heal through alternative methods. I was finally ready, willing, and able to let go of my own human mind and surrender to my Divine Mind. This was a big step.

I chose to let go of my human mind and follow my heart into the unknown. This choice felt like an insurmountable leap of faith, but I knew I had to let go and trust. So, I closed my eyes, took a deep breath and I jumped. I put my physical life and destiny into the hands of God, knowing I personally had no clue what I was doing or how I was going to do it. I just jumped.

This is actually good news. You don't have to know how to heal in order to heal, but your human mind will think it does. Your human mind wants to figure out a plan before it moves forward. Your human mind does not like the unknown, because the unknown is scary and not safe. Your human mind can and will block you from moving forward. The human mind can and will block you from healing. However, with awareness and faith, you can move through your mind's fears and move forward with Divine trust and understanding. You do not need to have a human understanding of how every detail is going to work. In fact, it will work to your benefit it you do not fully understand the process.

Blind faith is a powerful tool, but very few choose to experience it. I'm Living Proof that blind faith has powerful potential. I had no idea how I would heal, I simply surrendered and trusted the One that did know. Here's how I jumped and put blind faith into action.

"OK, God, where do I start?" I asked.

"You already started," God replied. "You opened your heart and mind and allowed Me to be with you to guide you and to love you. Now you need to trust Me and follow the guidance you will receive. I will bring everything into your life you will need to heal your body and restore your life. Allow these things, people, and opportunities to come into your life. They serve a very specific purpose.

"Open your heart and mind to the messages they will deliver to you. Do not question them with your own mind. Take them into your heart and I will answer you. 'Love' will answer you and be your guide.

"Trust Me and trust your Divine intuition. We will lead you on your path and give you everything you need to heal, learn, and grow. Keep an open mind and follow your heart.

"Follow *love* and *peace* and recognize *fear* when it surfaces. *Love* and *fear* will direct and guide you to your answers. Use them as tools in your journey. When fear surfaces, acknowledge it, allow it to be with you and sense why it is there. Fear will surface to either guide you away from harm, or it will surface as a part of you that needs to be healed with love.

"Either way, allow fear to be with you, but not consume you. Listen to its message and follow its direction. If fear surfaces as a part that needs to be healed, heal it with love and acceptance. Love will heal fear and will guide you on your healing path. Always make your decisions in the state of *love*, not *fear*.

"Love will show you the way. I love you, and I will show you the way. I am always with you. Connect to love and you will connect to Me. Now, are you ready for your next step? I'd like to ask you a question."

"OK," I said, "I'm here and I'm listening."

"What is it that you really want to experience?" God asked.

"Well," I said, "I want to heal my body and restore my life. I want to fully live again."

"OK," God replied, "What does that look like to you? What does that feel like to you? Visualize and create an image in your mind. What does healing and restoring your life look and feel like to you?"

I took a deep breath and began to visualize what "vibrant health" and "fully living" looked and felt like. "Vibrant health" and "fully living" is want I wanted to experience, so I needed to create this experience within my mind. My body does not know the difference between an outer physical experience and a created experience within my mind through visualization.

I began to visualize living in a state of "vibrant health" and "fully living." I saw myself smiling and happy. I saw my body strong and vibrant. I saw myself laughing with my kids and meeting new friends. My physical body was glowing with radiance. My skin was glowing with life. I was happy and fully living every moment.

I enjoyed running and playing. I screamed with laughter. I loved to move, jump, and skip. I felt like a child again, free and playful, uninhibited and exuberant. I saw myself running through open fields, full of fragrant flowers glistening with dew. A sweet fragrance filled the air, like fresh spring buds after a gentle rain. I reached down and touched their delicate petals. A drop of dew rested on my fingers; it felt like a tender kiss from heaven's gate.

I sat on the top of the ridge and looked into the sunset. The sky filled with golden rose light and engulfed me in sweet sensuous love. I felt the warmth of the sun on the horizon as it glimmered and glowed. The sun's affectionate rays filled my entire body with radiant love. I could finally breathe again; a peace beyond human understanding settled in me as the sun gently met and blended into the horizon.

My husband sat by my side. There was no need to talk, we just sat with each other in silence knowing how much we loved, cared, and honored each other. No words were necessary. Life was simple and pure. I enjoyed the moment of just being.

I felt the peace and love and comfort of home, simply being one with myself and my surroundings. There was nothing I needed to do or have or want. I was simply happy and content being me. I was completely fulfilled in the moment and the expression of now. I was completely filled with life, love, and happiness. I became one with all there is. I lost myself in this moment. I lost track of time and didn't care. Time didn't matter, nor did it exist. I could have stayed there forever.

As I came back to my physical reality, God said, "Now you know what life is like fully alive. You now know what it is like to live healthy and whole as one with yourself and one with Me. This is what you really want, isn't it?"

"Yes!" I exclaimed. "There is nothing I want more than to live life and feel life in this expression. It was amazing!"

God said, "Yes, Mary, what you just experienced is life. You can live this life in this physical expression you just experienced in your mind. You create your reality by visualizing it in your mind and then feeling it within your body. Carry this energetic expression with you in your daily life and it will become you.

"Think, feel, and be healthy and whole and healthy and whole will become you. It is in this physical expression and Divine alignment that you will fully heal and live. It is this expression of your being that directs life itself.

"Be the energetic expression of what you want, not what you don't. It is this energetic expression that will heal and restore your life. Carry this energetic expression with you throughout each moment of every day and it will draw to you all that you desire. Be the energetic expression of health and life, and health and life will become you.

"I will be with you. I am always with you and I will draw all that you need into your life, as long as you continue to carry Me with you. You always have the choice. You choose whether you are connected to Me or not. It is up to you to keep the door open between us.

"You can choose to live with Me and through Me, loving and experiencing life through My eyes, My heart and My wisdom, or you can choose to live by yourself, separate from Me, struggling and fighting your existence.

"Both experiences will serve you, but one will be filled with love and connection while the other will be filled with fear and disconnection. You get to choose. I am always here with you and for you."

God then became silent and allowed me to process what I just seen, heard, and experienced within my own mind and within my own being. I wanted to fully live, and I wanted to live through the expression of God and the experience I just visualized. It was so magical and wonderful. I wondered if life could really be like that. Could I experience what I just visualized in my current physical reality?

For the time being, cancer completely left my mind, as well as all the worry, anxiety, and fear. I was taken to a place of pure bliss, a place where cancer didn't exist, a place beyond the human body, human thoughts, human emotions, and physical world. Is this a way to heal cancer? To enter a state of consciousness where cancer cannot and does not exist, where the physical world and physical limitations do not exist, and then draw that new expression into this physical reality through an energetic expression and state of being? This concept was too expansive for my human mind to relate to, so my human mind remained quiet and still.

I simply sat with my new energetic expression and allowed it to sit with me and become me. I silently pondered these questions, "How can I be an energetic expression of life and health? What would that look like and feel like in my current physical reality?" While I didn't have all the answers, I kept enquiring and feeling into the question, "How can I be the perfect expression of life and health?" Even though I had no clear idea, I knew that I was going to find out. I could feel an energy inside of me awaken and I allowed it to stir, move, and run free within me. I was open to learn and discover what this meant for me.

I knew God was with me, loved me and was holding me close in this journey. All I had to do was open and receive the messages and follow through with inspired action as I was instructed. That was my lesson for that day.

I knew more lessons were going to follow if I simply kept following God. I decided to retire for the evening and allow this new information to sit and process with me through the night. Tomorrow would be a new day. Tomorrow I would revisit this question and start living my life with a new outlook and a new energetic expression of life and health.

Healing through Energetic Expression and Inspired Action

The next morning, I woke up and immediately revisited several questions in my mind, "What does the energetic expression of health and life look and feel like to me? What will I be and do each day to hold that energetic expression with me? What does life look like and feel like as a whole, healthy, human being, fully living and fully alive?"

I sat on the edge of my bed, silenced my mind, and began to visualize what my life looks like healthy and whole. Here's what I experienced and saw:

I saw myself eating whole and natural foods. I ate foods provided by God in their natural form, not processed or genetically manipulated by man. Everything I eat and put into my body is an act of love to heal, nourish, and restore my body. Food is my medicine.

Everything I eat will be in an effort to support my body and will not cause a toxic burden. My body needs to reserve energy to heal. I don't want to burden my body with having to detox chemicals and pesticides. I eat living foods grown from the earth. Foods that had been nourished from the sun and soil by Mother Earth Herself. These foods nourish me, too.

I see myself walking and breathing in fresh air. I walk bare-foot; my feet touch the ground. I feel an intimate connection to the earth. I feel Her loving support. I look around and feel the energy of nature surrounding and holding me. Everywhere I look, God is all around me. I breathe in God's love through fresh air. This breath of life brings life into me and sustains me. I feel the sun on my face and God's warmth fills, nourishes, and heals me. I am happy and content.

I see myself calm in the midst of stress and work. I am at peace. I see myself making conscious choices to be peaceful and I do not engage in arguments. I am able to step away from heated situations, maintain my composer, and respond rather than react to situations. I am peace in the middle of chaos. I have the power to choose how I want to be in relation to any person, place, or thing that shows up in my life.

I began to feel more deeply into this new life and this new state of being. I am at peace. I am peace. I feel deeply loved. I feel supported. I feel empowered and strong. I sit with these feelings. I breathe them in and allow them to take over my entire body. I am alive. I am whole and I am complete. I am healthy. I am strong.

This is the state of being from which I will live my life. No matter what was going on around me, I chose to think, feel, and *be* this way. I have the power to consciously choose, live, and be in a grounded state of love, peace, harmony, compassion, and healing presence. This is a healing state of being. This is how I choose to live.

I continued to feel and breathe into this state of being, so it would become me. I knew through conscious effort I could choose to revisit and become this state whenever I wanted. It felt so good and it felt so alive. Nothing else mattered in this state, not even cancer.

I knew I needed and wanted to bring this energetic state into my physical world and so I made a commitment to myself to be this state of being as much as possible. I needed to learn how to become this state of being every day and integrate it into my life. If I could be health and life, health and life could become me.

I began each morning with a visualization and experience of perfect health and my perfect life. I consciously and intentionally became that state of being each day. In all that I did, saw, heard, touched, and experienced, I engaged in an act and ritual of love and support. When I went to the store, I purposely chose foods that would nourish and support my body. I intentionally prepared every meal as an act of love for myself. Before every meal, I visualized the food nourishing my body to heal. My real-estate job became an act of love so that I could afford high-quality food and supplements. When interacting with my family or any relationship, I chose to interact with love, kindness, and peace. I became the living expression of love, nourishment and support in all areas of my life. My life became a living intention of love, peace, health, and healing. Every evening, I revisited my day and bathed myself in gratitude for life and for one more day to live in the expression of health, healing, and restoration.

All of my actions were inspired by this new energetic expression. I began to see my life shift and change before my eyes and I began to experience health and life in my physical world and my physical body. I began to heal from the inside out. My body, mind, spirit, and Soul became fully aligned with each other and created what I truly desired because I became what I truly desired.

When you are fully aligned and in total coherence with all parts and aspects of who you are, and when you are in full alignment with God and the Universe, miracles simply happen, and life simply happens for you. By living in the state of perfect health, perfect health became me. This is how I energetically and physically healed my body. Your body heals when it receives the energetic information to do so through your interior state of being in complete and full alignment with Divine guidance, love and support.

Creating Your Own Energetic Expression.

My energetic expression and state of being co-created a state of health within my physical body. Creating your own energetic expression will have a huge impact on your physical reality as well.

The first step in creating your own energetic expression is to get very clear on what you really want. What do you want in your life, your health, your relationships, your work, your finances? What is it that you really want? Remember that life brings you want you think, feel, and are. Your state of being is the energetic signal and request you send to the world. When creating an energetic expression or state of being, create what you really want, rather than creating what you don't want. You will create and attract into your life whatever signal you put out, so choose your thoughts and feelings carefully. They are the key to barely surviving or fully thriving in your life. In order to thrive, your energetic expression must match the energy frequencies of thriving (Divine frequencies) rather than the lower frequencies of survival (human frequencies).

Last but not least, there needs to be an alignment between your mind, body, and heart (your thoughts, feelings, and actions). When one of these three things are out of alignment, your energetic flow and signal gets distorted and sends out an incoherent signal. Your outer world receives this mixed signal and gets confused about which message to follow, so your life reflects the dysfunction.

Your first step is to get crystal-clear on the signal you want to send to your body and your physical world. This starts by setting a clear intention and aligning this intention to your Divine thoughts, feelings, and actions. In order to uncover your Divine thoughts, feelings, and actions, you need to connect and discover the deeper desires and wants from your Soul, not your human wants and needs. I've designed the following worksheet to help you create your Divine Energetic Expression and align your thoughts and feelings.

See Diagram H: Creating Your Own Energetic Expression.

Diagram H: Creating Your Own Energetic Expression

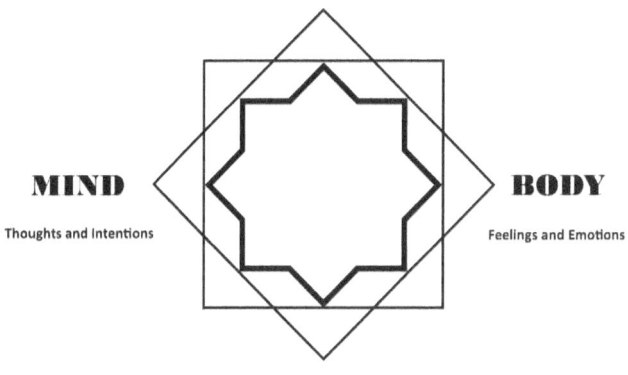

What Do You Desire?
(Thoughts and Intention)

_____
_____
_____
_____

Why?
(Your Why Should Make You Cry)

_____
_____
_____
_____

How Does It Feel?
(Divine Feelings and Emotions)

_____
_____
_____
_____
_____
_____
_____
_____

© 2018 Mary Rust, Inc.

Creating Your Own Energetic Expression Exercise: Find a time and space for yourself where you will not be distracted or disturbed. Use the Energetic Expression Worksheet and choose one area of your life you desire to shift and change. It is easier and more effective to work on one area of your life rather than multiple areas at one time so that your energy is clear and focused.

Energy directed to multiple areas gets diffused multiple times. You will be trying to manifest your outer world with diffused energy rather than focused, full, clear energy. Stay focused on one thing at a time and you will have more energy at your disposal.

Pick one area of your life you want to change. Here's a few areas to select from: health, family, career, finances, romantic relationship, spirituality, community, friendship. Choose your main focus and stick with that **one** thing until it manifests. My main focus was, of course, health.

When you have decided on your main intention, write a symbol in the star at the top of the worksheet that represents your intention. For example, if you want to work with your health, you may put an "H" in the star to represent health. If you have a heart condition, you may put a heart in the star. If you want to work on finances, put a $ in the star. Put whatever symbol resonates with you and your desired intention in your star. Whatever you put in your star will be the "heart" of your energetic expression you wish to create.

Stillness of Your Being Exercise: Now, prepare yourself for an inner journey. You will be diving into the depths of yourself through your senses, thoughts, feelings, and your inner eye. Find a comfortable, quiet location where you will not be disturbed. Sit down, close your eyes and align your spine. Take three deep breaths in. Exhale fully and release all emotions, thoughts, and voices running rampant in your mind and body. You must clear your mind and body of your own thoughts and emotions to make contact with the stillness of your being and connect with your Soul. *Be still and know that I am (you are) God.* Breathe out and let your mind and body go. Continue to breathe in and out in this manner until you are calm, peaceful, and silent.

Now breathe into the center point of your head at least 3 times, releasing any voices or thoughts with each exhale. Breathe in Divine knowledge, wisdom, and counsel. Breathe out human thoughts, chatter, fears, and anxiety. Continue to breathe until you experience a calm stillness within your mind.

Now move down to your heart center and breathe in through the center of your heart three times. As you breathe in, feel Divine energy flow into your heart center and fill your entire core with love and peace. Feel your heart expand and grow with each inhale and exhale. Do not let this energy dissipate on the exhale, but instead allow it to grow internally and stay contained within you.

Next, move down to your feeling center, the center of your belly approximately two or three inches below your belly button. Breathe into this space three times and feel your energy expand and grow with each inhale and exhale. Breathe in Divine safety, protection, and strength. Allow this energy to stay with you.

Now breathe into both your feeling center and your heart center at the same time. Do this for several breaths. When you feel they have joined and aligned, add your thought center (point in the center of your head) and breathe into all three centers at the same time. This will help to align your mind, heart, and body as you ask your Higher Self and internal guidance to lead and help you discover your deepest desires and wishes.

You will be creating a new energetic expression in alignment with the love and support of your Divine being and Divine Source. This is the unity from which you want to create and it is the unity that accesses your highest state of being and creative capacity. When you align with the Divine you are able to access energies that transcend the physical world.

You create from a level of energy and frequency you cannot connect with through the physical world alone.

Divine energies have the power to access a deeper level of healing because they understand all of who you are, why you came to this world, and what needs to heal so you can fully live your life experience and all that you desire. These energies have the power to heal you instantaneously if that will serve your highest and best purpose.

Open and allow yourself to experience and feel this energy flow to you, through you, and with you. This energy is pure love and light. This energy heals and restores your life, but it can only work through you if you ask, open your heart to receive it and allow it to flow through you.

You should be in a centered, aligned, connected, and peaceful state within the stillness and fullness of your being. It is from this state that you have access to your Divine Self. You have connected to the Stillness of Your Being. This is place where you will continue creating your Energetic Expression.

When you feel you have let go of your human mind and have opened to and aligned with the Divine Mind, ask yourself, "What do I really want? What do I really want to experience in my life in this moment? How do I align with my intention to heal my (health, relationship, career, finances (fill in the main focus that you put in your star.)"

Stay in the silence of your being. Do not let your human mind interrupt you and answer this question for you. Feel and allow the answer come to you through your heart. Your human mind is in the habit of interrupting the silent whispers from your Soul. Be aware of this. Choose to stay within your stillness and listen to your heart.

Feel and sense the answers as they come to you. Your answers may come as a picture, a sound, a color, a feeling, or words. Feel and sense the messages as they come. Do not force the messages.

If your human mind tries to enter, simply acknowledge it and ask it to step aside. You may even visualize walking your mind through a door into the next room with other human minds, so it will not be alone. Close the door and let your mind rattle in the room next door, so you can maintain your stillness in the space where you are. You will only be able to hear, feel, and receive messages while in the stillness of your being. When your mind begins to chatter, Divine messages will not be heard, felt, or sensed.

Let your mind go and stay within the stillness. This may take some time. This is a practice, but it is a practice worth perfecting. Be patient and steady. This is a skill that will come to you and come much more easily each time you choose to connect to your Divine Self.

Your Divine Self will always lead you on the path that serves your best purpose. Your Divine Self will lead you to healing and wholeness. Trust this path and continue to seek. You will find your answers. When you have received the message of what your Soul really wants, write down what you received under "What I Desire" on the Energetic Expression worksheet. Keep your answer short and simple. Your Soul's desire is short and simple. FYI, if your desire is complex or complicated, you may be communicating with your human mind rather than your Divine Mind.

Now close your eyes, take three deep breaths, get into the stillness of your being again and ask yourself, "Why do I want this? Why is it so important that I experience this event or healing in my life?" The answer to this question will stir emotions and feelings in you. Your "why" should make you cry. It should lead you to a space of deep emotion and feeling.

Keep asking yourself the question, "Why do I want this?" Go deeper into feeling the response. As each new answer flows to you, keep going deeper into your "why" until it makes you cry. Your "why that makes you cry" is rooted in deep emotions and feelings. The answers that come to you that do not have this deep emotion is not your true "why." Keep asking until you are at your deepest "why." Your deepest "why" is your

Soul's "why". Your Soul's "why" is the feeling and emotion from which you want to create your new energetic expression.

Your Soul's "why" is in alignment with the Divine Mind and Divine feelings. Divine thoughts and feelings are what you want to create your new energetic expression from because they have a deeper and stronger healing capacity than human thoughts and feelings. Do not stop asking yourself "why" until you reach your deepest emotion.

Your Divine feelings and emotions will give you the strength and passion that will lead you through the difficult times when your human mind wants to give up or take over and run the show. Your Divine "why" will help you move through fear and allow you to move forward with inspired action rather than contract in fear. Your "why" that makes you cry has a deep passion, feeling, and emotion fueling it. You must have that deep emotion to fill you, guide you, and attract what you really want in your life.

You will know you are connecting to your Soul's desires when you feel deep-seated emotions rooted in Divine feelings of unconditional love, acceptance, belonging, peace, joy, bliss, gratitude, connection, community, freedom, purpose, and fulfillment. These are the deep frequencies and energies of love, and they are powerful energies that can fully fill and restore your health and life. These are the emotions that are the deepest desires of your Soul. Nothing can totally fulfill you but these deep emotional life experiences. They are the experiences that your heart and Soul are calling for.

Now open your eyes and write down your "Why" on your Energetic Expression worksheet. Your why should make you cry.

Next, write down the deep feelings associated with your why. What is the "feeling" you really want to experience? Joy, peace, connection, belonging, freedom, unconditional love, full acceptance? What is your deepest feeling associated with what you want and why you want it? Your feelings will be your guide and tool in your physical reality to show you if you are living in the energetic expression of what you really want or what you don't. It is these deep feelings that carry the power to hold your energetic expression that you will deliver to your outer world. Your new state of being is created with these Divine feelings.

Keep your Energetic Expression worksheet close to you. Use it as a tool to remind you about your intention, your why, and what you need to "be" in order to manifest your deepest desires in your outer world. It is a powerful resource for you.

My Personal "Why" with Cancer

I want to share my personal experience of connecting to my Soul's "why" after I was diagnosed with cancer. This is how I discovered, created, and set my own healing intention and energetic expression in my real-life circumstance with cancer.

First, I asked myself what I really wanted, and allowed the answer to surface. I then asked "why" I wanted this, and I allowed each answer to surface until I received my deepest "why," my Soul's "why." Here's how it played out for me.

I began by asking myself, "Want do I want to experience in my life given my current situation?"

The answers began to surface, "I want to heal from cancer. I want the cancer gone."

Then I asked myself, "Why do I want to heal from cancer? Why do I want cancer gone? Why is having cancer gone so important to me?"

"Well," I replied, "I want to live."

"Why do I want to live?" I asked and continued to dig deeper.

"I want to live for my family, so they don't have to live without a mother. I don't want them to be without their mother."

"OK, what else?" I continued to question and go deeper, "Why do I want to live for my kids?"

I replied, "I want to experience more life with them. I want to love them and experience more time with them."

I continued to ask deeper, "Why was it important to have more time with them?"

I continued to answer, "I want to experience more of life with them and with me. I want to live for my life. I want to fully live and experience more love, more peace, more joy, and more happiness. I wanted to fully live all of my life and have more experiences."

Tears began to well up in my eyes as I internally recognized that I actually wanted to live for me, not for someone else. This was the first time I have ever wanted to live for me. In the past I have always lived my life for someone else. I wanted to make them happy, experience their joy and help them succeed. I always put myself aside for someone else's happiness, needs, and wants. I put their needs, wants and desires before my own. I rejected myself for someone else.

My Soul knew that I was rejecting myself for everyone else. My Soul was calling to be heard, loved, and accepted. For the first time I finally realized I needed to live because my life was worth living for me. I want to love life again and I want to fully live for me because I am worth it. I'm precious and valuable. I am loved and appreciated. I am finally enough!!!

Do you see how I kept asking until I reached my deepest why and desire? My true desire was not to get rid of cancer. Getting rid of cancer was what my human mind wanted. My true desire was to fully live life again in love, peace, joy, happiness (which are all Divine feelings and emotions) and I wanted to live it for me. I wanted to experience more joy, more peace, and more happiness for me. I wanted and needed to be loved, valued, and appreciated by and for me.

My Soul was calling me to acknowledge who I really am and live for my purpose and my life experience. My Soul was trying to save me from living someone else's life and living from superficial human desires that led to discontentment, fear, anxiety, disease, suffering, and disillusionment. My Soul wanted to experience the higher frequencies of joy, happiness, peace, unconditional love, connection, bliss, purpose, and fulfillment. My Soul wanted to fully live, finally live, and for the first time, live for me. My Soul needed me and I needed my Soul. I could no longer abandon myself.

At first, my answers were directed toward my children and their needs. I wanted to live for them more than I wanted to live for myself. I needed to bring my intention back to myself, not from an egotistical point of view, but from a place of unconditional love and acceptance. I needed to love and accept myself completely and fully before I could fully love them or my life.

All healing journeys and intentions must be for your own growth and healing first. True happiness, joy, contentment, peace, bliss, and unconditional love must come from you, for you. You are your answer to everything in your life. Your Soul knows this and will guide and direct you to you.

This is how you create your new energetic expression that aligns with your Higher Self. Keep asking yourself what it is you really want until you get to the heart of your desires. Health and healing start and stay with you. This is your journey; no one else can choose it for you or do it for you. You are your answer.

Set your healing intention in what you want, not what you don't want. Continue to ask your Soul "why" you want this intention until you get to your deepest "why." Your deepest "why" will make you cry. Don't stop asking until you cry.

Your Soul's "why" will be for you, and you alone. "Whys" created for and focused on outside things, people, places, or situations are not your Soul's "why." Once you reach your Soul's "why," you will create your state of being from this place.

Your Soul's why will direct your thoughts, feelings and inspired actions that have the highest energetic frequency to heal and restore your health and life. This is the state of being you will begin to live your life from. You will create your intention from a high-energy emotion and feeling that is full of life, not scared of death.

Where your mind goes your body will follow. They are intimately connected. Your Divine thoughts and feelings will create your new energetic expression and you will live from this state of being as you live your physical life. From this state of being, your body has no choice but to follow. You must become your new reality as a state of being, before your new reality will come to you.

Healing Through Inspired Action

Now that you have discovered and created your new Energetic Expression, you can connect to this expression to create and visualize your daily inspired action. Start by closing your eyes, take a few deep breaths and *feel* into your new expression. Feel into the Divine Feelings you just uncovered in the Energetic Expression Exercise. How does it feel to be in love, in hope, in happiness, in joy, in freedom in your new life experience? Feel that emotion and breathe it in.

Place your left hand on your feeling center (center of your belly, two or three inches below your belly button) and breathe in that emotion through your feeling center three times. Place your right hand on your heart center and breathe in that emotion through your heart center three times. Keep your left hand on your feeling center, your right hand on your heart center and breathe that emotion in through your mind (middle point in your head). Focus your attention back to your heart and breathe it in. Drop down to your feeling center and breathe it in. Repeat this breathing pattern several times until you can breathe through all three centers at once continuing to feel your Divine Feelings.

Now embody and align your new energetic expression through your entire being by breathing the feeling in through your entire body. Feel it in each cell of your body. Let it grow and expand through your entire body. Visualize each cell glistening in gold, sparkling light throughout your body. Breathe this new life into your body, hold it and allow it to hold you.

Love and embrace this new expression with all your being. Be with it and allow it to be with you. Get very familiar and comfortable in this new feeling and energetic state. Own it and embody it. This is your new energetic state that inspires a new state of being that you are going to consciously shift into throughout your day.

Now that you are familiar and are experiencing your new energetic expression, ask the Divine wisdom within for your inspired action. Ask yourself, "What am I doing in my physical reality when I am connected to peace, love, joy, etc.? What am I physically doing and experiencing in my life? Who am I with? What does my world look like? Begin to visualize this experience in your mind as a virtual 3-D reality.

What does my work look like? How am I interacting with myself and my co-workers? If you are a stay-at-home parent, you might ask, "How am I interacting with my children? With my spouse? What kind of relationship am I experiencing in this state of being? How am I interacting with my friends? What activities are we enjoying together?"

If you want to heal your body, ask yourself, "What am I eating in order to love, nourish, and support my body? What physical activities am I doing? How much rest does my body need? What activities would love, nourish, and support my body to feel healthy and strong?"

Ask yourself the questions that connect your new energetic expression to your current life and situation. How would you like to "be" in relationship to your current reality? If your current reality is not in alignment with your new energetic expression, behave (be-have) as your new reality, *be* your new reality, in order to *have* a new reality. Visualize and experience your new physical reality within your mind that matches your energetic expression.

Once you can see and visualize your physical reality, now it's time to bring in your five senses and fully experience it. Experience this moment as if it were already yours. Make the picture you see in your mind as "real" as possible by including your senses. Experience every detail. What do you see, hear, taste, smell, sense, and touch?

Make this vision in your mind as real as possible. Your mind and your body do not know the difference between a created thought and visual experience in your mind and a thought and a physical experience from your physical world. When you create a realistic thought and experience in your mind and then experience it in your body, the body will act as though it is real and has already happened.

This is how you use your mind to create a different experience in your body and your physical world. Where you mind goes, your body will follow if you create and hold an energetic expression that the mind and body *think* and *feels* is real. The language of the mind is thought. The language of the body is feeling, the language of your outer reality is an energetic state of being, which is created through thought, feeling and action. Are you starting to connect to this concept and how all things are interconnected?

Let's connect this concept to your physical health. If you are struggling with health issues, create an energetic expression of health and healing. Align your energetic expression with what you want, rather than what you don't. Too many people focus on the illness and their desire to get rid of it. When you want to get rid of an illness, you resist it. When you resist the illness, it persists. That is not what you want. You want health, not illness.

First, consciously acknowledge, accept, and thank the illness for showing up in your life. There is always a reason an illness shows up in your life. By acknowledging and accepting it, you are acknowledging and accepting the message it came to deliver you. Give thanks for the opportunity to heal.

Next, focus on the feeling of health and healing. Focus on loving, nourishing, and restoring your body to health rather than the fear of dying or suffering in sickness. Ask yourself, "What does whole and healthy living look like in my current reality? What does it look and feel like to live in a healthy, whole body? What are you doing in this new body? What are you experiencing? How does this new body move? How does this new body feel? What activities are you able to do in this new whole body? Are you walking? Are you running? How are you walking? How are you running? Where are you walking? Are you in the mountains? Can you climb the mountain? Are you walking, running, and playing on the beach? Are you swimming in the ocean? What are you doing, loving, and experiencing?

Now that you have created a clear picture in your mind, how does it feel to be living in this new, whole, healthy body? Feel and live this experience through all of your senses as if it were your current reality. Be with this experience and allow it to become you.

Now ask, "What does it look and feel like to take care of this new body? How am I nourishing this body? What foods am I eating?" See yourself choosing foods that will love, nourish, and support this glowing, healthy, vibrant, alive body. See yourself preparing the foods as an act of love. You love to take care of your body and your body responds with love and takes care of you.

Visualize eating the foods you have prepared. How do they taste? How do they smell? How do they feel within your body? Feel the love and nourishment they provide for you. You choose to eat whole, alive foods because they love and nourish your body. They provide you with the energy you need to fully live and participate in life. These are healing, nourishing, and loving foods. Thank yourself for loving and nourishing your body in this way. Your body thanks you as well.

If you have a physical condition and need to make choices regrading treatment options, ask yourself, "What treatment plans are going to heal, restore, love, and nourish my body?" Allow the messages to come to you. Do you see a person, doctor, or friend come into your life to support you? Do you see a book or other tool come into your consciousness? What treatment, plan, program, or person is coming to you?

Sometimes Divine messages will come as symbols. Do you see a color or an object or an energetic frequency come into your vision? Do you hear a sound? Do you just sense a feeling or energy moving to and through you? Embrace and accept this information. It comes to serve and heal you. It comes to guide and to love you.

Do not judge or resist what comes to you and through you. You may not understand or comprehend the information. That is fine. Simply allow the messages to flow to you. Receive and accept them. They are working even if you do not understand them. Allow them to be with you. Trust that the perfect message is coming to you and is guiding you toward the best plan to heal and restore you. Trust their guidance. Visualize yourself participating in this treatment plan in its fullness and know that it comes to serve and heal you. There is no fear with this plan. There is only love and support.

Feel your internal guidance supporting your body to heal, whatever that looks like and feels like. It is coming to you and working for you to love and support you. Feel the love and support in your body now. Feel it healing you now. Open and allow its healing capacity to consume you. This energy has the power and potential to heal at a much deeper healing capacity than the physical world can offer you. Open and allow it to heal you. Let go and allow healing to become you.

Remember, your mind and body do not know the difference between a visual thought experience and a physical experience in your reality. Experience healing now in your mind and body and it will become you. Allow your mind and body to heal. Heal now in this moment and hold onto this experience as your physical reality. It is yours. Accept, love and honor it. Feel it. Live it. Love it. Own it. Breathe it into you and embody it. Sit in healing presence now and enjoy it.

Now thank the Divine for offering this beautiful, wonderful experience. Say these words in total and complete gratitude, "Thank you. Thank you. Thank you." Offering gratitude is your way of acknowledging that it has already happened, and it is already provided for you. Thank the Divine again and surrender your physical healing back to Divine. You are able to let go and give your body's physical healing back to the Universe because you know it is already yours. You know that healing has already happened for you, so you do not need to hold onto it. It is already yours. You are healed. You are healthy and whole, and you are able to fully live your life from that knowing.

The more you can live from the knowing that you are already healthy and whole, the more you can draw that experience into your life. Your physical reality will reflect your inner reality back to you. You feel whole, so life reflects wholeness. You feel healthy, so life is healthy. You are the energetic expression of that which you know, and your life reflects the knowing you already are.

Now place your right hand on your heart and your left hand on you feeling center (center of your belly, two or three inches below your belly button). Breathe into both of these centers to fully embody this healthy, whole energetic expression. Take three deep embodying breaths. Open your eyes and observe the world around you, knowing and feeling you still contain and hold a new inner energetic expression of health and wholeness. Take three more deep breaths as you observe your world. Look around you and observe that world. You are in this world, but not of it. Feel that you carry a new energetic expression within you that has the power to influence and change this outer world that you are observing.

Now stand up and begin to walk into your new life, carrying and holding this new expression of yourself. If you are not able to walk, visualize yourself walking into your new energetic expression. Walk and participate with life in this new state of being.

Repeat this exercise every morning and walk into your new state of being every day. Connect to the messages you receive and follow through with daily actions in alignment with your new energetic expression. Make them a part of your life, living, feeling, and being them.

Remember and remind yourself of this new expression and state of being often. Set reminders for yourself on your phone or make a habit to connect within before meals or every time you drink something. Create sticky notes and place them around your home or office to remind yourself of your intention to live with inspired action. Be creative and make this a simple, easy practice. You have the ability to revisit and hold this energy anytime you want by simply closing your eyes, placing your right hand on your heart center and your left hand on your feeling center. Take three deep breaths and embody this energy once again.

The more you practice this exercise and shift your state of consciousness, the more it becomes you and you are more easily able to live from this state of being. Match your daily actions with this energetic expression you just visualized and experienced. The more you practice shifting into this state of being and following through with inspired action, the more your physical world will become you.

Write down what you just experienced, thought, felt, and saw on the back of your Energetic Expression worksheet. Your new energetic expression and state of being will eventually become a habit and your body will become the mind and automatically create the energetic expression you desire to create and experience in this world. Your outer world begins to shift and change to match the state of being you are sending out and receiving. This is how to fully attract and manifest the life you desire and deserve. This is how to heal from the inside-out. This is how spontaneous healing and miracles happen. If they can happen for me, they can happen for you, too.

7
WORKING WITH YOUR MIND TO HEAL

Stages of the Mind Through Your Healing Process

It is important to work with your mind through your healing journey with love and compassion. Your mind will go through several stages during the healing process. It is helpful to be aware of these stages so you can recognize and move through them as you heal.

Let's start with a very basic concept: Whether you think you can heal or whether you think you can't heal, you will be right either way. This is how powerful your mind is. Not only do you get to choose your healing path, you get to choose whether healing will work for you or not. This power of choice is in your mind. Your mind will either help you through your healing process or it will hinder you from healing. It is wise to work *with* your mind, so you can move into a healing state of mind.

When working with the resistance in your mind, you will go through several stages as your mind expands its capacity to shift and flow toward your goal. It is helpful to understand these stages because I have seen people get stuck in one stage or another and never reach their full healing potential. In fact, I have seen the mind completely halt or sabotage the healing process altogether.

The first stage the mind must travel through is the initial *desire to heal*. If you do not have the desire to heal, then healing will be nearly impossible. Illness and disease comes into one's life for many reasons. One of these reasons is life transition. Illness can come into someone's life as the final stage, which allows them to transition home because it is their time to move on. They have completed their life lessons and they are ready to go home.

Transitioning home is a natural phase of life and we will all go through this life experience. It can be a peaceful, light, and gentle transition if we recognize and honor this part of life. We were never meant to stay in this body forever. Honor your life by honoring your death and welcome your transition home when it is time to do so. When you are connected to your Soul and the Divine within, you will know when it is your time to go and the process will be beautiful and peaceful. When you are at peace with death, there is no resistance to it and there is nothing to fear because you know and sense that love will carry and welcome you home.

My mother's passing was a peaceful transition home. Being with her as she passed taught me that death can be Divine. If you have a loved one who is ill, and this illness is an end-of-life transition for them, honor their life by honoring their death. Comfort and love them through this process. Your love and support will be the best gift you can give them.

Other times, an illness comes into someone's life because the conflict within them is so great they feel like they can no longer tolerate their life. They want out of this physical experience. They are sick and tired, and they have no desire to heal and continue living. This is a difficult circumstance to witness from an outside perspective, especially when you love someone. Disease and illness may come into their life as an "opting out" and it is a way to transition home. Again, the best gift you can give them is to love and support them. Your love and support may be enough to initiate an inner desire to live again. Love, support, and honor their process. It is not up to you to decide their destiny. We are all on our own journey. Allow each person to choose what they need to experience, always loving and supporting them.

In both circumstances mentioned above, their minds do not have a desire to heal. Accept and honor this choice. Love them. Going home may be in their best interest, whether you want that or not, or whether you understand that or not. There is always a higher purpose or lesson that is calling to be experienced. Let them go.

It's usually family and friends who have the hardest time with this transition. The family member or friend has the desire for them to heal, but the individual does not. This can cause a lot of pain for everyone. Trying to fight for their life only causes conflict and struggle within yourself and with them. This does not serve either one of you. Surrendering your personal desires is the highest act of love you can give yourself and them. It's not an easy thing to do, but it is the most loving and supportive thing you can do. Love them and allow them to figure out what they want to do or don't want to do.

Feel free to talk to them about it, leaving your personal desires aside. Remind them that this is their own journey and they are allowed to make their own choices. Work with your own feelings and emotions on your own time. By doing so, you can fully love and support them without your own fears getting in the way. There is nothing worse than having someone pressure you or tell you what they want you to do when you are sick. Set them and yourself free by allowing them to make their own decisions, then accept and support their decisions. This will be a gift to them.

The second stage in healing is the belief that *you can heal*. You must believe that you can heal before the body will follow that instruction. If you don't believe you can heal, then the body will receive that message and it can't, because you are telling the body that healing is not possible.

You must have hope to heal. If someone does not have hope, and they don't believe in the possibility of healing, they have already set the stage that healing is not possible for them. You must believe you can heal before you will be able to heal. You might have the desire to heal, but if you don't have hope, you will not be able to move forward.

The third stage of healing is the thought that *you are healing*. In this stage you are telling the body, "I am healing." It is a stage of action and transition. When you believe you are healing, the body receives the message it is in the process of healing. This is an active stage, and healing is actively happening within the body. Healing is moving and flowing through the body in this stage. In this third stage of healing, you have the *desire to heal*, you believe you *can heal*, and you are now in the *active process of healing*. The body is changing and transitioning from a diseased state to a whole, healthy state, but it is not fully healthy now because the mind has not gone to that thought process yet.

The third stage of healing is the state of mind that so many people get stuck in. They can get their minds into an active healing state, but they never transition to a state of mind that they are fully healed. They stay in a continual act of healing. This is a permanent mind-body circuit that can never complete the healing cycle because it stays in the process of healing rather than moving to the final state of whole and complete health. People will experience and be in the process of healing year after year after year after year. The healing process never ends. Illness and disease never moves through your body because you are still in an active healing state rather than moving to a completely healed condition.

The final state of mind is, *I am healed. I am healthy and whole*. It is this state of mind that has the most power because when the mind moves to the belief that says, *I am healed*, the body can then move to a fully healed state. There is no more healing to do. Everything is already healed, you are healthy and whole. You have unraveled the Veil of Illusion enough to connect and use Perfect Source Energy within you.

This is why, in all of the visualizations and exercises I use, I ask that you visualize and experience a perfect, healthy, completely healed and whole state of being. Even though your current physical reality does not mirror the finished intention, it is important to visualize and experience the full healed state of being because that is want you really want, right?

When you visualize and experience a lesser state of completion, the body will only move to the lesser state. The body will only move to the state of mind from which you are able to create. Work with your mind where it is at and visualize what it is able to process. If your mind puts up a lot of resistance visualizing a complete state of health, honor your mind by accepting where it is at, but then ask your mind if it is okay to move forward. Allow your mind to adjust and grow through incremental stages, moving into a full, complete, whole state of being in your visualizations.

Throughout my journey I experienced these stages gradually. My mind needed time to process each state of being. I could not trick my mind into thinking it can fully heal when my mind couldn't embrace that fact. I had to move through each one of these concepts. I needed to ask and honor what my mind could expand to in the current moment, then allow my mind to move through these states gracefully.

You will eventually want to create and visualize *complete health* rather than a state of healing that is in process. Do not let your mind talk you out of visualizing and experiencing a complete state of health and wholeness forever. Your mind needs to grow and expand with you to create and visualize a complete state, the final state, and feel as though healing has already happened. If you visualize healing happening in the future, your healing will never end because the body has been instructed that it is still in the process and will never completely heal. Where your mind goes, your body will follow.

Make sure the instructions you give are full and complete or the body will never get there.

Give your body the clearest mind you can and move through the mind's healing states to the best of your ability. Trust this process. You must have the *desire to heal*, the belief *you can heal*, the physical action that *you are healing* and then the full knowing that *you are healed*. You are healthy and whole; then healthy and whole will be you.

Meeting Your Mind Where It Is At

Meeting your human mind where it is at is another important part of your journey. Get to know where your mind is before making decisions regarding treatment plans and options. Your human mind will not budge from its own thinking until and unless it feels safe to do so. You are the bridge that will introduce new concepts to your mind and support your mind to open up to larger possibilities. When you reject or tell your mind it is stupid, or its thoughts are not welcomed and need to go away, your mind will reject you and reject your healing process.

Healing your human mind is an imperative part of the deeper healing process. To heal the mind, you must be willing to accept, love, and gently move your human mind to the greater capacity within your Divine Mind. If your human mind gets hung up on a certain treatment plan and believes that it needs a certain thing to heal, meet your mind where it is at. Your mind can completely stop and reject your healing process if it does not feel safe, honored, and accepted.

Your personal healing and treatment plan will be different from everyone else's plan because we are all working from different mindsets and past experiences. The external treatment plan is not as important in your healing process as the inner alignment of your mind, body, and spirit. What works for one person may not work for another due to the past programming and unconscious patterns within one's own mind. Be real and honest with yourself and your mindsets. Go within and ask your heart for your next best step.

When I was trying to decipher which treatments were best for me, I had to get honest with where my human mind was. My mind and every one of my past experiences played an important role in selecting my personal-treatment plan. I had several conscious and unconscious belief systems within my mind that I needed to be aware of before I could make the best choices for me. I needed to choose a treatment plan that integrated my heart's desires and my human mind's ability to move through its fears. I needed a plan that honored me, all of me, mind, body, and Soul.

Because of my past experience with my mother and her cancer journey, I had a belief that chemotherapy and conventional treatment would destroy my physical body. I saw my mother's physical body transform from a healthy, vibrant, women to a weak, depleted cancer-patient. I witnessed a chemical attack on her body as she slowly died in suffering and pain due to the toxic exposure of the treatments. In my human mind, chemotherapy, radiation, and drugs kill and destroy the physical body. That was my mindset and I needed to honor that belief in my treatment plan.

My mother's struggle through cancer broke my heart and left a lasting impression that these treatments would kill and destroy me rather than help me heal. I set my full intention to heal my body, not to destroy it. Conventional therapies did not align with my personal healing intention, nor my mind's ideas on healing. Therefore, the conventional system did not align with my personal-healing protocol.

Another mindset I was aware of had to do with my conscious and unconscious beliefs from fitness training and competitions. I knew, from fitness training, that my body responds quickly and easily when I give it the proper nourishment and exercise. If my body responded quickly and positively from fitness training, why couldn't it do the same thing with alternative cancer treatments? I had the belief in my mind that if I can support my body with healthy foods, supplementation, and detox protocols, my body would be able to adapt to heal and restore itself. My human mind was connecting my past experience from fitness training to a new healing potential with cancer. I trained my body to build muscle and change its shape through diet, exercise, and supplements, why can't my body heal from cancer if I provide the same love and support for healing? My human mind began to align with the fact that my body can heal, if I provided the environment for it to do so.

A new level of conscious awareness began developing in my mind that said, "My body can heal if given the proper support and system to do so. It is my body that does the healing, not the treatments themselves. The treatments are tools to help support my body, but it is my body that actually does the healing. When I cut myself, my body heals by itself. I accept the fact that my body can heal, and the body does its job. There is nothing I have to do to heal the cut, my body heals the cut. If I use a Band-Aid or ointment, they are used as tools to assist my body, but they do not do the actual healing. That means that all treatments are outside tools to help assist and support my body. It is always my body that does the physical healing, not the tools themselves."

That was a new and expanded concept for me. My old program was that I had to go to the doctor when I was sick. The doctor would prescribe a drug, pill, or ointment to heal me, then I would get better. It was the drug that I needed to heal. Now I was questioning the validity of that thought. My mind was opening up to a new healing concept.

Then I thought to myself, "If we (the human species) needed prescription drugs to heal and restore our body, we would have been extinct years ago because we didn't have drugs years ago. Our bodies healed themselves because that is what they are designed to do. Everything else in the physical world is a tool to assist healing, but exterior tools are not the actual cause of healing. *We* are the cause of healing."

My mind continued to process my new revelations, "Maybe my body does have the ability to heal? Maybe my body already has everything it needs to heal, I just need to find the best way to support it to do so."

My mind was beginning to unwind past programming from society and doctors and get onboard with my heart. It began to embrace the belief that my body has a powerful healing potential and capacity within it that goes beyond human potential and physical resources. My body has everything it needs to heal and restore by itself if I give it the chance to do so.

I felt my mind aligning with my heart and body. I knew if I could love, nourish, and support my body by providing the tools my body needs, my body could and would heal itself. I didn't need to do any toxic treatment to heal, because my body already had the capacity to heal. If my body created cancer it could *uncreate* it as well.

This is why I made the decision that every treatment I would use would love, nourish, and support my body to heal, not to destroy. This choice made sense to my mind and it finally felt safe to move forward with alternative treatments. I met my mind where it was at and then gently guided, loved, and supported my mind to align with my body and heart.

Resistance Will Happen ... Do Not Let Resistance or Fear Sabotage Your Healing

I wish I could say that when I made the choice to follow my heart and let go of my mind that my healing journey and process was easy and smooth sailing. It wasn't. I had many unconscious patterns and programs that began surfacing. As each old pattern and thought from my human mind surfaced, I needed to go through the process of surrender, love, acceptance, and reorganizing.

Healing the human mind is an on-going process in this regard. Continuing to love and accept all parts of your being is the inner journey of the Soul and is only way to unravel and heal the mind. Healing the human mind is like pulling teeth. The process can be painful and it is not easy, but after you begin to remove the decay within the human mind, it no longer causes problems and you begin to heal.

There is usually much resistance in this process. The human mind is strong and persistent. It wants what it wants and thinks what it thinks, and it is always right … wrong, but it *thinks* it's right. The human mind is stuck in patterns of fear, survival, and past programming. It thinks it is keeping you safe, but in reality, it is slowly killing your life force and keeping your very limited state of being in this life experience. It is only when you move through the programming of the human mind and integrate it with your Divine Mind that you can fully heal, restore, and live your life within your highest potential.

After I chose to move forward with alternative treatments and reject the conventional treatments for cancer, I was faced with a lot of resistance. I was not only faced with resistance from my own thoughts and fears within my human mind, but I also had to deal with resistance from external sources and influences. This is an example of how our outer world is a reflection of our inner world. My inner resistance was showing up in my outer-world experiences.

After I decided to use alternative treatments, I had to call and cancel my appointment with my oncologist and additional surgeons. These calls were challenging because they were an external declaration of my internal decision to move forward and find another way to heal from cancer. I knew I would be ridiculed and questioned by everyone and everything that did not agree with my decision.

When I thought about making the calls, I could hear my human mind saying, "Are you sure? Are you really sure you want to move forward with this decision? You are going to be on your own. You will not have the support of the medical community and doctors. No one will help you or be there for you if you go forward in this decision. No one will be there for you if you fail." My mind questioned everything because it was scared and was trying to protect me from what it did not know or understand. I chose the road-less-traveled and there was still a part of my mind that was unsure and uncertain about the decision. It didn't feel completely safe.

I also had to call my friends and family and let them know what I decided. I knew they loved and cared for me, so I wanted to keep them in the loop, but these calls were forbidding. I could sense and feel their personal fear regarding my decision before I ever dialed their numbers. I knew they were not going to agree with my decision and they were terrified of losing me.

I specifically remember the call with my Dad. He knows how aggressive cancer can be. We shared the same cancer journey with my mother and he was concerned for me. He didn't want me to go down the road I had chosen, and he was sure I was making a mistake. We both know what it feels like to lose someone you love because we both lost my mother to cancer. I knew he couldn't bear losing his only daughter to cancer as well. He still believed the only way to fight cancer was through chemotherapy, radiation, and drugs. My choice to not fight cancer through the conventional system was like I had already lost the battle because I wasn't going to fight to live. I was daddy's little girl, and this was devastating for him. He didn't want to lose me and he was afraid he already had. My conversation with him was difficult, but I stood my ground and stayed strong in my decision to heal with alternative methods. My heart broke for him, and for me, as I reluctantly hung up. I knew my dad could not support me in my decision.

My human mind chimed in again to remind me, "Are you sure you are making the right decision? You are scaring the crap out of people and they are telling you that you are making a big mistake. This mistake could cost you your life. This is your life you are risking. Is it worth risking your life?"

Standing my ground and standing in my decision to find another way to heal was incredibly difficult with friends and family. I knew they loved and supported me, but I also knew that they didn't support my decision. Even if they didn't voice their opinion that I was making a mistake, I could feel the fear behind their words or their silence from not knowing what to say. The dead silence was actually harder to deal with than the physical words of disapproval. The silence was awkward and uncomfortable, but I knew I needed to be able to stand strong in my decision if I was going to heal.

It was becoming apparent to me that this was going to be a solo journey, and I needed to be comfortable within the discomfort around others. I knew I had to be strong for me even if no one else could or would stand with me. I also needed to honor where they were, so I could honor where I was, and be okay with it. They still cared for and loved me, and I knew they would continue to pray for me. Maybe the fact that I chose the "risky" path made them pray even more? In all honesty, that probably worked to my advantage, but the reality for me was that I was surrounded in fear. Fear was not the support I needed to surround myself with if I was going to move forward in my healing process.

The exterior fears didn't just stop at my friends and family. It attacked me from many angles. Everyone had their own opinion and they all felt they needed to tell me about it. I even had a dentist corner me and tell me that I was being selfish; I should think of my children. He looked me directly in the eye and belittled and chastised me saying, "How are your kids going to feel when they lose their mother? You are going to die, and you are being totally selfish!"

Wow, I couldn't believe the fear people were projecting on me. He had no clue how much I was thinking about my kids and how much I loved them. My sole purpose was finding a way to live and he was telling me I was going to die. He told me that I was making the biggest mistake of my life and I was being selfish. The external resistance was coming at me from every direction.

To make matters worse, my human mind often agreed and supported this resistance. I realized that I needed to find my own healing space and support system, both within myself and outside myself. As you can see, they go hand in hand.

I created loving boundaries by limiting my interaction with the outside world, so I could focus on my own healing and not be surrounded and attacked with fear. I had to distance myself from outside sources of fear, which included some of my best friends and closest family members.

I also needed to find a loving tribe that did support me. There were a few people who believed in me and were able to support my decision. This small group became my healing tribe. They were able to let go of any resistance they had within themselves and energetically back my healing expression. They became my supporting angels through this process, and I am so grateful they were in my life.

For everyone else, I decided to write a blog that would keep them in the loop, but I wouldn't have to deal with their fears in person. It was so important to create boundaries for myself and surround myself with love and support. Along with creating boundaries in my external world, I also had to create boundaries within myself so that I could move through my own fears.

EFT - Moving Your Mind through Resistance and Fear

I needed to find a tool that could help me reconnect to my Divine Mind when my human mind, thoughts, feelings, and emotions wanted to run the show and freak out in fear. I couldn't physically separate myself from my own mind, as I did with people, so I needed to find a way to coexist with it. I needed to accept and heal what was coming up in my mind and move through my fears. I couldn't reject and ignore my fears because they were strong and needed to be heard or they would block my healing progress.

My human mind was not going to go away during this process, so I needed to pay attention and let my mind know that I heard it, loved it, and accepted it. I also needed to let my human mind know I was choosing a different path and we were going to move through this together. I needed my human mind to feel safe and move forward with me, so we could heal together.

I knew that my body cannot be in a healing state when it is in a fight-or-flight stage with my mind. I needed my mind to let go of the fear and transition into a relaxed, healing state. I needed my mind to let go, but it didn't want to do that. My mind was scared shitless and terrified to let go. I needed to find a tool that would help my mind feel comfortable letting go and allowing me to move forward.

My Soul heard my request and sent me a simple tool called EFT. EFT (Emotional Freedom Technique) provided a way that allowed the thoughts in mind to surface and be with me as I loved and accepted them. By loving and accepting them, they could feel safe and let go. This was the way I could move through the fear and lovingly and openly accept and integrate my fears into my Divine Mind, so I could move forward with healing.

EFT works by saying an affirmation to things I feared or didn't want in my life and allow myself to accept and love them instead of rejecting them. By accepting and loving my fear, my fear could feel safe and move through me rather than staying stuck.

When you reject your feelings and/or your fears, you create a state of resistance in your body. When you reject anything in your life, your life becomes a state of resistance. What you resist, persists. It means that anything you reject and don't want in your body or your life stays with you. What you resist stays within the body as an energetic block because it cannot move through you. What you don't consciously recognize and accept in your life, your body will carry for you and eventually it will cause a disruption of the energetic flow and information within your body field. When the body's energetic flow and information is disrupted or distorted, the body becomes disrupted or distorted and the body can't function or operate correctly. This block in flow then creates disease.

So many of us, including myself, carry unconscious patterns, programs, thoughts, and beliefs that we do not accept in our lives. We think certain actions or thoughts are bad or immoral, so we reject them. We also bury past trauma and emotions. Many of these traumas and emotions happened in childhood and we buried them as a means of survival. Our body will carry these past emotions and traumas as a survival mechanism until the time comes that we are able to heal them. Our body carries these past emotions, traumas, and experiences for us because it loves us.

When we are ready and able to process them, they will surface in our life as a message to heal. If we recognize the message and heal them, these emotions and trauma can move through us. However, if these past emotions, traumas, and experiences are not recognized and healed, they continue to be held in the body and cause many of the chronic illness we are experiencing today. When chronic pain and disease manifests in the body, it is a call for deep internal healing.

This is what happened to me and breast cancer. My cancer developed because I was carrying past programs and patterns within my body that eventually manifested as cancer. This is why it is important to recognize emotions, feelings, past trauma, pain, and chronic illness when they surface and assist them to move through you. It is not healing or helpful to avoid, stuff, or resist them. Instead, acknowledge, accept, and love them.

EFT is a tool to help you do this. EFT uses an affirmation that says, "Even though I have/feel _____, I totally and completely love and accept myself." You can fill in the blank with whatever is coming up for you at the time. It can be a fear, a situation, a physical ailment, a relationship challenge, business challenge, etc. Whatever is showing up in your life that you don't want, or you think is unacceptable, needs your love and acceptance. As you say the affirmation to yourself, you are also physically tapping on energy release points on your face and body to help release fear and resistance.

Remember, what you resist, persists, so if you don't want something in your life, you must change your mind about the situation. You must fully accept and love it, instead of reject and hate it, so that you can move through it. This is not the typical response with which our human mind functions or how most people live their lives. If something is in our life that we don't want, our immediate reaction is to fight, fix, and reject it. We want it to go away, but that is not how things heal from an energetic stand point. In fact, it works just the opposite.

When you focus on what you don't want and focus on what you reject, it stays with you. Instead, you must accept it, not reject it. Allow it to be in your life and love it so it can feel safe to move through you.

One of the first things I worked on using the EFT method was cancer itself. My mind didn't want cancer in my life. My mind wanted it to go away. My mind would be perfectly fine to ignore cancer and hope that it went away. Obviously, that train of thought was not going to work! In order for cancer to go away, I needed to acknowledge it was here -- because it was here -- and I needed to accept it into my life. I needed to be alright that cancer may be in my life forever so that there would be no resistance within me if cancer stayed. This was not what my mind wanted to do. In fact, accepting cancer meant that it was okay for cancer to be there forever and that was the last thing my mind wanted. Being okay with cancer was not okay with my mind. I needed to find a way to be okay with not being okay. My mind wanted it gone, but my Soul wanted it to stay. My Soul knew that cancer had come into in my life as an important message for me and I needed to accept it, love it, and restore it.

My human mind chimed in, "How the hell was I going to find a way to love cancer? Cancer sucks! Cancer took my mother from me. How am I ever going to love cancer? That's a stupid idea and completely insane!"

My Soul knew differently. I had to find a way to love cancer. I needed to love cancer because it contained an important message for me that would help me move through my old patterns that kept me living in fear and survival. I needed to love cancer so that it would bring me thorough new patterns that help me live in love with life and thrive instead of barely survive. Cancer came to save my life, not destroy it. I needed to find a way to love cancer.

I wasn't able to love cancer right away, nor did I discover the deeper message it held for me until much later in my journey (which I will get to later in this book). For the time being, EFT gave me the tool I needed to move through the process of acceptance, love, and restoration. EFT did what it needed to do, even though I didn't have a comprehensive understanding how it worked. I simply used the method as a bridge to a later understanding.

The affirmation I used to acknowledge, accept and love cancer went like this, "Even though I have cancer, I completely and totally love and accept myself." I repeated this affirmation as I physically tapped on my body's energetic release points. This practice helped me move my mind through cancer. EFT helped my mind accept cancer and feel safe to move forward with the healing process. It helped me release my inner resistance, so energy and information could flow again.

I used EFT for everything that came up in my mind when I felt resistance or fear. I used EFT to move through every fear, every worry, and every doubt that surfaced during my healing journey. Much of the time, I didn't even know what I feared or doubted, I just felt fear and doubt. In that case, I simply said, "Even though I feel scared (or I entered any other emotion, feeling or life circumstance), I completely and totally love and accept myself."

It doesn't matter if you don't know why you are feeling the way you do; simply acknowledge the emotion or circumstance and accept and love it. Your Soul knows the details and that is good enough. You can create your own affirmation for anything that is bothering you, even if you don't know why you are feeling the way you do.

You can also use EFT for any situation, circumstance, or person that appears in your life and you have no idea what to do with it or them. Simply acknowledge it or them, accept and love it or them. You do not need to understand or have a conscious awareness of the deeper emotional charge behind the situation or person, simply do the exercise with the intent on releasing and letting go of the energetic charge. It works.

There is also a series of points on the body that you tap while you are saying your affirmation. I find that you don't need to tap on the body points to have this exercise work for you but tapping on your body while saying the affirmation can help ground the information into your body. It helps get you out of your mind's fear and helps the fear move through your body. It is also a way to let your body know you are present with it. The tapping is like knocking on the door to your body and waking it up to move the energy through you. The tapping is saying, "Knock. Knock. Hello, body, are you there? Are you listening to me and hearing that I am acknowledging these fears and I am ready to move them through me?" It's a little wake-up call for your body so it can work with you to move stagnant energy through your body to help with the healing process. This is why many people refer to EFT as "tapping."

If you are interested in using EFT in your own life, there is a ton of resources and information online that you can look up. There are several different tapping locations on the body you can use when repeating your affirmation back to yourself. The tapping points vary slightly, depending on which resource you find. Use the tapping points that feel comfortable for you.

You can also visualize the tapping in lieu of actually tapping on the points if you are doing the exercise at work or are surrounded by a large group of people. Tapping on your body while other people are watching might make them think you are losing your mind, (even though losing your mind is what you are doing), and you don't need people to think you are crazy. Visualizing gives you the option to tap without physically tapping.

The points on the body that I used were: the top of my head, top of my brow, temples, under my eyes, under my nose, under my mouth, collar bone, side of my ribs (where a bra strap would go) and both wrists. You can use EFT for any fear, anxiety, feeling, or personal circumstance or situation you find yourself resisting. It is a simple and effective tool to help heal your human mind and accept all circumstances in your life so that you can move into a healing state of mind. I have included a detailed exercise and diagram for you to follow in the back of this book.

Use EFT to assist you in moving through your mind's fears, blocks, and emotional programming so that you can begin to integrate your human mind with your Divine Mind. If you are not able to acknowledge, accept, love, and move through your fears, they will hold you back from healing and living the life your desire and deserve. Your mind is a powerful tool that will either assist you or resist you. You have the power to observe your mind and recognize when it is out of alignment with your inspired healing intention. You have the power to integrate your mind with your Divine Mind through acceptance and love. This is how you help yourself help your mind. EFT is a powerful tool to assist you.

8

WORKING WITH YOUR BODY TO HEAL

Love and Acceptance

Besides loving, accepting, and healing your mind, you also need to love, accept, and heal your body. Your body is a valuable tool and resource in your healing journey. Your body is a physical representation of your inner world. If your body is holding pain, illness, disease, or any physical symptom, the symptom is an indication there is some internal dysfunction or disruption within the body.

At the heart of all matter, there is energy and information. When this energy and information is out of alignment, the body manifests physical symptoms that are out of alignment. Just like the mind, healing begins with acceptance and love. After acceptance and love, you can move forward with inspired action to nourish and restore the body back to health.

One simple and effective tool I used to begin the process of loving and accepting myself and my body is through mirror reflection. You, too, can use this simple exercise morning and night to access deep inner love and acceptance that initiates healing and alignment in your body, mind and spirit. The two most powerful mirror affirmations are, "I love you, (your name)" and "I accept all that is in my life right now."

To begin this exercise, write the first affirmation (I love you, "your name") on a sticky note and place it on your mirror. Look into your own eyes and tell yourself you love you, just as the sticky note says. Say the affirmation as if you really mean it. Feel unconditional love from within you as you say the words.

The "I love you" exercise may feel very uncomfortable at first. It was uncomfortable for me for a long time. I was very good at telling others I loved them, but I never told or felt love for myself. As you look into your own eyes and feel love for yourself, you may sense deep and intense emotion and/or pain surfacing. There may be a deep emotional pain within you that has wanted and needed to hear and receive love from you for a very long time. Allow these emotions to surface. Allow the tears to surface and love yourself through this process. These feelings are intimate and real. They are calling to be healed. You will heal these pieces by loving yourself unconditionally.

If the ability to feel love for yourself is difficult, close your eyes and think of someone or something that is easy for you to love. Visualize them in your mind and connect to the love you have for them. Feel this love deeply within yourself. When you can feel deep love, open your eyes, look at yourself in the mirror, feel this love and tell yourself, "I love you." This is one of the most powerful exercises you can do to heal. It is vital that you fully love yourself so that you can move forward through the healing process.

Complete the "I love you" mirror exercise morning and night, for at least one week or until you can fully and deeply feel unconditional love for yourself; then you can move onto the acceptance exercise. Complete the acceptance exercise in the same manner until you know in your heart that you fully and completely accept your body's condition. You need to accept this condition, even if your condition is going to stay with you the rest of your life. You do not want to be in resistance to your body.

Healing is not a fight with your body, it is working with and loving your relationship with your body. You do not want to be at war with your body, so you do not want to be in resistance to it. Just like your mind, you need your body to work with you, not against you. Healing is being at peace with your body and at peace with its condition -- all of its conditions. You will be at peace with your body when you can fully love and accept what is showing up in your body and life.

Once I was at peace with myself and my body, I was in a state of being that could fully accept, love, and nourish my body back to health. I knew I needed to carry this energetic expression with me throughout the day if I was going to heal. Love and acceptance are powerful energetic healing frequencies. By staying within those frequencies my body received the energetic message to heal.

Remember, your outer world is a reflection of your inner world of thoughts, feelings, and actions (state of being). Your body is an outer expression of your inner state of being. Your body is a valuable tool to show you if you are aligned within your mind (thoughts), body (feelings), and spirit (inspired action) or if you are out of alignment. I used my body as a tool to help me regulate how I was doing and where I needed to make adjustments so I could stay fully aligned within my thoughts, feelings, and actions. I used my body as a healing tool.

Intimate Relationship with My Body

I chose to have an intimate relationship with my body and used it as a guide to show me how I was doing. My body and I became one whole unit in this journey and we were in it together. I chose a treatment plan, diet, and supplements that would love, nourish, and support my body rather than choosing a treatment plan, diet, and supplements that would add a toxic burden my body had to heal and repair. This is how I gauged everything that went into my body. I would physically ask my body, "Will this ____ love, nourish, and support you?" I would wait for the answer in the stillness of my being, a quiet mind and knowing heart.

I would also pay very close attention to how my body reacted with any food, treatment, or detox protocol. I would always ask my body for guidance and feedback. When I was able to go within and ask my body, I would receive the best answer for what my body needed. I carried the energetic expression of health and so my body would respond with the best answer to create health in my body. My body knew what it needed to heal, and it knew what it didn't need. I trusted my body. I became so connected with my body, that even the sight or smell of something allowed me to know if my body needed it -- or not.

This is the same concept and theory used in muscle testing. The body knows what it wants and what it doesn't. If you ask your body, it will tell you what it needs. My body's reaction to diets also let me know what worked and what didn't work.

One day I was researching how great vegan diets were to heal cancer. I asked my naturopathic doctor if I could go vegan and she said, "Well, if you really want to. You can give it a try, but I wouldn't recommend it for very long because vegan diets are highly detoxing and it's hard to get all of the essential nourishment you need to heal." I decided to try it anyway, because it made sense to my human mind.

After two weeks on a vegan diet, I lost a lot of weight and my hair began to fall out. Apparently, my body did not like this diet and was letting me know, in no uncertain terms, to stop. I listened and immediately added protein and clean meat back into my diet. I felt great within days and learned a valuable lesson. My body needed meat and protein. I knew I needed to listen and trust what my body was telling me.

Just because I read something that worked for someone else didn't mean that it was going to work for me. In fact, someone else's plan might prevent my own healing efforts. I learned to trust myself and my body. My body knows. Honestly, I was relieved that I could eat meat because a vegan diet was really hard for me to follow. I think my Soul knew that, too.

As a society, we have become detached and disconnected from the innate wisdom our bodies contain. We have lost touch with this valuable resource. By reconnecting to my body and having an intimate relationship with it, I was guided to the perfect solution for my perfect health. If I had a negative experience, I would ask my body, "What is this reaction about? Was this a detox reaction or did you not like or need what I just offered you?" My body always knew.

It took time for me to get reacquainted with my body. The last time I had a similar relationship with it was when I was competing in Fitness. I worked with my body and listened to what it needed to grow and build muscle. I trained hard and worked my body to the point it was exhausted, but not over-exhausted. I listened to my body and honored where it was. My body told me when it was time to push and when it was time to stop. I also took a break and rested when it needed rest. I tried different supplements to see how my body would respond to them. If I noticed a positive change, I knew they were a good fit; if not, I would discontinue using them.

I never pushed or over-stressed my body more than it could tolerate. Pushing always led to sickness or injury that would defeat my purpose. I saw too many gym rats push and push through their pain or fatigue because they lived by the concept, "No pain, no gain," but I found this concept debilitating. Pushing though, past the point your body says "stop," is unwise and sets your efforts back through undue fatigue, sickness, and injury.

Training for fitness competitions taught me how valuable our body is as a healing and teaching tool. I was grateful I had this experience and the wisdom it offered. It gave me a glimpse of how valuable my relationship with my body is and what this relationship can do to for my physical health.

LIVING PROOF

Trust Your Body

Too often we seek outside advice from trainers, doctors, books, or other health gurus to tell us what our body needs and wants. We take their advice as the "Word of God," so to speak and ignore advice your body offers you. While the information you receive from outside sources may be helpful, always run the advice by your inner-guidance systems. Always ask your body what it needs and wants. You will receive your answer through the stillness of your being and your heart. Your body and heart will lead and guide you to the answers you really need.

Following outside advice without inner consultation can knock you off your healing path and leads to much trial and error. When you seek, trust, and put faith solely in advice and resources outside yourself, they will eventually lead you to limited success and eventual failure. Trusting only outside sources is a quest of constantly seeking and "maybe finding," but never truly solving your situation. It is a quest that leads you in circles and an endless journey of seeking. What works for one person may not work for another. We each have different bodies, different life experiences, different emotional patterns, and programs that affect our physical being. This is why you will never find the perfect diet, supplement, drug, pill, or potion that will heal you because we all have unique past experience and operate from different Veils of Illusion.

We are constantly evolving and have come for our own Soul experience. We are on our own unique journeys and we all have our own past life experiences, so we will react and respond in our own unique way to foods, supplements, and treatments. You are unique in this regard. You are also constantly evolving. What worked and nourished you at age 6 will be different at age 20 and age 40 and age 80. This is life's evolution. You are changing, growing, and evolving. What nourishes your body and life will change with life itself. Just when you think you have found life's answers, life inherently changes all the questions.

You need to grow and flow with life. You need to meet life where it is and know that you are changing and growing with life as well. Life is much easier and simpler when you flow and grow with it, rather than against it. Seek answers where they can be found, which is from within. Your body, Soul, and spirit can guide and lead you to what you need in the moment. They are designed to transition and flow with you, and they act in synchronicity with each other to deliver messages and signs you need for your personal growth and well-being.

Stop looking outside yourself for what you can find within yourself. Begin to develop a personal relationship with your body and the world around you and in you. You will find all the answers you seek, and the answers will lead you to your heart's desires.

Connecting and Integrating Your Inner Body to Your Outer World

My diet played a huge supporting role in my healing journey and process. My diet was a way to integrate my inner body and my outer physical world. I used my diet as a way of loving, supporting, and nourishing my body back to health. Eating whole, healthy foods was an outer reflection of my inner intention to heal and restore my body back to wholeness and health. I intentionally chose foods that would heal my body rather than cause a toxic burden my body had to mitigate.

I knew if I wanted to experience health, I needed my actions to reflect an inner intention of health. Eating clean, healthy, whole foods was one of my "Inspired Actions" that I visualized. I needed to bring these experiences into my life to draw in the effect I desired. I used my meals as a time to connect and remember my intention to heal. The more I could connect to my intention to heal and align to that energetic expression, the more I could and would draw it to me.

I used meals to connect with and remember my intention. You can also use meals as a time to reconnect to your desired intention. We all have to eat throughout the day, so why not use this time to reconnect to your own intentions and energetic expression so that you can draw more of what you want into your life? Remember, life is integrated so you must find ways to integrate your intentions into your life. Simply thinking and feeling your intention will not complete the job. You must integrate your intention with action ... inspired action.

Here's how I did it and how you can do it, too. Reconnect to your Energetic Expression worksheet. Place one hand on your heart and the other hand on your feeling center (two or three inches below your belly button). Connect to the thoughts, feelings, and inspired actions from your worksheet and visualizations.

Close your eyes and take five deep, slow breaths and breathe into these thoughts, feelings, and actions before each meal. Take five more breaths and repeat this affirmation with each one, "I love, nourish, and support my body and my life with inner love, nourishment, and support from my Soul." When you have finished your affirmations, finish with a feeling of gratitude that your intention has already been granted. Thank the Divine and your Soul for your inner love, nourishment, and support.

Now you can eat your meal as an outer reflection of your inner intention, knowing that you are fully loved, supported, and nourished from the inside out. The more you can connect to your inner intention throughout the day the more you can draw it into your life. Meals are an easy way to implement this into your life.

I used my diet as a ritual of healing and reconnecting to my perfect source within. The foods I ate were an outer action of my inner energetic expression I wished to experience. The way I ate, and the foods I ate, were outer expressions of love, nourishment, and support that sent a signal to my body to heal.

MARY RUST

When I aligned my inner intention with my outer expression, I sent a message for my physical world to follow.

9
WORKING WITH YOUR SPIRIT AND SOUL TO HEAL

Perfect Health: The Way Life was Meant to Be

The definition of *healing* is: to restore to original purity or integrity, to make whole again. This is the truth of your being. Your original state of being is perfect health. This is how God originally designed your body. Remember, you are a piece of your creator. God is perfect, whole, and complete, as are you. You have simply lost this connection and belief that your true essence is perfect, whole, and complete.

Your human mind has done a great job of telling you how imperfect and dysfunctional you are. When you are able to unravel these concepts within your mind and begin to connect to who you really are with God and in God, you begin your inner restoration process, because you reconnect to the original purity and essence you are. If you want to fully heal and become whole again, reconnect to your Divine essence. Healing is not about getting rid of a physical ailment or wanting or needing something different in your life. It is about restoring what has been lost and reconnecting to all that you have ever needed or wanted.

Everything you have ever needed or wanted is already with you and in you. Your human mind just distracted you for a while. You have been and always were created in perfect health. Perfect health is your natural *state of being*. It was only when you began to accept and believe your human programming, patterns, past trauma, and concepts that you began to experience what you are not.

Living What You *Are Not* to Discover What *You Are*

You might ask, "If my true essence is pure and perfect, why would I ever want or need to experience pain and suffering? Why would my Soul want to experience illness and disease if my natural state of being is perfect health? That doesn't make sense."

Yes, I agree, it doesn't make sense that your Soul wants to experience disease, illness, and dysfunction in your life, when your true essence is opposite of these experiences. Why not experience health, love, and happiness instead? Isn't health, love, and happiness what you really want? Isn't that what your Soul really wants to express? Yes, it is. So why do you come to this world and experience the opposite? This a great question that deserves a great answer.

The truth is you need to experience the opposite of who you are in order to fully know and understand who you really are. Experiencing crisis, disease, pain, and suffering actually serves your Soul's purpose to learn, grow, and understand through experiencing contrast. Just as a diamond is rubbed on all sides in order to be polished and reveal its shine, we, too, are triggered and roughed up on all sides by undesirable circumstances so that we awaken our inner light, joy, and pure desires. You came into this physical world to experience a full range of feelings and emotions. Feelings and emotions are the language of the Soul. Your Soul experiences itself through the language of feelings and emotions. Your Soul desires to know what it feels like to experience grief, pain, loneliness, suffering, fear, shame, deception, and many other negative feelings and emotions. You Soul craves to experience relativity. You can only know one thing when you see and experience another. You know what joy is when you have experienced suffering. It's your suffering that gives depth to your joy.

This concept didn't make sense to me at first, because I was trying to understand it from my human mind. My human mind was questioning why I would want to experience unpleasant things when my innate nature is love, abundance, freedom, joy, etc. My human mind wants to experience comfort, joy, and peace, so why does my Soul want to experience the opposite?

Then my Soul chimed in and said, "You will never understand spiritual matters or concepts from your human mind. Your human mind was not designed with the capacity for spiritual understanding. That is not its job. It is designed so you can have a human experience of duality and survive in the physical world. Let me explain from a spiritual perspective why your human experience of duality (good and bad) in life is so valuable to your Soul and why it is important to honor and love it all.

"In the spirit realm, good and bad do not exist. Good and bad is a concept held and created by your human mind to label, classify, and create an experience of duality that doesn't exist in the spiritual world. Duality, though, must be created in the physical world to have a fuller understanding of an experience. Think of it this way, how can you explain or understand *hot* if you don't know and have never experienced *cold*?

"Here's a challenge for you: With your best capacity, try to explain and define the word *hot* without using any word or combination of words that describe hot's opposite. Go ahead, try it. It's impossible to know and explain *hot* without knowing *cold* or using *cold's* opposite characteristics. In order to fully explain and understand *hot*, you need to use and have an experience of *cold*."

That's when a light bulb when off in my head. In order to learn grow and discover myself as a Soul, I needed to know and experience the opposite of who I really am. That means that pain and suffering has value and serves my Soul as an important part of my experience, growth, and evolution on this earth. We live in a physical dimension that provides all degrees of love and fear, hot and cold, happiness and sadness, so that we can understand, grow and evolve as a Soul. Our experiences here give depth and meaning to our Soul.

Imagine your Soul in the spirit realm where everything is based and experienced in love and bliss. How could you really know and appreciate the true value of love and bliss until you experienced its opposite? It's the "degrees of the opposite" that enrich the experience of each other. It is the experience of opposing degrees and duality that enriches our life. Both and all degrees are important and have great value in this human experience.

Loving and Accepting All of Life. All of Life Serves Your Soul

Part of the healing process is to accept and be able to love all experiences in life. From a spiritual perspective there is no experience that is bad or good, right or wrong. All experiences serve to help your grow and evolve your Soul. That is why it is important in the healing process to love and accept all of life and all that is in life. That is how you learn, grow, and move through the lessons of life for the benefit of your Soul.

Your Soul calls for these experiences and creates them in your physical world, not to harm you, but to help assist you to learn, grow, and move forward. Once you embrace and accept your circumstance, you are free to move through it because you no longer resist it. You are open to the message it has for you and you are free to move forward in new and positive ways rather than staying stuck in your current dilemma.

Once you have accepted your circumstance, the next step is action. Love and acceptance alone is not enough to move forward. Action must be applied. Take your circumstance in and move with it, in the direction it's pointing, which is toward more health, purpose, and Soul desires. Ask yourself, what thoughts, beliefs and actions can I integrate into my life to move from my undesirable circumstances to a more preferable experience?

Every experience, thing, or condition that is in your life contains a valuable message or lesson for you. Life is constantly providing you experiences that point to your highest good. When you know this and work with your life to learn and grow, you can move through life much easier. When one lesson has been learned, you are free to move on to the next. Life flows and you are free to flow with it to your best and highest good. Having a conscious awareness that you came into this life experience to learn lessons helps you accept what is showing up in your life and let go of the resistance to it so that you can move through it. Once the lesson is learned, the symptom or condition moves along because it is no longer needed.

Many times, your illness or disease goes away once you learn the lesson it came to teach you. Other times, the condition will stay because it is part of a larger lesson and part of your Soul contract and life plan. If a condition does not move through you, it is a sign there is still more for you to discover. Continue to trust and seek the wisdom the situation has for you. There is always a deeper reason and message for you. Continue to seek so you can evolve and grow.

Before you came into this physical world, your Soul had a very specific purpose for this life experience. You made a contract with your Soul to learn specific lessons for your own growth. These lessons are incredibly valuable to you and your Soul. When you came into this physical world, you forgot all of your Soul agreements and contracts, so you could experience life in the moment of now. If you had retained knowledge of everything your Soul wanted to learn you would not have been able to experience the lesson in the moment and you would not have been able to learn and grow from it.

If I would have had prior knowledge of my financial collapse, challenge in motherhood, or cancer diagnosis, my human mind would have made different choices in advance to try to avoid these situations. Had I avoided these challenges, I would never have learned their valuable lessons. I would not have had the opportunity to have grown from the experience and become who I am today. I would not have the knowledge I know today. I would not be able to live my life in its fullest expression. I am grateful, and I honor all that has showed up in my life and all that will continue to show up in my life.

Life with the Divine Mind

Albert Einstein once said something like this, "No problem can be solved from the same level of consciousness that created it." Cancer came into my life as a call to make some big changes within the concepts of my own mind. I was being called to move from the limited consciousness within my human mind and begin to create and live my life from the unlimited consciousness of my Divine Mind. I had been living life with the limited understanding of my human mind and my physical existence, instead of the unlimited knowledge and wisdom within my Divine Mind.

When I was able to let go of my own mind and reconnect to my Divine Mind, I was able to live in the freedom, expression, and with an expanded consciousness that loved me more, knew me more, and was able to help me more than my human mind ever could. I was able to connect and heal from energies that transcended the physical world and heal from a spiritual realm where anything is possible. This is the realm of miracles. This is how to heal the body beyond the body and the physical world. Universal laws transcend physical laws. They are able to provide "miracles" where everything else has failed.

So, the question is, "Which mind would you rather create and live your life from? The human mind or the Divine Mind?" I chose to create my health and life with my Divine Mind. Creating and living life from the Divine Mind is mysterious and miraculous because it creates from an unlimited, full-potential state. As a co-creator with my Divine Mind, I am no longer limited by my human mind and all of its limiting beliefs and concepts (Veil of Illusions).

When I created my intention from the Divine Mind for perfect health, my Divine Mind knew exactly what I needed because it knows perfect health. I aligned my Divine Mind's concept of perfect health, meditated on what perfect health felt like, integrated perfect health into my body, then moved forward with inspired action. Everything I did, said, ate, felt, and experienced aligned with the energetic expression of perfect health. I became a living energetic expression of health.

When my mind, body, and spirit were aligned with my perfect health, I was able to be that perfect expression of health in my daily life. I was the "living expression" of perfect health. This "living expression" then drew everything I needed into my life to support and create health in my physical reality. All of my daily actions were aligned with the spirit within me and we co-created health together as one. Everything I needed in my outer world was drawn to me through my interior "state of being" in thought, feeling, and action. Everything I needed to heal and restore my body was provided to me. Life and my healing plan simply flowed to me because I was energetically drawing it into my life through the Divine expression of perfect health. I was a living expression of perfect health; perfect health became me.

This is how you create and experience life with the Divine Mind. It is not really a struggle. The hardest part was getting my human mind and its concepts out of the way and getting my human mind to trust the process. Once I was able to become the perfect expression of health, it became my daily state of being. It was this state of being that intimately guided and directed perfect health to me. My body had no choice but to follow the guidance of my thoughts, feelings, and actions. My body healed because it was receiving the energy and information of health and healing. The energetic instructions I was sending were easy to follow because perfect health is our natural state of being.

Life with the Human Mind

Your human mind doesn't know what it wants because it doesn't know what it is. It is only through Divine Mind and understanding that you can fully know who you are and how to heal your body. The human mind's thoughts and concepts are created through your past experiences, which are limited compared to the vast knowledge and understanding of eternal truth.

The human mind only knows and interprets life from its limited understanding of itself through past and current physical sensations, which it interprets as "hard fact" of what is and what was and will always be. It tries to understand and explain life through its past programs and concepts, none of which are based on eternal truth. The human mind wants to know, but it simply does not know.

It is no wonder our lives get so messed up by our human mind. Our human mind is so busy trying to figure out who it is that it keeps us very busy in the process of working, thinking, wanting, wishing, having, and doing. It is programmed to believe that if you want anything in this world, you need to work for it. The more you want, the harder you have to work. The human mind doesn't realize that everything is controlled and granted by the Divine. You can work your heart out, busting your butt day and night, but if it is not in your best interest to achieve something, you will not receive it. On the flip side, if you work hard and achieve a lofty goal, the true cause of achieving the goal was not entirely based on your work. The human mind wants to give all attribution of your success to your hard work and effort, but in truth, it was still your alignment with the Divine that allowed and ultimately provided it to you and for you.

Your Soul provides all of your experiences that you receive and all experiences that are taken away from you. I've experienced both ends of the spectrum. I have been blessed with much success and many failures. It wasn't the quality or amount of work I put into them that caused my success or failure. It was ultimately a choice of my Soul and the experience It wanted to provide. If it is in your best interest to have something taken away from you, your Soul will provide that life experience as well.

For example, my husband and I worked our butts off to build our first company and business. We continued to work our butts off trying to salvage it from falling and crumbling, but all of our hard work was of no use. The business failed, and we were left with substantial debt. Our business failed not because we weren't working hard. Our business failed because our Soul was calling for change. There was nothing we could do about it. There was no amount of hard work we could do to change our circumstance. It was destined to fail, and so it did.

The human mind also keeps us busy thinking. It is busy thinking because it thinks it knows but it really doesn't know much compared to the eternal mind, which knows all. The human mind can think all it wants, but it will never know. The human mind will make you think you need to know more because you do not know enough. You go to school and get degrees to prove to the human mind that you know more, and that knowing more is better. The human mind does not realize you already have a Divine Mind that knows all. There is no amount of education you can learn that will compare to the wisdom of Divine Mind.

The human mind wants more because it thinks that the more you have, the more you are worth. How many people are trying to "keep up with the Jones's?" Who are the Jones's anyway? Where does this thought come from that we need to compare ourselves to one another in order to prove our worth?

This thought comes from the human mind that does not know you are already enough. Each and every one of us is already enough. There is no need for any of us to compare ourselves with each other because we are all equal and we all have intrinsic value -- because we exist. We are all born on this planet with unique gifts, quests, and desires for life. This is our birthright. The roots of "not enoughness" spur from the cultural belief that attending to or appreciating the self is selfish and that we must toil our lives away in order to be worthy of our shelter, food, and community. This simply isn't true. Nature does not do this, why do we? The human mind does not understand that you are already enough and so it tells you you want more, you need more, and you must have more in order to prove you are enough. You will never be enough for the human mind.

The human mind will keep you in a prison of itself if you let it rule your life. The human mind keeps you busy in its programmed reality until you are ready and willing to break free. Which life would you rather live, the Divine life or the human life? The choice is entirely up to you.

Be-ing Who You Are

When you break the unconscious patterns in the human mind, you will free yourself to be and live from a state of consciousness of who you really are (Divinity) rather than who you are not (Veil of Illusion). You don't need to want more because you already are more. You don't need to think more because you already have access to the knowledge of all there is. You don't need to wish for more because you already have access to the dreams you can fully create with your Divine Mind. You don't need to work more because you already have the love and support of the entire Universe. The Universe willingly provides everything you need. You just need to learn how to connect to it and use it for your own benefit through Divine thoughts, feelings, and actions.

The human mind keeps you so busy trying to do more, have more, and want more that you forget that your greatest power and access to all of the Universe is to simply *be*. *Be* the energetic expression of what you want, and the Universe will bring it to you because that is the energy and information you are sending out to the Universe. We are not human workings, human wantings, human doings, human wishings; we are human *be*ings. It is through our *being* that we create, express, and experience our greatest self and the most fulfilling life. It is through our state of being that we can heal and restore our body and our life.

This is exactly what happened to me when I chose to *be* the perfect expression of health through my thoughts, feelings and actions – state of *be*ing. When I physically became the perfect expression of health, my body followed that instruction and I simply healed. My body had no other choice but to heal because that was the energetic information I was providing it.

My body responded quickly and easily because I was aligned with the Universe and the Universe had my back. I was aligned with my body and my body had my back. I was aligned with my Divine Mind and the Divine had my back. Life is magical and miraculous when you are in complete alignment with the Universe and all that is. When you are aligned with all there is, "all there is" is already yours, and there is nothing you will ever want or need again.

10

WOO-HOO! I'M CANCER FREE ... NOW WHAT? MY HEALING JOURNEY CONTINUES

My Physical Healing

By living in the energetic expression of health and aligning my daily actions with my intention, my physical healing happened quickly. Within three months of my diagnosis, my diagnostic tests indicated that I was cancer-free.

I was on my way to work and my phone rang. I grabbed my phone and immediately recognized the number. It was Linda. I knew she was calling to discuss the results of my cancer-profile test. My heart immediately jumped out of my chest and I began to hyperventilate. I didn't want to get bad news. What if the results were worse than before? What if the cancer was continuing to grow and take over my breast and my body? Though I felt fine, I had no idea if what I was doing was working. Was I winning or losing this battle? This call would determine my fate. Given the impact of the call, I decided to pull the car over before answering. Whatever the answer was going to be, I knew I better not be driving. I found a safe place to pull over and answered the phone.

"Hello," I said apprehensively. "Hi, Mary, this is Linda. I have your test results back and I have some good news."

"What?" I said shocked and surprised, "Did I just hear her say *good news*?"

My heart skipped a beat and I fell silent. I didn't think good news was a possibility at this point. All I knew and was experiencing up to this point was bad news. All I had heard was cancer, cancer, cancer and you are going to die. I had gotten in a habit of hearing bad news. I expected bad news and I didn't even know what good news was anymore. I didn't know how to react, so I just went blank. I couldn't and didn't say a word.

"Mary, are you there?" Linda asked. Linda thought she lost me and we had gotten disconnected.

"Yes," I said, "I'm here. Did you say that my test revealed good news? What does that mean?"

"Yes," she said, "You are cancer-free!!!"

Linda was never the one to beat around the bush. She simply calls it as it is, and today she called to tell me that I was cancer-free. Just as with the phone call I received from my oncologist that told me I had cancer, I went numb. I wasn't able to process what she just said.

"What?" I questioned, "What do you mean when you say *cancer-free*?" I still didn't know what that meant.

"Yes," she said, "cancer-free. You did it! You are cancer-free. The test results indicate that you are within normal ranges and you are cancer-free!"

I was still numb. I was in shock and couldn't believe what I just heard. While I dreamed and hoped for this day coming, when it came I was just numb and dumb.

I had gone through so many different emotions, fears, hopes, and dreams. I was conflicted and I did not know if I could trust this new information. Part of me wanted to scream and jump for joy but the other part was frozen in silence. My mind was in a state of shock, and for once in its lifetime, it was completely silent. Yes, for the first time my human mind was speechless. (Thank God, I thought. This was one of the few times in my life I didn't have to consciously still my mind. It was already silent.)

I kept repeating the words, "*Cancer-free, cancer-free, cancer-free.*" What does that really mean? I had no idea what those words meant or how I was supposed to feel.

The great news of being *cancer-free* wasn't the reception and celebration I was hoping for. I thought I would be excited, overjoyed, and relieved. I thought I would scream and celebrate for joy, but that's not at all what happened. I was melancholy and unsure. Once again, I was scared and uncertain. I had prepared to live and heal from cancer. That was my purpose and passion in life. Now that I didn't have cancer, I wasn't sure what life was supposed to look like. I didn't know how to feel about the news. What was my purpose now? I also questioned if I could really believe and trust this new diagnosis?

Then there was a silent voice within me that said, "Yes, Mary, you are physically healed, but your physical healing is only the beginning of your larger healing journey and purpose. There is much more for you to discover and learn. Give thanks and gratitude for your physical healing. Enjoy some time and celebrate your life. You are off to a great start, but you have so much more to learn. The path ahead of you is a long, narrow, winding road that will continue to lead you on your healing journey and journey home. This is only one part of your journey. Rest now, breathe, and take some time to enjoy this milestone. It will be one of many milestones on your path home."

I had no idea what this voice was talking about. I was still trying to process my *cancer-free* diagnosis, but something within me knew I was headed for a deeper healing journey than I was able to consciously understand in this moment. This voice knew something I didn't know.

But here's what I did know. I knew this voice would be with me now and forever more. I knew this voice would guide, love, and lead me to whatever journey I needed to follow. I knew that I could and that I would trust this voice. I knew this voice would lead me home ... whatever that meant. For now, I was simply being asked to enjoy living my life ... *cancer-free*.

Living Cancer-Free

I spent the next few years of my life, living life. I continued to question if I was really *cancer-free*. My mind was having a hard time accepting it. Physical healing was too easy, and it happen too fast, according to my human mind. My mind kept questioning, "Am I really cancer-free? I can't really be healed, can I?"

While my mind was busy questioning everything, my heart was leading me to a deeper understanding of the healing process and how to fully live my life. I healed physically but I didn't have an understanding or comprehension of what I did to heal. My mind thought that healing occurred due to the physical things I did, such as the diet, supplements, and detox treatments, but my heart was leading me to a more expansive awareness and understanding of the healing process.

My human mind was trying to connect my healing with something outside of itself in order to understand the reason for my miraculous healing. My mind cannot and could not comprehend anything outside the realm of this physical reality being the cause that healed my cancer because the human mind only thinks in terms of the physical world. It is designed and programmed to help us survive a physical reality and does not know or understand life from a spiritual perspective.

The human mind thinks it lives in a physical reality and that the physical reality is all that exists. I have since learned that belief is far from the truth. The essence of our physical reality and our life experience is spiritual in nature. The physical world is created from spirit for spirit so that our Soul can have a physical experience. This is a baffling concept for the human mind, so it continues to argue with the Divine Mind and Its knowledge and understanding.

For many years after my "cancer-free" diagnosis, I thought and believed it was the physical things I did that healed me, but my Soul knew more. My Soul knew that the diet, supplements, and detox protocols were "tools" I used during my healing journey, but they were not the things that healed my body. It was a combination and integration of mind, body, spirit, and Soul that healed me. I just didn't know how all the pieces were intertwined with each other, nor did I know that the healing process runs much deeper than just physical healing.

There are mental, emotional, and spiritual elements to the healing puzzle, as well. That's what the next ten years of my life were going to uncover for me. My original desire was to physically heal. I did not know there were going to be other parts of me that needed healing as well. But my Soul did.

My Soul had the full intention on teaching me what "whole healing" was all about. I wasn't aware that my healing journey was going to be a full-blown spiritual journey to self-realization and life restoration. My Soul knew I needed to heal all parts of me, not just my physical body. This was all part of my Divine plan and Soul contract for this lifetime. I was being led and guided by my Soul to untangle the illusions, perceptions, beliefs, programs, and patterns in my human mind and reconnect to my Divine Self as a way to initiate the inner journey to my Soul.

I never consciously knew I was going to go down this road, nor did I think I needed whole healing, but that is what I received and I'm so glad I did. My Soul knew I needed more and it took me gently by the hand and solemnly guided me on the journey of a lifetime. I fully and completely healed because I trusted and followed the inner healing path to my Soul so that I could experience "whole" healing. My human mind thought physical healing was enough, but my Soul knew I needed more. My Soul wanted me to experience eternal healing and not just Band-Aid fixes that cover up internal wounds that never really heal. I had no idea what was coming, nor did I know what was in store for me.

It didn't matter that I didn't know how healing unfolds. There was always One within me that did know. All I had to do was open my heart and mind to Its guidance, receive Its messages and follow through with Its inspired action. That is all that is required to heal. I asked for healing, I became it, and I received it. I asked for life, I lived my life, and I found it. Ask and you shall receive, and boy, did I receive!

I received much more than I ever thought humanly possible, but that what's happens when you let go of your human mind and thinking. When you let go of your human mind and thinking, you get to experience life and healing beyond the human mind, beyond the physical world. Instead, you enter the world of unlimited possibilities, a world of powerful potential that the physical mind and physical reality does not know or understand. This is the realm of miracles and a way to live life that transcends the physical world.

I would not have believed it unless I had the opportunity to experience it for myself. That's the gift cancer brought to me. It brought me a miracle to experience life from an unlimited and transcendent experience. My healing wasn't just about the diet, supplements, and detox protocols, but so much more. Much, much more.

Three years passed, and I was still *cancer-free*. My human mind was beginning to accept my *cancer-free* status. As my mind opened to more possibilities, I began to question and dig deeper into my internal healing journey by getting curious and asking more questions, "What was it I did that caused my physical healing? Was it the diet? Was it the supplements? Was it my mindset and positive attitude? What was it? Why did I heal and others who have gone through similar diets and treatments did not? Why do some people who go through conventional treatment heal and others don't?"

These were the questions I wanted to discover if I was going to be a healer and teach others "another way" to heal.

My human mind wanted a better understanding to how I did it and how other people have done it. What is the common thread between us all?

I knew if I could find the answer to this one question I would be on the right track to uncovering the healing truth. I was still on the journey of finding "another way" to heal and I wouldn't stop until I got answers. My mind wouldn't stop until it was satisfied (it takes a lot to satisfy my mind; it is annoyingly persistent).

In researching alternative options to heal I read several articles about the mind, body, and spirit healing journey. I really had no idea what that journey was about, but I thought it would be interesting to investigate all of these aspects and what they meant to me.

Mind, body, and spirit healing sounded so much like a cliché. Is mind, body, and spirit healing something people just said because it sounded virtuous, or was there something more to it? I never found a comprehensive explanation of mind, body, and spirit healing, but I knew I needed to find out. What does mind, body, and spirit healing really mean? How do I apply this in my physical reality? How do I apply this to my own physical healing? Why does it matter? I had a sense that all of these questions were worth further exploration.

The Power of Your Mind

I thought I had enough information about healing the body, since I used physical things to heal my body, so I decided to explore the concepts of my mind in more depth. I began to ask questions like, "How powerful is the mind?" I knew that it is a constant battle to sort through the voices and thoughts in my head but, "How powerful are these voices and thoughts when it comes to healing?" I continued with my questions, "What is more important, the mind, or the physical tools I used? Which is more important and contributed the most to my healing process?"

These questions seemed like a good place to start to understand the healing process in greater detail. At this point, I was comfortable enough in my physical health and healing that I could play with my diet and supplements without having a negative effect on my health. I felt safe to experiment with my body.

I had practiced enough with my mind to be able to hold a consistent intention by focusing and believing in a desired outcome. I used various supplements through my healing protocol during cancer. My human mind thought that the supplements were a necessary tool in healing my body. I used supplements while training my body for the Olympia competition, so I assumed they would be helpful healing my body from cancer. I formed a belief from my past experience that I needed them to heal my body. But now, I was questioning if they were really necessary or if I just *thought* I needed them. How important and necessary were they in my healing process?

I began to experiment with supplements. If supplements are necessary for my health, my health would decline once I stopped taking them, right? I decided to convince my mind to believe they were not necessary to feel healthy and whole. I began to practice and visualize feeling and living healthy and whole without them. I hated taking them anyway, so I really didn't mind the thought of reducing my supplements every morning and night.

When I knew my mind was in alignment with the belief that I no longer needed them, I physically stopped taking my supplements. I made a note on how I was feeling prior to stopping the supplements, so I could have a bench-mark to compare my findings. After I stopped taking them, I continued to visualize feeling great without them. My mind, body, and heart were in alignment with this thought, so I was able to hold and carry the energetic expression of health, whether I was taking the supplements or not.

The next few weeks, I continued to feel great. The next month, I felt better than ever. The next three months I was still healthy and strong. My blood tests all came back normal and my health was just as I had envisioned it. This was enlightening. My body maintained a healthy vibrant state without supplements.

I then began to experiment with adding supplements. I researched the main benefit of a new supplement. For example, I experimented with a supplement that claimed to provide more energy. I visualized and convinced my mind that this supplement would give me more energy once I took the new supplement. After taking the supplement for a few days, I began to experience more energy.

After a month, I changed my visualization and pictured the same supplement not working for me. I visualized taking the supplement but not receiving any benefit from it. In fact, I decided to visualize that I received negative effects and reactions to the supplement. After a few days, my energy began to decline and I started to experience adverse reactions to the supplement. Once I stopped taking the supplement, the negative reactions went away.

Wow, this experiment blew my mind. My intention and belief in the supplement worked both ways. The supplement stayed the same but my belief in it – or not -- caused a physical reaction. If I believed the supplement would work, it did. If I believed the supplement wouldn't work, it didn't. Where my mind went, my body followed.

I then tried a similar experiment with a different supplement. I researched the main benefit of the new supplement, but instead of visualizing the supplement benefitting me or reacting poorly to me, I decided I would stay completely neutral. I visualized no intended action or reaction to the supplement. I wanted to know for myself what would happen if I left my mind and beliefs out of the entire scenario and just let the supplement do what it wanted to do. What kind of reaction or action would I have in this scenario?

What I discovered is that when I left my mind out of the process and maintained a neutral position, I had a neutral experience. I had no experience or change at all. I discovered that my mind was still part of the process even when I set no intention. Setting no intention was the intention. Wow. This was mind blowing.

My mind was the driving force behind any healing tool I used. It was and is the driving force behind the effectiveness of the healing tool itself. It is impossible to take my mind out of the healing equation. Where my mind went my body followed. Once I changed my mind, I changed my outer reality and physical outcome.

All of the dieting, supplementation, and detox protocols worked for me because my mind believed they would. It was my mind that was the greatest tool and influence in my healing protocol, not necessarily the tools themselves that helped support my body to heal. They work synergistically together. All the while my mind thought I needed the diet, supplements, and detox protocols but really what I needed was the *belief* in them that allowed them to work.

It is the beliefs and concepts in my mind that held the healing power for them to work in my physical reality. That is where the magic happens. The magic begins in the mind. This experiment also explains why the placebo effect works. People heal when they are given a fake pill, surgery or treatment, not because of the exterior tool, but because they believed the tool would heal or benefit them. It was their belief that changed and healed their outer condition, not necessarily the tool itself. It wasn't the physical tools themselves that caused my healing, it was the belief in them, as well as the belief that I could heal, that caused my healing.

This is one of the reasons why there will never be a simple ten-step program to heal your physical body. Whether something works for you or not is directly related to your internal thoughts, beliefs, and life experiences. We all have different thoughts, beliefs, and experiences so it makes complete sense that we have different ways we need to heal.

That is also why you need to go within for your answers. Meet your mind where it is at. Follow your heart that knows your mind and Soul intimately; it will lead you to your next best step. Your human mind will keep you in fear and fight-or-flight mode, which does not support your physical healing. Your human mind is limited by its knowledge because it can only draw from past experiences. It does not know all of the unconscious thoughts, patterns, and programs that you hold internally because they are hidden from your mind -- but your Soul knows. Your Soul knows you completely and knows exactly what is required to heal you.

Look within, not without, for your answers. There will never be anything, anyone, or any situation outside yourself that knows you better and can heal you better than you do. Your mind is a powerful part in this process. It is your thoughts and beliefs about the exterior tools or situations that have a massive effect on the outcome. It is not the outer world that controls the inner world. It is the inner world of thoughts, beliefs, and feelings that control the outer world.

We will never find a cure for cancer outside of ourselves, because the true answer for cancer is found within us. The answers are already there but we keep looking for answers outside of ourselves in the next drug, treatment, or cure. We already have the answer for cancer and all chronic disease if we will start looking within. The answer is so close, yet so far away. If we all began going within for our answers and healing from the inside-out, we would eventually discover our own solutions within. They have been there all along.

You are your own placebo. You already are the placebo. Whether you know this or not, you are your own answer. There is nothing outside of yourself that heals you. You heal you. If we needed something outside of ourselves to survive generation after generation we would have been extinct long, long ago. Your power lies in your belief. Your power and everything you experience in life lies in your perceptions regarding life itself.

Change your mind, change your belief, change yourself, and change your world. Your power is within you.

Redefining the Spiritual You

Once I had a deeper understanding of the power of my mind, I felt there was much more to learn. I began seeking into the spiritual realm and how my healing was connected spiritually. When I asked for guidance, I was led to several books on the subject (Yes, the Universe continued to provide all I needed to learn and grow. When I was in Divine alignment and asked, I received). My mind was beginning to grasp the workings of the mind and body integration, but what was this spiritual piece about? Besides connecting and trusting my intuition, what else was there to discover about my spirit? What did it have to do with healing?

One of the first books that opened my mind regarding spirituality was *Conversations with God, Book 3,* by Neale Donald Walsch. Neale originally wrote three volumes about his personal Q & A sessions with God. He asked God questions and received answers. *Conversations with God, Books 1-3* is the total of all of his questions and answers from God.

I thought, "How cool would it be to have a direct conversation with God? I would love to ask any question I wanted and get an answer directly from Source. This would be like finding and holding the Holy Grail!"

Little did I know, I was already having my own conversations with God, but I didn't realize it. My entire healing journey was directly guided and inspired by conversations with God, but they came as gut feelings, or instincts, not physical words. God spoke through a feeling of "knowing" and "intuition," but I didn't realize I was actually communing with God at the time. Now I am able to interpret these feelings into words, but that happened only when I let go of the thought that I was crazy to communicate with God. I just couldn't believe it was possible to talk with God ... until I finally believed and accepted it as truth.

Again, the power of the mind is always working! If you think you can, you can. If you think you can't, you can't. This reminds me of one of my mother's favorite sayings. She always said, "Can't, can't do anything." As a child, I never understood what she meant, but now I know. You can't do anything if you think you can't. On the flip side, you can do anything if you know you can. My mother was and still is full of wisdom I never really knew, until I knew.

Now back to the book, *Conversations with God.* There were many concepts in the book that were in opposition to my current thinking on spirituality, life and God. My human mind questioned, "Were these new concepts really true? How would I know if they were true?" I was willing to open my mind to the concepts presented because I was extremely curious. Were the concepts in the book right and maybe I was wrong? What if I was wrong?

My Soul was continually guiding me to question all concepts and truths I held within my mind. The healing process is a continual unraveling of the Veils of Illusion we create within our human mind. I was being called to unravel many of the religious, moral, and ethical concepts formed and created in my mind growing up in Catholic and Christian churches -- as well as my social and familial environment.

I learned right and wrong from my family, society, and the church. Everything I thought and did had to fit in the box of religious, ethical, and moral standards. I lived my life from this box and I could only live within the confined borders of this box. If I went outside this box, my human mind judged me as bad, wrong, and in need of correction. To avoid feeling guilt and shame, I never stepped outside the box or questioned the box. I simply accepted it as my truth.

I had also been taught that God is something outside of myself. God is distant and separate from me. God watches from "out there." God watches over the world with great conviction. He judges the living and the dead and if I didn't meet God's expectations, I was surely going to hell. If I didn't live my life "right," I would face the Wrath of God. I lived my life in a bubble of perfection and safety, following all the rules and being a good little girl. I stayed in my box and I condemned myself for even considering stepping outside the box. I actually judged myself more harshly than I thought God judged me.

If I was "good enough," and stayed in the box, I might have a chance to be loved and accepted by God. I might earn my angel wings and go to heaven someday. If I stepped outside of the box, I would certainly go to hell. Growing up, this concept was very real to me; I dared not step out of the box. I was able to expand the box slightly as I grew up, but the majority of my life I still lived within the box which kept me contained in the guilt and shame of my upbringing. *Conversations with God* inspired me to open my box of religion and question its validity.

I began to question and reframe religion and spirituality. What does religion and spirituality really mean to me? What were they all about? What was this entire journey of life about and what was I supposed to do about it? Who am I in relation to God, life, and spirituality? Who is God, really? Is God an entity outside of myself looking down, judging me if I am good or bad?

This is what my religion taught me, but it didn't feel right anymore. I always tried to live my life as a good person, but what does "good" mean? Who is the entity judging good and bad? Is God the one judging me, or am I judging me? Why am I judging me? Am I right or wrong in my judgment? Who is the judge anyway? Who's right or wrong? What's good and what's bad? Who's the one going to decide whether I go to heaven or hell? Is there a heaven or hell?

Anyway, you get the point. I started to question everything I thought I knew or held as my truth. When I began to question everything I thought I knew, and open my mind to new information, miraculously answers began to come to me. I discovered that most of the concepts I thought were true, were not really true. The concepts in my mind were misunderstandings and misaligned with who and what God really is. I had been living much of my life misinformed by my own mind and by all of the past programming and patterns my mind thought were real.

I wasn't good or bad. I wasn't right or wrong. My truths are only my mind's interpretation of the truth. My truth was limited by my human mind and its concepts and perceptions. It wasn't until I questioned everything I thought I knew that I was able to learn more, grow more, live more and open up more to the real Truth of God.

When I let go of my own mind, I was then able to open up to Divine Mind, Divine Wisdom, and Divine Love. Everything opened up to me when I opened up to everything. The world I had created and perceived through my human mind's conception and perception was limiting me. My mind could not and did not fully understand the capacity of God's mind. It never will.

I knew right then and there that I would spend eternity growing and learning more. I know now that I don't know anything through my own mind, but I have the ability to know, grow, and expand exponentially when I let my mind go and connect to the Divine Mind within me and all around me.

The Divine Mind knows all, is all, and loves me unconditionally. The Divine Mind is unlimited and is the creator of all there is, all that has ever been, all that will ever be, and has the power and potential of eternity. As a piece of Source God, I have all these attributes as well, not because I am God, but because I am a part and a piece of God. God created me in God's image and because I am created in that image and likeness, I have all the attributes of God, my Creator.

I am a child of God, as are you. We are all children of God. We are one with God and God is one with us. We have come to this world for an amazing experience to learn, grow, and become more of what we are, a living piece and divine expression of Source God, one with God and all the gifts God provides for us. But you will never come to this realization or experience the gifts of God until you ask and open your heart and mind to receive them.

You must let your human mind go and open and allow God's gifts of wisdom, knowledge, peace, joy, and freedom to be received. They will be provided for you because you already have them; you just haven't been accessing and using them. Your human mind (Veil of Illusion) has gotten in your way. Dissolve the misperceptions of your mind and you will experience life in a whole new capacity as one with God, at one with God, all of us one with God, and all there is, because that is all there is.

Life separated from God is a misconception of your human mind and it is keeping you stuck in the illusion of pain, suffering, guilt, crisis, and many other life conditions you find yourself in. From a spiritual sense, there is no good and bad, there is no right or wrong, there is no heaven or hell (unless your human mind creates one). There only is.

God is. Life is. I am. You are. Any other word you put behind *is*, *am* or *are* is a judgement of the human mind trying to explain or categorize something it doesn't understand. God is the great I AM. I am that I am. God is and that is all there is. You are and that is enough. We are and therefore we are enough. We are all there is. There is no need in the eyes of God to strive to be anything other than what you are in the moment. You exist, and life exists because you are a part of God. You are life itself.

This is atonement (at – one – ment). Atonement is being "at one" with God and "at one" with all there is. That is all you need to be. Simply be at one with God, at one with yourself, at one with life, at one with each other and at one with all that is. This is a simple concept, but it is not easy for the human mind to grasp. The human mind makes this simple concept difficult because it does not understand. It is impossible for the human mind to understand. The only way to understand this truth is to fully experience it in life itself.

How would your life and world change if you were to fully embrace these concepts? What if you completely accepted yourself, your neighbor, your life, and any experience that came to you as a perfect part of your life's evolution? What if you never judged yourself, judged another, or judged anything in the world again? Would it not be heaven on earth, peace on earth? This is the world as God sees it. This is the world God originally created. It's our human minds and misconceptions that have distorted the truth of what is.

God sees and knows the world in complete freedom from judgment. There is no judgment, no good or bad, no right or wrong, there only is, from God's perspective. God is perfect. God is love. Judgment cannot exist in the full presence of Love. Judgment is a human condition, not God's condition.

This world is a gift for you to experience all aspects of life. You are free to experience it anyway you choose. Free will is a gift. How do you choose to be in relationship to yourself and the world around you? Do you want to judge and condemn it, or do you want to love and accept it? Judgment leads to condemnation, guilt, pain, and suffering. Acceptance leads to love, joy, freedom, and bliss.

If you removed judgment from your mind, there would be only the experience of what is. You would have no need to judge life, you would simply have the freedom to experience life. You would accept everything in your life and appreciate it for the beauty and loving lesson it came to bring you. There would be no resistance or conflict. There would be no dis-ease. There would be no war, no fighting, no hatred, no bitterness, no resentment. We would all know who and what we really are, as children of God, created in God's image of love and light.

There would be no need to struggle for anything because we knew we already had all, know all, accept all, and are all. We could live in the freedom of pure "being." We could all live in a perfect expression of God as a human "be"ing, honoring, learning and growing in this experience called life. There would be no conflict within or outside of ourselves.

This is what happens when you begin to question your human thoughts, perceptions, and concepts. It frees your mind so that you can live in the fullest expression of who you really are as a perfect embodiment and expression of God. When you realign your mind, body, and spirit with your Divine Mind, you are free. You connect to the whole truth of all that is. You connect to the whole truth of all that has ever been, all that is now, and all that will ever be.

This is the Truth and the Truth will set you free … but only if your human mind will allow it. Life is so much more than you think it is, and only as much as you think it is, thanks to your human mind. Remembering and living from who you really are can and will change everything in your physical world; it has to, because that is the Truth of who you are.

The World Begins to Communicate with Me

I was discovering and opening my mind to new concepts and ideas every day. My conscious awareness was growing and expanding, and my physical reality was changing and shifting right before my eyes. I was experiencing a deeper understanding of myself and my world around me. Life was unfolding many mysteries and I was experiencing life in a greater capacity than I could before. By opening my mind, the physical world was opening up to me.

The next question I was curious about was the role my diet played in my healing process. If the mind is so powerful, did my diet matter as much as I originally thought? Did my diet matter at all in the healing process? What foods are best for healing, and which ones are not? What role did my diet play in the healing process and what role does it play now? I didn't understand the role of diet in my healing process, but I had an insane curiosity to find out more.

My daughter is a book enthusiast and she loves the written word. We visit book stores on a regular basis and I'm drawn to the health-and-wellness section. Every book store I've been to is filled with a plethora of books claiming to have the next best answer on diet, nutrition, and detox programs. With all of these books and programs available, don't you think we would have found the one that works by now? How many diet trends do we need to go through and need to experiment with until we find the one that works? We should have found it by now, unless … it doesn't and will never exist. Therein lies the truth. There will never be a perfect diet or nutritional program to address your diet dilemma.

This is good news and bad news. The good news is, you can stop going from one diet to the other trying to find the perfect solution to your diet needs. You can stop the insanity of starving then binging, losing weight then gaining it back again. You can stop putting faith in programs guaranteed to be your next solution only to end in failure. This is the crazy diet roller-coaster ride that needs to stop. It's time to get off that crazy ride. That's the good news. You can stop driving yourself crazy with all these diets.

The bad news is you will never find the perfect diet to solve your diet issue in one simple solution. It is not and will never be that easy. So, what is the answer? What is the truth about diets? How should we eat to heal and restore our lives?

After contemplating these questions over and over in my mind, I heard my inner Voice of Wisdom say, "Stop trying and thinking so hard. You are beginning to drive yourself crazy with all these questions. The diet that is most helpful will be different for everyone. Everyone's past experiences, thoughts, concepts, and programs are different, so they will have different needs and lessons to learn. Everyone is at different stages of growth and learning in their life experience. It is more important to build a relationship with your body, reconnect to your Soul, and allow them to guide you. Your diet and your needs will change as you move through life.

"Your diet is another reflection of your inner world and health. When you choose foods that are not in alignment with your natural state of being, it is a sign that you may not be aligned with your natural state of being. There may be something more for you to discover in your inner world if you constantly choose foods that do not love and nourish your body.

"This is another example of how everything in your outer world is designed to lead and guide you to learn and grow. Your outer world can teach you messages of what your inner world is calling for. When you choose foods that are in alignment with your natural state of being, the foods act as tools and rituals of love and nourishment that support your body to move into a natural state of health and well-being. Your outer actions reflect your inner state of being."

Then Divine asked me, "What foods did you use to heal your body?"

"Well," I said, "I used whole organic foods. I ate clean, farm-raised foods with no preservatives, GMO, or pesticides. If it was grown and provided by the earth, I ate it. If it was not, I didn't. I also drank clean, pure filtered water."

"Yes," the voice replied, "You used foods provided by the earth, that were whole, clean, pure, and not changed or tainted by man (human mind). You ate foods that were provided by the earth and by nature, just as you are part of nature. You ate foods that the earth nourished, loved, and supported. Because the earth nourished, loved, and supported them, they carry the energetic expression to nourish, love, and support you, too. You drank clean, pure water that cleansed and detoxed your body from toxins?"

"Yes," I agreed, "That sounds right."

"Good," Divine acknowledged. "Now, look back on the foods you ate to heal. How do they reflect your healing journey thus far?"

I thought for a moment and repeated the words back in my head. "Whole, clean, pure, natural, provided and nourished by God, not man-made or altered by man." I then connected these words to myself and my healing journey.

I asked myself, "How do these words connect and apply to my journey of healing?"

I considered the first word: *Whole*. *Whole* is what my journey was and is about. Wholeness is about reconnecting to all of who I am as a mind, body, spirit and Soul. I was and continue to be on journey of interior wholeness and whole healing. I am learning how to heal all parts of me, not just physical healing, but healing, reconnecting, and integrating all parts of me. I was and am still on a 'wholeness' journey, so I ate whole foods."

"Yes, go on," said Divine.

"OK," I said, "next words are: clean, pure, and natural. I was on a journey to discover the real me, the original me that God created; this was a journey of my true identity. A clean, pure discovery of my Soul, not the identity that my human mind created. I wanted to know who I was as God created me and see my world, myself and all of my life through God's pure, clean eyes, not my own. I wanted to reconnect with nature and see myself and know myself as one with it because I am a natural being. Nature has taught me so much about myself by observing it and recognizing that I am part of nature. My natural state of being is perfectly healthy and whole."

"Yes," Divine asked, "what else?"

I continued, "I ate foods that God made and supplied. I chose not to eat foods that were tainted or altered by man. I avoided GMO's and foods contaminated by chemicals, preservatives, or pesticides. I ate organic and free-range meat. I avoided processed foods. If it was made in a factory I avoided it, if it was made and provided by the earth, I ate it. My healing was a process of connecting to Divine Mind and releasing my human mind, my man-made mind. The GMO's, pesticides, and chemicals represented my human mind and its desire to control and manipulate life. Natural and whole foods represented my Divine Mind and the journey to get back to nature and the wholeness within me. The clean, pure water represented the pure and clean consciousness and connection to Divine Wisdom. By reconnecting to Divine Wisdom and allowing it to flow like water through me, it cleansed and healed me."

OMG! My entire diet and way that I ate was a reflection of my inner healing process. Eating clean, pure, whole foods was an outer ritual of love and nourishment to support my body back to its natural inner state of being a perfect state of health. I had no idea that my diet was reflecting and acting as a ritual of the whole, natural healing process."

I sat stunned and still for a moment allowing this message to sink in. This is a new revelation. My diet reflected my entire healing journey. I had no conscious awareness that my outer world and diet was a reflection of the inner healing process I was going through. I chose to eat clean, whole foods at the time because it simply felt right and made sense to my human mind. I just did it, but I had no idea of the deeper messages my diet contained until this moment, eight years later.

Then Divine said, "You have come a long way in your journey. You are now able to understand the deeper messages of your life because you have expanded your consciousness to know more.

"There are signs all around you, but you had not developed the broader consciousness to recognize them or interpret their deeper meaning until now. The world around you is going to continue to get more and more magical for you because you are opening, learning, and growing. You are open to growth and you will receive many messages from your world. Continue to be present and open to them.

"Everything you have needed and everything you will need has always been available to you. Stay open to the signs and messages in your outer world and use them as a tool for your inner healing and growth process. Life is opening up to you because you have opened up to life. Live life. Love life. Be life and life will become you. You are life itself.

"You are life and you are a magnificent creator and observer. You are now conscious to this and will be able to experience life from a whole new level than before. Your human mind is dissolving, and the veil is being lifted for you to discover and experience more life from and through your Divine Mind.

"Enjoy your life, enjoy your world. It is all here for you, for your growth and for your expansion. You are becoming one with your world and the world is becoming one with you. You are awakening to a whole new world. Your old life has died, and you are birthing a new life, one created with God and one with the Universe. You are never alone, you are loved, and you are becoming whole."

"Whoa!" I gasped, "All I asked was a simple question regarding diet and I received so much more!"

This is how life began to respond to me. It responded with so much more than I could have ever expected or anticipated. Life grew exponentially that day and I began to observe and see the world from an entirely different perspective. My outer world became my inner teacher. I began noticing things I never noticed before; they had an entirely different meaning and message for me. Information began pouring into me and I was beginning to experience "Ah-Ha" moments each and every day.

Divine messages and understanding were coming in much more frequently, even when I didn't ask for them. It was like the world was speaking a new language that I was able to hear and translate. I was able to sense energies I didn't have access to before. The world shifted and changed because I shifted and changed.

My consciousness had been expanding and growing through this healing journey and I was now able to hear and experience life from an entirely different level of consciousness -- and it was incredible. I began to experience life from an expanded consciousness and know and understand from an entirely different perspective. I was no longer limited by the perspective of my human mind and was able to see, hear, and enjoy life from a Divine awareness.

Heaven on earth was beginning to unfold right before my eyes because I could see life through God's eyes rather than my own. I was able to interpret life from God's understanding rather than my own limited understanding. I was able to solve problems from an expanded consciousness and awareness. Problems weren't really problems for me anymore because I was able to see and understand them from a new perspective. From God's perspective, they were simply new experiences in my life; there was no problem, only a new experience. I was excited each day to see, hear, feel, touch, and experience the world in a whole new way. I felt like a child again and began to explore everything from my Divine Mind and highly attuned new senses.

Life is so full. Heaven is already on earth if we are willing to expand our consciousness enough to see and experience it. It's like waking up from a bad dream into the reality of heaven on earth. When you break free from the human mind and human consciousness, when you break free from your own perception of reality to God's perception of reality, you begin to live life, see life and experience life in an entirely new way. Life is magical and miraculous if you choose to see and experience it that way.

Come back to the wholeness that you are. Recognize that you are nature and your natural state of being is already perfect and whole. Experience life through your Divine senses, perceptions and reality and your whole world will change. You will begin to see life and the world from a whole new perceptive and life will begin to teach you everything you need to know in order to learn and grow. You will fall more in love with yourself, your life, and your world.

The kingdom of heaven is within you, whether you know it or not. You just need to recognize and follow it. You have the power of the Divine within you. When you connect to it and work with it, you have the power to change everything. You had it all along . . . you just disconnected for a little while.

When Life Repeats Itself ... Messages Through Patterns

After this deeper discovery into self-realization, I began playing with life and noticing all the messages it had for me. I noticed that messages and lessons come through as repeating patterns. Have you ever noticed a time in your life where a certain situation or problem continues to resurface? Even when you thought you had learned the lesson at hand or moved yourself away from the problem, it keeps coming back to you?

Any time you recognize a repeating pattern in your life, the pattern reappears as a sign that there is something more for you to discover. There is still more for you to learn. Perhaps there is something within you that is not paying attention or listening. Maybe you heard the message and thought you were done with it, but because the pattern resurfaces, there is still a deeper lesson calling to be learned. Sometimes life patterns repeat themselves as a test or challenge for you to apply what you have learned. Remember, life is a school for growth and development. There will be lessons to learn as well as tests and challenges for your personal growth and development.

One of the patterns that repeated in my life was the collapse and financial fall of my business. (Ugh!!! I wish my Soul could leave this one alone, but apparently, I needed to go through this again for my own growth.) Yes, there was more I needed to learn and discover. I also had a sense that this pattern was repeating itself as a test and challenge to see how I would apply all that I have learned through my healing journey so, my Soul gave me another round of financial collapse. Well, here we go again.

Whether I wanted it or not, another financial collapse was on its way. How would I handle it this time? What would I choose? My Soul was giving me a test to apply all the lessons

I had learned. I knew this time was coming and I was now called to face it. There was a part of me the secretly hoped my Soul would skip this challenge and move on to something easier, something fun, but that wasn't going to happen.

There was also a part of me that wondered what I would do. How was I going to handle financial crisis this time? Would I be able to apply all the lessons I had learned over the last eight years -- or not? My Soul was giving me the exact life circumstances that led to my final breakdown and cancer diagnosis. I was given the chance to live through it again. Would I choose to thrive or barely survive?

My Soul delivered this test right after Ed and I reached the point of financial recovery from the first collapse, loss of business, foreclosure, and separation from friends and family. We had rebuilt our lives and life was good. Ed restored his construction company to a seven-figure business and had just invested in a large-scale development project with 200+ home sites. I grew my real estate company from one agent (myself) to nine full-time agents. I purchased an office building and had just finished an extensive remodel, inside and out. Between the new building, remodel, and subdivision development, Ed and I had invested most of the money we created and saved over the last nine years. Last, but not least, we had finally built another dream house and just moved into it. Life was thriving, according to my human mind, and we had finally survived the first collapse. We were back on track and life was good ... for roughly one month ... and then the coal and oil industry collapsed (does this story sound freakishly familiar?)

The Gillette market and economy crashed fast and hard because the coal and oil industry was the main economic producer and all this tiny town had. When coal thrived, Gillette thrived. When coal didn't, the town goes bust, and bust it did. The market went down fast and furious. No one was buying or building new homes. In fact, most people were losing their homes. The majority of the town lost their jobs and people began leaving the area in droves.

I stood in silence and stillness because I knew exactly what was going to transpire. I had just gone through this same situation in Colorado 10 years before. Just when I thought my luck and my life had changed for the better, it changed again. All I could do was stand and watch as the market and economy crumbled. Are you fucking kidding me!

The majority of our money and savings was again tied into investments and property that was losing value each and every day. We couldn't sell our homes or investments because no one was buying them. All we could do was watch our financial empire dwindle and diminish to nothing but expensive liabilities. We still had loans on the real estate building, development project, and our personal home. Each day was like burning a pile of $100 bills and there was no end in sight. Shit, now what?!

Then the Voice in my heart whispered, "OK, Mary, now what are you going to do? You are now faced with the same situation you were faced with before you got cancer. Are you going to take what you have learned and apply it, or you going to withdraw and hide from it? What would you like to do?"

"Ugh!!!" I growled at the voice in disgust, "Are you kidding me!?"

"No, this is no joke, what would you like to do?" the Voice replied in a sweet and calm manner.

"Fine," I groaned with apprehension, not in complete agreement with this new life lesson and circumstance. In my heart, I knew this collapse was a life-lesson I needed to go through. There was no fighting or denying it. I knew this was part of my healing journey and spiritual practice. I needed to choose whether to trust this plan or fight it. I had a lot to process, but I knew I needed to trust and learn the lessons I was faced with. Was I going to barely survive this situation or was I going to find a way to thrive?

"Ok," I said, "I choose to trust you (even though I don't want to). I choose to thrive. Please show me how."

I then made a choice to accept the situation as it was. I chose to see and learn the lessons that would come. I chose to accept all of the material loss as it came and accept all of the challenges I was going to face as my material world crumbled (again). I chose not to fight the situation and I chose peace instead. I continued to be patient, loving, and kind to myself despite my exterior world crumbling around me. I openly accepted each challenge as it came up. I didn't judge or stress about anything (at least not for long) and I trusted that I would be led, loved, supported, and guided by the Universe. The Universe would provide for me, no matter what happened. I trusted that everything was happening for a reason. Everything was happening to serve me, not to harm me. It wasn't easy, but the choice was simple. I knew what I was called to do and go through.

I was surprisingly shocked how calm I was able to be and how I was able to maintain a steady peace in the midst of crisis. Crisis didn't affect me, and I was not entangled in it or with it. I was *peace* in the middle of crisis and I was not bothered by it. I was like the eye of the storm. I was the calm in the midst of the hurricane.

I learned that crisis and stress is a choice and I had the power to choose how I wanted to be in relationship to it. I had the choice to be engulfed in it, or not. I can choose my response in any situation I face. This was empowering. My power is my choice. My human mind labeled this experience as a crisis, but I chose not to *be* in crisis. I chose *peace* instead, and that was what I experienced.

Eventually, I worked through this financial collapse and deepened my trust and relationship with my Soul by trusting my internal guidance and not getting entangled with my outer world. I learned that I could choose to *be* whatever I wanted to experience despite what was happening around me.

"Interesting," I thought. "What an insightful lesson. I can choose my experience and my relationship to life. Whatever I choose, I will experience despite what is going on around me. This is powerful!" I thanked my Soul for the lesson and I continued on.

11

COMING HOME -- DEEP INNER HEALING OF MY SOUL

A Call to Come Home to the Land of Love ... Moving Back to Colorado

Ed and I knew that it would be a lost cause to stay in Gillette; the market was going to take a long time to recover. We began to explore other options and other areas to relocate. We looked at several opportunities and multiple locations, but nothing was coming together except for one option.

The only option that looked promising was to relocate back home, back to our hometown of Loveland. Yes, ironically my Soul was creating the path and calling me home. Not only was my Soul calling me back to my physical home, I was also being called back to my inner home, back to the love land of God, back to the love of my Soul, back to Love itself, back to the origin of who I am. My outer world was simply reflecting my inner world's call from my Soul. I was being called to come home, internally and externally. "OK," I said, "I'm coming home."

Ed and I left everything we had in Gillette. We left our personal home, the newly renovated office, my real estate business, Ed's construction company and an entire development project back in Gillette. Within two weeks after making the decision to move, we were back home in Loveland, CO.

My outer world was a perfect reflection of what my inner world was calling for. This, too, was part of my healing journey and discovery of my true self. Self-realization is a *coming home*. It was my Soul's purpose in life to discover more of who I am as a Soul by showing me the way home. I was coming back home to the heart of who and what I am as a perfect piece of Source God. I was coming home to myself and I was coming home to God. I was coming home to the heart of Love itself and I was now living in Loveland. I was being called to come back home, in many different ways.

"Thank you again for the message," I said, "you are completely blowing my mind."

"That is the point," my Soul replied. "Dissolving and letting go of your human mind is the only way to find your way home and the only way to fully heal, restore, and live your truest life." I could feel my Soul smile.

"Thank you again," I replied, in humble gratitude, "I'm sure there's more for me to discover, isn't there?"

"Yes," my Soul replied, "Much, much more."

Ed and I arrived back in Loveland and moved into a tiny rental, not fully knowing how we were going to make ends meet and rebuild our lives. Moving into a rental was another life message and sign of how my outer world was reflecting my inner world. The rental symbolized a period of transition for me, as a rental is a temporary home. Moving and changing homes also represented the moving and changing of my life and inner home. I knew the next stage in my life was going to be a transitionary and transformative stage. I was being taught how to come home and be at home with my spiritual world and authentically integrate it into my material world. How would I balance and integrate the two worlds of my inner home and outer reality? What would my life look like and feel like now?

Ed and I were starting over again. While the real estate/construction market had recovered and was going strong in Colorado, we were still faced with the dilemma of a broken bank account. How can we build a business on pennies, support a family, and make our lives work? Instead of fretting, as I used to do, I was able to let the situation go and place my trust in the hands of the Divine. If Divine led us here, Divine could find a way to support us here. I fully trusted that God would find a way to get Ed's business going and stay alive. I put his business in God's hands and kept my hands off. It was a relief to give this responsibility to Divine rather than holding on and getting dragged by the debilitating burden of it all.

I was also faced with another decision. My Soul was patiently waiting for my answer. The question was, what was I going to do with my career path? Was I going to go back into real estate and put my financial security into the real estate business, or was I going to put my financial security into the hands of Divine and follow Its guidance? The market was strong, and I knew I could make really good money. My human mind loved this idea. It made sense and was practical, logical, and smart. We needed money and this was a great way to get it quickly and efficiently. I already had my real estate license. All I had to do was start working and start making money.

While jumping back into real estate was a logical choice for my mind, my heart was calling me to go a different direction. My heart was calling me to build a business, share my story, and teach people how to heal and restore their lives. I knew this new business was my purpose in life. I had a passion to share my life and experience with others, so I could teach people another way to heal. I knew my Soul had been calling me to do this for a very long time.

I had actually made a deal with God shortly after my cancer diagnosis. Have you even made a "deal" with God? I did, and I knew I was being called to fulfill my end of the bargain. This was a "deal" that I wasn't going to get out of. It was one of my life lessons and purpose for being and living. There is no hiding from your Soul's purpose. The truth is, once you connect to the purpose of your Soul, and accept Its truth, there is no going back. I knew and had experienced too much to go back into unconscious thinking and living now.

The deal I made with God was that if I was alive in five years after my cancer diagnosis, I would learn how to fully heal and teach others how to do it. During this time of transition in Colorado, I was reminded of the deal I made years before. My Soul had provided an intimate healing experience so that I could gain a unique understanding of the whole healing process. Now I was being called to share this message and information.

I knew I was being called to step forward with this information and my Soul knew it, too. If I didn't listen to my Soul, I would not be fully living my passion for life. I would not be fully living my purpose in this life. I knew if I did not move forward with sharing my story and sharing this message, my Soul would begin to slowly die instead of fully live. If I did not choose to follow the path of my Soul, I would be tormented and conflicted from the inside out. My outer world would reflect my inner torment and I would be miserable.

The last few years I had placed multiple excuses and reasons ahead of my Soul's desire to share this message. Over the last eight years, I had kept myself busy running a real estate office, raising kids, supporting my husband's work, and rebuilding a financial empire and financial security. I had kept myself "too busy" to share my story, start a business, and help other people. My real estate company, my husband's company, my kids, all kept me too busy to pursue my Soul's passion and my purpose. Now my Soul had taken all of my "safe excuses" away and I was left with a choice. What am I going to do?

Am I going to jump back into real estate and make money or am I going to honor my Soul and share my message of healing and restoration? I knew what my Soul called for, but my human mind wanted me to play it safe and go back to real estate. The money sounded so good, safe, and secure to my human mind because it was scared and wanted a plan for immediate financial security. My human mind did not care what my Soul wanted or needed. My human mind did not care whether I would be internally tormented. It wanted what it wanted at any cost. But my Soul wanted more. My Soul knew more. I chose to love and nourish my Soul.

So again, I surrendered my human mind to the calling of my Soul. I reminded my human mind what happens when I neglect my Soul. When I neglect my Soul, life begins to neglect me. Life becomes hard and I struggle and fight for my life. Dis-ease can become a physical reality. I reminded my human mind how much Divine energy loves us and wants to take care of us. I reminded my human mind how much Divine Wisdom knows and wants to lead us into new ways of knowing and experiencing a Divine Life. I knew I needed to answer this call and I needed my human mind on board with me. We cannot be at odds with each other. Being at odds creates too much conflict. My human mind agreed and we were ready to move forward together again.

My minds were in agreement again and ready to move forward with creating a new business, but Divine said, "Wait, there is still more. You are missing one more piece of the healing puzzle. You must go deeper and heal and integrate the abandoned parts of your Soul." Once again, I had no idea what this meant or how I was going to do this. The only thing I did know what that there was more for me to discover. I was open and willing to discover more.

I spent the next year looking and seeking within myself. I began to sit in silence and channel messages from my Soul. My Soul was leading me inward on a deeper healing journey into my past selves. I didn't realize it, but I was still carrying past wounds, traumas, and unconscious feelings that were stuck in my body. My Soul needed and wanted me to come home and come face-to-face with each one of these past traumas.

My Soul wanted me to meet the dark, deprived and neglected inner pieces of myself, so that I could heal them through awareness and love.

The next year was one of the most powerful and life changing experiences I had ever gone through. I was able to touch into the deep layers of unconscious wounding, patterns, and programs I didn't know existed, but that I needed to heal and restore with unconditional love and acceptance. It was the next piece of the whole healing puzzle. It was Soul healing and integration. I wasn't ready for this final piece until now. I first had to move through healing physically, mentally, emotionally, and reconnect spiritually. I needed those other parts and pieces first to expand my conscious awareness before I was ready to heal and integrate at a Soul level.

My Soul had been guiding and directing this entire process through every single event in my life. I was able to move through the process by opening, allowing, and trusting my Soul through my personal journey. Most times, I had no clue what I was doing or how I was healing, but my Soul knew the whole time. It wasn't my human mind's understanding that healed me. It was my Soul's understanding, direction, and guidance that healed me. Thank God I didn't know what I was doing because I probably would have gotten in my own way. Most of the time it is the mind that gets in its own way, but I realized that you don't need to know "how" to heal in order "to" heal.

Healing is a process of opening, accepting, receiving, allowing, surrendering, and trusting the part within you that does know. It is so simple and so hard at the same time. But, I am here to say that healing is possible. Anyone can do it. If it is possible for me, it is possible for you. We are one and the same. It is a simple choice to stop fighting and start healing. Go within and allow your Soul, your heart, your Divine Mind, and the Divine to lead you home. You will find your home in the center of who you are. Your home is in your heart. It is your heart that can heal all things. It is your heart that also heals and integrates your Soul.

Heart as Home and Soul

I'd like to touch on the importance of your heart in the deeper healing process of your Soul. Why is your heart so important in this deeper healing process? Let's dive into this.

Your heart is the center of your Divine home. It is your connection to all things in your inner and outer world as well as your spiritual and physical world. You will find all the answers you seek when you connect to your heart. Feel and connect to your heart. Your heart is your connection to your Soul, the Divine, and the world around you.

Your heart's energetic frequency has a language that speaks to all things seen and unseen. It contains a frequency every single cell can hear and understand. It contains a frequency that everyone and everything in your outer world can hear and understand. It carries the energetic frequency of your state of being and your energetic expression. It contains the frequency that sends and receives messages to and from your outer and inner worlds. You send and receive messages through your heart. It is how your Soul speaks to you and how you speak to the world. Multiple studies have been done at the HeartMath Institute in California regarding the energetic field of your heart and how it is a powerful energetic messenger and receiver.

Your heart is the center of all things, including your thinking and feeling centers. Your thinking center is in the center of your head. Your feeling center is in your lower abdomen. Your heart center is the middle point between these two locations. The heart takes information from your thoughts (mind center) and feelings (body center) and integrates them into the energetic expression you relay to your body and your world. Your body and world then respond to the message your heart sends out and draws physical experiences to you based on your thoughts and feelings.

Most of the problems you experience are related to conscious and unconscious thoughts and feelings. The conscious thoughts you have you are aware of and familiar with but it's the unconscious ones that really hold you back from what you want to experience in your life and this physical reality. This is where the deeper Soul work comes into play.

Your heart has the innate capacity to heal all past programming and concepts that keep you stuck and hold you back from living your life to the fullest. The heart heals through acceptance, love, and compassion. There is no judgment, criticism, or denial from a pure, whole, healthy Divinely connected heart. There is only acceptance, love, peace, and compassion. The combination of these attributes contain a powerful healing capacity. All pain and past emotional trauma can and must be healed through the heart. It is not possible to heal emotionally through outside resources. While outside resources can help you understand and/or guide you to the inner healing process, this work is an internal job consciously directed by and for you. There is no trauma, pain, or emotional burden greater than the love and healing capacity of your heart. All can be healed from a Divine heart that knows all, loves all, and is all. There is a Divine heart within you that knows all, loves all, is all, and can heal all that is inside of you.

In order to heal unconscious thinking, feelings, emotions, patterns, and programs, you first need to become aware of them. They need to surface into your conscious awareness before you can accept, love, and restore them through your heart. You also need to be able to love and accept yourself. In order to love and accept painful emotions and past memories -- those you would just assume be forgotten and abandoned -- you must carry an immense inner capacity to love. Painful emotions and memories will only feel safe enough to come forward if they know they will be accepted and loved by you. You can no longer ignore or abandon them. I had to learn to love and accept myself before I could heal my deepest pain.

So how do you bring unconscious thinking, feeling, patterns, and programs into conscious awareness? How do you bring what is unknown into the known so you can heal them? This is where deep reflection and help from the Divine is absolutely necessary. And working with someone trained in these unconscious patterns is also very helpful. Another person who has done their own inner healing is more likely to recognize patterns and signs that show up in your life, because they have done their own work. They have walked into the unknown themselves and carry an energetic capacity to see and recognize unconscious thoughts and feelings you can't. When these unconscious thoughts and feeling become conscious, you can then heal and restore these patterns and programs. This the deep healing that happened for me during my one-year sabbatical.

Problems in My Own Home

Our marriage had gone through hell and back and hell again. It was barely hanging on, held together by a weak and tattered thread ready to break at any moment. I felt completely disconnected from Ed. I was still a single married woman but instead of raising infants, I was raising two teenagers on my own. Nothing had changed.

I began questioning everything about my marriage and our relationship. I didn't feel loved, honored, and cherished by him. He was distant, controlling, and harsh. He continued to drown his pain by working all day and then drinking from the afternoon until he passed out at night. Every night I left him on the couch; I was feeling abandoned and alone. Ed and I continued to manage our internal pain in our own dysfunctional ways. I buried my pain and tried to ignore it through positive thinking and numbing my feelings. Ed managed his pain through working and drinking. This was our life for a long, long time. This is how we survived. We were trying to manage the unmanageable and our lives reflected it. We were living in hell within ourselves, our family, our finances, our home, our lifestyle, and our relationship. Our inner worlds were creating our outer reality through our relationship.

I finally had to face my inner demons because I didn't want to live this way anymore. I did not need to be in a relationship like this any longer. I longed for a relationship where I felt loved and accepted for who I was and who I was evolving into. My inner wounds were ready to be seen and felt.

So as I opened the door to face my inner wounds, a bitter anger began to rise and awaken within me and I had the courage to feel it for the first time. Not only did I feel anger, I felt hate and resentment. These dark, dense emotions surfaced from deep within me and I did not push them away this time. Instead, I let my pain rise and be with me however it needed to be. I needed to get these feelings out. They had been buried a long time because my human mind could not face, accept, or honor the deep feelings I was carrying. The only way I could release these intense emotions was to project them onto someone else. Ed was an easy and rational target, so he got the brunt of my pain. I needed someone to blame and I chose him.

I projected all of my anger and resentment toward Ed. I deeply resented him for the fall of his business and losing all of our money. I blamed him for taking my security and safety away from me. I blamed him for our disconnected relationship. He was ruining our marriage, not me. Damn him! Everything was his fault. He was a good-for-nothing piece of shit, a loser who couldn't control himself or his life. He created hell in my home and I blamed him for it. It was his fault and I was not going to let him off the hook for what he was creating in my life. I was going through an explosion of my internal feelings that I had been holding back for a very long time.

Unfortunately, by blaming him, I was not able to see or heal my internal pain, emotions and personal responsibility for my life. I could never get to the root cause of my pain by projecting and blaming him, yet this was all I knew how to do at the time. The other problem I was creating by blaming my partner, was that it did not create a nurturing, loving, and caring relationship. Instead, I was creating a horrific, living nightmare. But in this moment, I didn't care. It felt good to blame him and blaming was all I could think of to do to make sense of my situation. The blaming gave me a sense of empowerment and control.

Deep down, I was scared shitless and I had no idea what to do. I had absolutely no control over my situation, my life, or my emotions -- and that terrified me. Who is this person I'm becoming? Never in my life have I felt such intense emotion and anger, but it was all coming to a head right here and right now. The flood-gates were open.

One night, after an "alcohol induced" argument, I finally snapped. I was tired of hiding and dancing around Ed's drinking problem. A reactive switch flipped within me and I exploded in a fit of angry rage. I finally braced him with the words I had needed to say for a long time but was too afraid to express.

I shouted, "It is time for you to deal with your own shit!"

He looked back at me, eyes glaring, and yelled, "No, woman, you are the one with the problem. I am just fine! You need help, not me!"

He slammed the door and trudged into the house. I steamed and stewed on the front porch in shock and disbelief. His reaction stunned me. How can he be so blind? Couldn't he see how his drinking was affecting us? Couldn't he see that we were beginning to destroy each other? Couldn't he see how his drinking was affecting our entire family?

I thought to myself, "Why can't he see what he is doing to himself, to me, and to the kids? I can't believe how unconscious he is. Why can't he see it?!"

I was frustrated and heartbroken. How could I both love and resent a man with such intensity? It's like my love and resentment were feeding each other and I was being eaten alive in the middle. What I didn't realize was that part of my anger, frustration, and judgment toward him was really an unconscious anger, frustration, and judgment pattern within me that was calling and surfacing to be healed. I did have a problem, but I didn't know it or see it. I was unconscious to my pain. The disconnected relationship between the two of us was a sign that there was a disconnected relationship within me and it was internally eating me alive. We both needed help and healing, but neither of us was able to admit we had a problem.

Ed's final remark continued to taunt me, "You are the one with the problem. You need help, not me!" I despised this remark. I despised Ed. I kept telling myself that Ed was the one with the problem, not me. He's in denial, not me. He's the alcoholic, not me. He needs to fix this, not me. I kept replaying our argument in my head and became even more angry, more resentful, more bitter.

Then suddenly a light went off within me. I realized the anger I felt was birthed within me, not Ed. *I* was the source of the anger. The anger was in *me*. I was choosing anger. In this moment, I recognized that this inner anger and bitterness did not serve me. It was destructive and I knew it would not help or heal my situation. I didn't want to be angry or bitter and I knew I could choose something different. I did not need to fight and be at odds with my anger, I could recognize, accept, and transform it. I did not need to have it consume me. Then something shifted within me, and I started to question: maybe there is something I am missing. Maybe I do need help. Maybe I am the one with the problem.

I sat in wonder and silence with this thought. This was a new concept I had not considered before. Was there something in me that needed help? I didn't think so, but perhaps I was willing to find out. I had nothing to lose by seeking help. Maybe there was something to gain. Maybe there is more to discover. Maybe I will try and see.

I finally surrendered to the idea of therapy for myself. I was willing to drop my ego and ask for help. I had to do something different and so I chose therapy. I chose to make the first step because I knew Ed wasn't ready, willing, or able to do it for himself or seek the help he needed with his addiction. This is what love does. Love called me to take the first step to initiate a healing process for both of us. I was called to be the change that both of us needed but only one of us was able to make. Would this act of love be able to save me? Save him? Save us? Save our family? I had no idea, but I knew I had to try. Humbled and broken, I made the choice to choose love.

After all that I had been through in my healing journey, I knew I needed to find someone special who would understand the process of my entire healing journey. I needed someone who had past experience with Soul healing, consciousness, and deep integrated healing so they could help love, guide, and support me through the inner journey I was already on. I needed someone who understood the whole healing process that includes all parts and aspects of me.

I didn't want to work with someone who kept me stuck in past stories and programs. I knew I needed to be released from the past, not encouraged to stay stuck in it. I have seen people spend years in traditional therapy and make very little progress. I knew the traditional route was not right for me. I needed someone who could work with "all of me" and help me understand who I am as a physical, emotional, mental, and spiritual being.

Where was I going to find someone like this? I had to go within and ask the Divine to find my therapist. My mind wondered if the Universe could really provide the answer. I'm not sure why I continued to doubt this process. After all, the Universe had always provided everything I needed when I needed it. I still struggled with doubt, but like everything in my healing journey, once I set an intention, people and things came into my life in the exact moment I need them to show up. I never have to work for it. I simply ask, trust, and allow the Universe to show and provide for me. This is another spiritual exercise that gets easier with practice and life experience.

Uncovering My Shadow, Meeting My Shadow, Healing My Inner Home

I began Googling "spiritual counselors" and I immediately found my spiritual guide and soul healer. His name was Jon McIntosh. His website was the first that popped up and I was immediately drawn and connected to it. I knew he had something to offer me. I called and set up a consultation and he agreed to meet with me.

Jon had more than 30 years of experience with inner healing and the deep unconscious patterns and material we carry within ourselves. He had gone through his own healing process and could recognize patterns and program within me because he had done his own work. He was the next human angel who came into my life and I am so grateful he showed up. Jon had the innate capacity to connect with my Soul and he held space for me to feel safe, loved, and secure so that I could revisit my past trauma, inner pain, and disintegrated pieces of my Soul.

Revisiting my past and trapped emotions was the most uncomfortable part of my healing journey. I had to be vulnerable with the most fragile and broken pieces of my being. I had to expose myself so that I could heal the pieces my human mind would just as well leave alone.

Deep Soul healing is challenging and uncomfortable. Very few people choose to go through this process because from the human mind's perspective, these hurts are better left hidden in the deep, dark recesses of the Soul. Your human mind prefers to keep them buried and hidden so you don't have to experience the pain and feel the emotions involved with allowing them to surface and be healed. It's a little like detoxing; often you feel worse before feeling better; we fear feeling worse as the feelings resurface to be cleared from our system.

Unfortunately, if you don't heal these parts and pieces, they will hold you hostage from fully living your life. You can try to keep them buried, but they will eventually insist on being heard. Unexpressed feelings and emotions stay buried for a while until they reach their tipping point. Then they manifest as an illness, such as stomach ulcers or a rash, etc., or they creep up on you when you least expect them, like a volcano building up intense pressure. When the right trigger happens, you explode in fits of anger, emotion, or overwhelming bursts of energy. They come out as expressions of emotion and feeling that feel foreign to you. In other words, you act out in ways in which you do not recognize yourself. This is what happened in my outbreak with Ed. I snapped and burst out in an angry rage. My volcano had erupted.

Unexpressed thoughts, feelings, emotions, and trauma stay within the body, trapped in a prison of fear. This prison keeps you from moving forward and expressing and experiencing your true purpose in life. You will be limited by your own limitations and you will have no idea why. Instead of living your life to the fullest, you will be trapped and paralyzed by fear, anger, loneliness, depression, frustration, pain, and suffering. This is not thriving; this is barely surviving. Unless you are willing to face and heal these buried emotions, they will continue to run and ruin your life. Stored thoughts, feelings, emotions, and trauma in the body have the power to keep you from moving into the freedom of fully living your life, physically, mentally, emotionally, and spiritually.

Again, deep Soul healing is not an easy process and your human mind will do everything in its power to prevent you from healing your broken pieces. Instead of allowing unconscious material to surface and heal them, your human mind wants to keep them buried. Your human mind thinks it is safer to hide from them rather than heal them. The problem with this method is that these unconscious thoughts become unconscious programs that run your life and potentially ruin your health. Unconscious thoughts, emotions, traumas, beliefs, and truths of you are part of the Veil of Illusion. If you want to fully heal, you must address the *shadows* of your Soul or they will continue to run the show. Burying your emotions is like burying parts of yourself and your Soul. It's impossible to love, accept, and heal all of you when you continue to reject certain parts of yourself. It is also impossible to hear further guidance and gain clarity on your purpose, desires, and your next best steps in life when you bury your emotions.

If I wanted to heal all of me, I needed to know, love, and honor all of me, including the messy and disowned parts. This meant I had to dig up past emotions and feel the shadow of my Soul. I needed to meet, greet, and love my shadow or it was going to continue to run my life. I loved myself enough to now discover and love the deepest, darkest, most painful parts of me.

Today was my first appointment with Jon, I met him at his office and he led me into his consultation room. It was filled with eclectic décor and had an eccentric feel. The walls were dressed in vintage wallpaper and there were two chairs; a leather recliner and a high-back antique chair covered in a maroon velvet. I could feel my human mind questioning if this was the right fit for me. The consultation room was dark and funky. An interior wall of protection began building up within me. I wasn't sure about the funky feel of the room and décor.

I slowly walked across the room and sat down in the antique chair covered in maroon velvet cloth. Jon sat down in the leather chair across from me. He sat in stillness and looked at me. His stillness was unusually uncomfortable to me and I didn't like it, yet there was something else about him that felt safe and comforting. His energy was confusing and conflicting within me. My human mind made the immediate decision that this guy was weird and this consultation would be the last time I see him. But my heart knew this confusing and conflicting energy was exactly what I needed to heal on a deeper level.

In an attempt to move out of my discomfort, I began to explain my situation and dysfunctional marriage with Jon. He quietly listened and accepted everything I had to say. My story probably sounded something like this, "Blah, blah Ed this and blah, blah Ed that." I'm sure everything I said was directed at Ed and how he needed to change, how he needed help and how he had a problem. Jon let me finish and lovingly said, "You know, every time you point your finger at someone else, there are always three fingers pointing back at you."

His comment shocked me. How dare he defend Ed! Couldn't Jon see that Ed is the problem? I came here for love and support, and he wanted to talk about pointing fingers at me. I was completely appalled! I wanted him to support me and share my opinion that this was Ed's problem. Ed is the one who drinks and avoids things, not me! My human mind wrote Jon off as an asshole and shut itself off from any further conversation. I was ready to leave. I politely finished our conversation, graciously thanked him for his time and walked out the door.

For some reason, however, my Soul was not at all offended by his comment. In fact, Jon's comment stayed with me for several days after our first meeting. I pondered, "Maybe Jon was right about the finger thing. What does that mean for me?"

I began to question what the three fingers meant for me. I knew they weren't pointing to a drinking problem because I didn't drink. So, what did they mean?

I sat in stillness and asked my Soul, "What do the three fingers mean for me? Why am I pointing fingers at Ed? What am I really triggered by *in him* that is a reflection *within me*?"

My Soul replied, "You are pointing the finger at him because he is not dealing with his own shit. Now, turn that question around for you."

"OK," I repeated, "I'm pointing the finger at him because he is not dealing with his own shit. Well, if I turn the question around, this means, I am not dealing with my own shit. That would mean there is shit within me I am not dealing with. There is stuff that I am hiding and not looking at."

"Yes," agreed my Soul, "there are parts and pieces, thoughts, beliefs, and emotions that are still locked up within you. Things you cannot see or recognize yet. There are parts within that want to surface and heal."

I didn't understand this answer at first, but there was something within Jon that did understand and knew how to help me. There was something about him, something in him, which contained a deeper understanding of the "shit" within me that I could not see and understand for myself. Maybe he wasn't the asshole I initially labeled him to be. Maybe he knew more than I gave him credit for. Jon intrigued me, and frightened me at the same time. Could I trust him? Could he help me? The only way I was going to find out was to work with him. I decided to give him another chance. Curiosity grabbed hold of me, "What does he know that I don't know?"

The next six months would uncover the shadows of my Soul. My shadow were parts and pieces of myself that I intentionally hid, so I didn't have to feel the pain they initially caused me. I didn't know it, but I was carrying a lot of baggage that no longer served me. I was holding on to past programs and patterns that were causing pain and suffering in my life and in my relationships. My shadow was surfacing and was coming out of the deep, dark crevices of my being because it was ready to heal. I had to face my shadow and the pain in my past, so I could finally live free in the present and future.

Ed was right, I did have a problem. Several of them, in fact. I had unconscious problems, but just didn't know it yet, because the problems were in my unconscious awareness. They were hiding in my shadows.

Heart-Center Meditation, Dreams that Heal, Life as Teacher and Healer

I worked with Jon for six months. He is one of the most caring, loving, and spiritually connected individuals I have ever met. Jon has the innate ability to hold a deep and intimate container of unconditional love and safety for you so that you can visit these darker aspects of yourself with as much ease and grace as possible.

Visiting and healing your shadow is not an easy process. It is uncomfortable. Most people never have the opportunity, nor do they purposely choose to heal these deep pieces because:

1. No one is aware of their unconscious material; and

2. No one wants to put themselves in uncomfortable, vulnerable situations and feel uncomfortable emotions.

Healing your shadow is an intimate, vulnerable process. No one really wants to expose themselves, but that is part of the healing process. You must be willing to be raw and vulnerable. Even if you become aware and know that you need to heal on this level, this type of healing is not readily available in our conventional system and very few people have experience in this field. It is a growing field, however, and I believe it is another missing piece to the whole and complete healing puzzle.

I have seen and personally experienced what deep Soul healing and integration can do. I've seen physical illness and life-long mental/emotional wounds simply disappear when deep healing occurs. I've witnessed miracles happen from deep healing alone.

If you feel you are being called to this healing work, I would highly recommend that you answer the call. If you know there is something within you that is ready and willing to heal these deeper pieces, feel free to reach out to me so I can meet you where you are and offer you resources and companionship to best support your own inner journey. There is no place too dark or too deep that cannot be healed. I am happy to share and hold this journey with you. I will walk with you just as other people have walked with me.

Jon was my inner healing guide and companion through this process. He knew all about the journey I had been on and where I was heading. He connected to my inner pain, patterns, and programs before I even knew they existed and he worked with me in a way that made me feel safe enough to go through my pain in order to bring those patterns and programs into my awareness so that I could accept, love, and heal them. Once I was able to heal these unconscious patterns, they didn't have control in my life because they become free to be and flow through me. He knew exactly what I was struggling with through past trauma and he knew how to connect to the energy of my Soul before I did. He had the capacity to love any circumstance or trauma I had in my life. He is and was a safe place to share and heal my past wounding.

I often describe Jon as an Eckhart Tolle on steroids. Jon is the full embodiment of Divine wisdom, love, compassion, peace, and healing presence. He has learned how to embody these qualities within himself and therefore he carries a high healing capacity and frequency within his presence. This was also the presence I was uncomfortable with in the beginning. I was uncomfortable with this energy because I had not fully integrated it into my being. Jon was there to help me connect and integrate the healing capacity of the heart center within me.

Divine wisdom, love, compassion, peace, and healing presence are attributes and energetic frequencies of the heart center. The heart center has the capacity and ability to integrate and heal past trauma though love, compassion, harmony, and healing presence. He taught me to heal my past through my own heart and heart-center mediation.

When I calmed my mind and focused on my heart center, I could revisit different times in my life that wanted to be healed. The most prominent themes that came up for me was the feeling of unworthiness and lack of self-love. My entire life had become a quest to find and fill my inner self-love, and self-worth bucket through outside things and resources. I went to the ends of the earth to be "good enough," including a world championship, but nothing was ever enough. I had to learn to love and accept myself wholly and completely from the inside out, not the outside in. I had to learn that it was necessary to reconnect to my inner child and allow her to play again, have fun, and be free. I had to learn that while it is nice to give love, it is also important to receive love. Opening and receiving love was not easy for me because I shut that door a long time ago, as I will share later in this chapter. I had to learn to "be" the love for myself that I so desperately needed and wanted. I had to go within to initiate this process and I did so with heart-centered mediation.

Heart-centered mediation is done by connecting to and expanding the energy of your heart. You too, can begin to heal through the practice of heart-centered meditation. Begin this mediation by calming your human mind through the stillness practice. When your mind is still, place both hands over your heart and connect to the energy of unconditional love, compassion, innate harmony, and healing presence. Feel the love and warmth of your heart. Feel its energy, warmth, and compassion. The heart has no judgment, it fully accepts all that is as it is. Feel and connect to that peace and presence. There is no other place you need to be, there is nothing you need to do, there is nothing else you have ever wanted or experienced more than to be in the full presence of your welcome, open heart. It is from this place that all is welcome, all is allowed, and all can heal. Allow yourself to sink deeper into the love and safety of your heart. Simply being and sitting in this peaceful blissful state is, in itself, healing. However, if your Soul begins to bring in memories, feelings, emotions, pictures, colors, sensations, or other energetic expressions, let them come in and be healed by this powerful energy. Allow them to be with you and you with them. This relationship, between you, your Soul, and your pain, is a tender, loving intimate experience that has the power to heal all wounds and integrate all of you with your Soul.

Besides heart-centered meditation, Jon and I also worked with my dreams. Jon taught me how to interpret my dreams and work with my dreams to uncover hidden messages from my Soul. It is no surprise that I initially dreamt of carrying a lot of baggage and dealing with a lot of shit (literally), both within myself and others. There is rich and valuable information in your dreams. Dreams can heal and bring unconscious patterns into conscious awareness. Dream work was fun, insightful, and uncomfortably revealing! The process of deep inner healing is uncomfortably revealing as you work to peel back layer after layer of unprocessed material.

The more I worked with my dreams, the more curious I became. My dreams and I formed an intimate relationship and I became a student of my dreams. The more I worked with them, the more benefit and value I received and the more clearly I saw and interpreted my inner and outer world. It was as if my Soul was working out the unconscious beliefs and patterns in my mind through the dream itself. These patterns were keeping me from the truth and purity of who I am. Dreams are like a movie, restructuring the psychological details within my mind that are seeking a new perspective.

The more I worked with my dreams, the more I began to see the patterns in my dreams reflecting messages back to me and shifting my physical reality. My dreams were working and healing me and my entire life; I just didn't have conscious awareness of the intimate relationship and guidance between my dreams and my physical life until then.

Dreams have a genuine purpose. Dreams are an incredible healing tool. You dream for many reasons. Most importantly, you dream as a way to integrate your life experiences and heal past psychological trauma. Dreams truly have the power to uncover the mystery of life and the lessons of your Soul. When you work with your dreams you can uncover and unwind your unconscious psyche. Dreams have the power to psychologically heal your mind and send messages to you from your Soul.

You can begin the process of dream work by setting the intention to remember your dreams at night then, as soon as you wake up, write down what you remember. Write down every detail that comes to your mind even if it feels vague or unimportant. It's the small details that can contain the most vital messages from your Soul. Do not try to interpret your dream as you are writing it down, simply allow the words to flow. When you are finished, still your mind through the stillness practice, and revisit your dream from a quiet place of inspiration. Notice different symbols and words you used to describe your dream. Symbols and words have very specific and personal meanings for you. Allow your personal experience and personal meaning of words to help you interpret your dream. Allow your Soul to unfold the messages and feelings within your dreams. Your human mind will overthink this process, so allow your heart and Soul to speak. Your dream journal will become a living memoir of your Soul's earthly experience and lessons. You can refer back to your journal many times throughout your life and it will have new messages and new meanings for you as you grow and expand into a fuller conscious awareness.

Jon also taught me how to become a master observer of my life and see how my life shows me everything I need to know to heal. My life is my personal self-help book, just as your life is your self-help book when you learn and know how to interpret it. Life is constantly delivering messages through signs, people, books, nature, synchronicities, and many other forms to lead and guide us in the most beneficial direction to grow and evolve as human beings in this life experience.

Jon expanded my awareness and understanding on how my exterior world is a reflection of my interior world. Anything that triggers me or catches my attention is a signal that there is more for me to discover about myself and my relationship to life. Life signals are personal indicators that there is another lesson to be learned. Once I learned to become a master observer of my life, I became a master of the messages that were flowing in and out of my life. I became my own master interpreter and teacher of my life. My life experiences were meant for me and my self-growth. I am not here to change, manipulate, or control others. I am here to work on my own growth and self-development. My job is for me, their job is for them, and we are all on our own journeys of self-discovery and self-realization, each one of us contributing an unique energetic expression to the collective whole (One).

Make No Judgments, Make No Comparisons, and Eliminate the Need to Understand

Once I became a master of my life and took ownership in my life, I stopped the habit of projecting my own inner conflicts and issues at or onto other people. I learned that all judgment is really a form of self-judgment. When I point the finger and judge someone or something else, that judgment is really a reflection of my interior world and my interior judgment that is calling for a deeper level of healing.

Judgment became a tool and a message for me to investigate further within myself and become curious what my Soul wanted to bring forth. The more I worked with Jon, the more I healed from the inside out and the more magical life became. I was able to work through judgment of others as a tool to heal the judgment within myself.

I also saw how I was defeating myself through the act of comparing myself to others. I would judge my worthiness based on other people's accomplishments, social status, financial abundance, physical looks, or well-being. Before doing the deep healing work, I did not see myself as a complete whole person, so I used others as a tool of self-assessment and measurement. I habitually saw myself as better than, or worse than, everyone I met. This was a trip up and down the rabbit hole, a useless tool that never served me. I never experienced full acceptance within me because I always saw myself on one end of the spectrum (a self-righteous deity) or the other (a worthless piece of dirt). That assessment may sound harsh, but ask yourself, with kindness and love, if you have found yourself in the same position. Any time you compare yourself to someone or something else, you set yourself up for self-rejection or self-inflation. You will be directly rejecting yourself or you will be rejecting someone else, which is ultimately a sign of hidden self-rejection or self-inflation you are not aware of yet.

The "comparison" pattern was formed in my early childhood and formed a deeply rooted internal thought that I was unworthy. My mind was trying to prove its worth by comparing myself and my circumstances to others. This method always led to failure and more misery because I would always find someone or something better than me, wiser than me, richer than me, more successful than me, etc. I would never find my worth for myself by playing the comparison game. I realized my need to compare myself with others was not working and I never filled my self-worth bucket by thinking or needing to feel better than another or have more than another. I needed to fill my own self-worth bucket from within and heal my disillusioned thinking pattern that I wasn't enough.

Nothing outside myself could ever fill the self-worth, self-love bucket. I had to go within to heal my unworthy wounding. Once I connected to my inner source of love and self-worth, I was able to fill and keep refilling my self-worth and self-love bucket with the unlimited love from God and my Divine Self. Once I recognized and healed self-love, there was nothing I ever needed outside myself to feel worthy or loved. I was loved all along, I just wasn't connecting or receiving it from within. I was looking for love in all the wrong places -- and never finding it.

Your heart is your connection to God and your Divine Self. God and your Divine Self have more than enough love to go around. God is love. You are love. Fill your love bucket from within and you will never need or want acceptance, approval, worth, or love from anything outside yourself again. You already have it *in full abundance* and life will constantly and continually show and bring love to you through your life when you know with all your heart that you are love.

These were a few examples of the unconscious patterns that I was able to unwind and heal by working with Jon, my Divine Self, and the insight provided from Divine Source. I discovered how the patterns and programs of my human mind are not in alignment, nor do they have the capacity to understand my internal pain and life lessons. But the fullness and wisdom of Divine Mind has that capacity – and more. I came to the realization that my human mind has a plethora of misinformed information that flows through it and affects my life. My human mind is always trying to come up with a rationalized concept of life because it does not, nor will it ever, fully understand all the mysteries of life from its human understanding. It will never fully know because it does not have access to the full knowledge of the Universe and life itself. It gets confused in its interpretations because it has limited access to full knowledge. My mind can only interpret life from its past experience in this lifetime. It does not have access to all of eternity. My human mind is limited. My Divine Mind is limitless.

The truth of our existence and life experience is so complex, mysterious, and magical that the human mind will never be able to fully understand and know how the Universe works and is designed. No matter how hard it tries, how hard it studies, or how hard it thinks. Knowing that it is alright to not know, gave me great freedom. By knowing I didn't need to understand it all, I was able to release the "need to know everything." This truth gave me full permission to simply live life instead of fighting and struggling to understand it.

Experiencing, cherishing and living each moment of life is all that is required. Life is meant to be simple and free. The human mind is the only thing that complicates it.

Looking for Love in All the Wrong Places

Jon and I worked at great length to revisit past programming from my early childhood. By revisiting my childhood programming, I uncovered multiple wounds and unmet desires for unconditional love. I deeply wanted to feel and be loved, but I never fully received it from my outside world. I tried everything and worked very hard to fill my internal love bucket from outside resources, but outside love never fully found or completely filled me. I continued to feel lonely, isolated, and abandoned by love.

I thought I could fill this empty hole through other people, places, and things, but every time I tried to fill my needs from outside sources, I only dug a deeper, darker hole until it became an endless abyss of loveless lies and loneliness.

I had been programmed by my competitive family to believe that I had to work for love and acceptance. Love and acceptance was earned through achievements, grades, awards, and good behavior. Since I didn't innately feel worthy of love, I worked really hard to become worthy of it. I became a lifelong perfectionist, but nothing I ever did was enough to win the prize of love.

In grade school, I was so focused on earning my family's love and appreciation through good grades that I refused to bring an assignment home to my parents unless my grade was 100%. A grade of 99.9% wasn't good enough for me. I could only be loved and accepted if I was 100% perfect. If I wasn't perfect, no one would love me. This, of course, wasn't true, but I believed it was and so I kept living this lie for a very long time.

This lie was my truth and I internalized and embodied it. This lie put so much pressure on me and my system that

I ended up breaking out in shingles as a second grader. The pressure and pain was so great within me that it needed to find a physical outlet, so my body literally broke out in a seething, oozing, painful, blistering rash. I still have the scars on my body to remind me of my past pain. What you are unable to heal or deal with consciously, your body will carry for you and your body will deal with the distorted energy any way it can. Shingles was my body's way of releasing and dealing my unconscious pain.

I also tried proving my worth for love and acceptance through athletic achievements. I was a good athlete and I began to receive positive affirmation through sports. I liked the praise and acknowledgment that I received when I won. I thought to myself, "Maybe winning awards is the way I can receive love and prove my worth. If I win, I would be loved."

I was a natural athlete in gymnastic and track. I only participated in sports I knew I could win. Each time I won, I received temporary acknowledgment, a golden badge of approval, but it still wasn't good enough to receive the love I deeply needed and desired. I played the "best athlete" game a long time, too. I kept trying to win the ultimate prize for love through accomplishments and winning until I became the fittest women in the world. In 1999, I won the Fitness Olympia. Surely that would be enough to win the love I deeply desired and deserved. Nope. Even that was not enough to heal the inner pain and my inner truth that I was never good enough for love. I was never worthy enough for love.

Another game I played to win the love I desired was through the pretty-perfect little girl game. I thought if I was pretty enough, put on a radiant smile, had a magazine cover body, and acted in a lady-like fashion, surely someone would love me. Everyone admired models and their beauty. If I was beautiful, maybe I would be loved. Even though I was one of the pretty and popular girls in school, it was never enough to feel loved.

Not only did presenting a perfect image not work well, it actually back-fired on me. I put so much pressure on myself to maintain a particular status that I completely lost and destroyed myself in the process. I dared not be less than pretty and popular. Everything I did or didn't do in school was to protect myself from judgment. I needed to make sure that anything I did or didn't do wouldn't make me unpopular. If I wasn't pretty and popular, no one would like me, and I couldn't bear the thought of being rejected or disliked, so I became reserved and quiet. I kept to myself in fear that if I said or did the wrong thing, I would be judged and ridiculed.

I became an island unto myself from the fear of not being liked. I became lonely and isolated, but I thought that was what I needed to do to protect my fragile self from not being liked or loved. I didn't dare do anything out of the ordinary to piss someone off. I thought that would keep me safe and prevent anyone from not liking me. That train of thought back-fired as well.

I heard people say that I was stuck-up and I didn't talk to or hang out with anyone I didn't like or who didn't measure up to me. This was the furthest thing from the truth. I was hurt by those comments and so I hid even more. I guess I wasn't doing a good enough job at isolating myself, so I decided to isolate more, thus spiraling down further into loneliness, isolation, and lack of love.

Despite my walls of isolated protection, I managed to stay hopeful for love with individual people. In eighth grade, I fell in love for the first time and thought I had finally found the deep intimate love that I desired and deserved. For the first time, I felt that I found a love that would last a lifetime.

Jason Robinson took me by surprise. I wasn't looking for a relationship because I was too busy isolating myself and staying within my self-created walls of perfection protection. Despite my best efforts to avoid life and love, Jason found me and swept me off my feet. I had no idea what was happening.

Jason was kind and humble. He was a simple, hard-working farm boy with a tall, strong stature, sandy-blond hair and deep-blue eyes that immediately shattered my walls of protection. I felt oddly safe with him and it confused me. Jason was also the school's top athlete and honor-roll student. He excelled in everything he did and was greatly respected by students and teachers alike. Everyone seemed to know everything about Jason, except for me. I knew nothing about him. Who was this kind, gentle, talented, simple, beautiful boy and why was he interested in me? Would he be interested in the real me, or was he only attracted to the perfect me, the image of me that I was trying so hard to create in the world? I didn't know which "me" to be.

Over the next six months, he was the one person who was able to break down my structured walls and see the real me. For a few short months I was able to relax, let down my guarded walls and simply be. I could breathe again. I felt appreciated, honored, and cherished. I felt accepted and loved. He was able to connect to the real me and I started falling in love for the first time. I began to fall and I fell hard because I let go of the walls I was clinging to for so long. I let him in and opened my heart to love. We had a great relationship and I felt as though I had found my soul mate.

Our young love was sweet and innocent, precious and perfect, but it wouldn't last forever. Our relationship ended as unexpectedly as it started. The ending took me by surprise and knocked me off my feet. I had no idea the breakup was coming.

Jason was a teenaged boy with a bright future and other opportunities to explore. He was a year older than I and would be going to high school the following year. He had no interest in holding on to a girlfriend from junior high, so he broke up with me as soon as school was out. I died that day. I had torn down my walls of protection, opened up to love, and now there was nothing left to protect me from the wretched pain of heartache. When he broke up with me, love broke up with me as well, and I was left broken and alone. I opened up to love and love abandoned me.

"I will never open up to love again!" I vowed, "It just hurts to deep and too much. My heart is permanently scarred. It isn't worth it. I would rather be alone and loveless than go through that again!"

I ceased dating until after high school. I distanced myself from anyone or anything that represented love. My walls of protection were rebuilt and reinforced with cold, hard steel, so that no one could ever harm or hurt me again. I refused to open up to love or let anyone in. I gave up on love. It wasn't until I began doing the self-healing work with Jon that I was able let go and let love back in. This was not an easy or simple process. It took a long time to feel safe enough to expose my vulnerability, take down my walls of protection and allow love back in.

After the breakup, my human mind decided to take over. My heart was dead and destroyed. It had nothing left to give or contribute. I was a mess. I was a teenaged girl with an unstable mixture of raging hormones who had just had her heart ripped out. All I had left was my human *teenaged* mind, which was a recipe for disaster. The way my teenaged human mind assessed my situation was to tell me that the breakup happened because there was something wrong with me. Jason wouldn't have broken up with me unless there was something tragically wrong with me. My teenaged mind concluded that I must be too fat to be loved!

"OMG, that's it," I thought, "I'm gaining weight and I'm too fat! Clearly that was why Jason broke up with me. I must lose weight so that one day (if I ever open up to love again) I will be loveable."

My teenaged human mind got the best of me and ate up the delusion that I was too fat to be loved, which of course was a lie, but it was my lie and my truth at the time. I quickly took my weight problems into my own hands and stopped eating altogether. The pain from the break-up was so deep that

I literally began starving and depleting my body of any love and nourishment. My outer world was reflecting the inner pain I could not heal or deal with.

For several months, I suffered from anorexia until I reached a mere 97 pounds. I hated myself mentally, physically, and emotionally but didn't realize it. I was dying from the inside out and losing control of my life. The only thing I knew I could control was food, so I stopped eating. I starved myself because I was starved for love. I thought I was unworthy of love and I never wanted to experience the pain of love again so I stopped loving and nurturing myself to avoid love altogether.

I remember the day I looked into the mirror and saw a girl I didn't recognize. Her eyes were drawn, cheeks receding, and she was thin as a rail. There was no sparkle or life left within her. She was gone. I reached out to this girl with my hand and she reached out to me. Our hands met and it was a perfect match. OMG, this girl is me! I jerked my hand back as my whole body began to tremble and shake. Fear rose within me as I began to feel the emptiness within her and a hunger to save her life. I chose to eat again in an attempt to save this dying girl.

At first, it was hard to eat. I didn't want to lose the one and only thing I had control over in my life. I also wasn't sure I deserved love and nourishment, but I continued to feed my body and it started to feel good. It felt good to not feel hungry anymore and food became my source of comfort. Food relieved my pain. Food and feeling full again gave me temporarily relief, but I was still afraid I would gain weight and get fat. No one would love me if I got fat. I began throwing-up everything I ate, so I could control my weight. Now, bulimia got the best of me.

I ate to feed my pain and I threw-up to control my weight. I became lost in an endless cycle of despair and desperation, filling up with food for comfort and throwing up because I felt guilty and ashamed. I was falling deeper and deeper into the pit of my own misery, further and further away from the love I so deeply desired and longed for. My life became a mismanagement of food, weight, perfect grades, and an inner struggle to put together a pretty, perfect little package on the outside while all along I was dying and decaying on the inside.

I learned how to survive within the pit of hell. I became a brilliant master of survival. I gave myself a grade of 100% in the study of survival. I told myself that I could survive anything, and I could do it all while keeping a perfect-pretty smile on my face. I made sure that no one knew how scared, lonely, terrified, and shitty I was on the inside. If anyone knew that I was dying on the inside they wouldn't like me, let alone love me.

I got so good at hiding and stuffing my emotions, I stopped feeling altogether. My feelings and emotions became unconscious to me. I didn't and couldn't recognize or acknowledge them. It was too painful. They remained buried within me. I made sure that no one, not even myself, could ever see my pain.

"OMG," I thought, "I hope no one sees my pain! No one would love me if they saw how broken I am."

This was the story of my life until life became too much for me to handle. Cancer was the straw that broke me to the point that all of me was broken. Finally, I had to give up the struggle and begin to heal. I had to take a real look at my life and all that was happening in it instead of hiding and stuffing the pain.

I had to lose everything I thought I loved in order to find the love I have always been looking for. I had to lose my job, my home, my financial security, and my health in order to find the love I so desperately needed and wanted. I had to stop looking for answers and love outside of myself and find the love within. I needed to reconnect and receive the love that was always there for me, I just never knew it was there and how to connect to it or receive it. I had to lose it all, to find it all again.

This is the dark night and the journey of the Soul. This was my portal and the entry into my healing journey. When I was finally able to let go of all the illusions and misconceptions in my human mind and reconnect to eternal love, I was able to heal. Love is the most powerful healing source and presence there is. Divine Love has the power to dismantle all misconceptions of the mind and open the door to whole healing.

Crisis Came to Heal ... Messages of the Body

My multiple full-blown crises broke me to the point where I was finally able to let go of my human mind and open and allow healing to happen in my life. Crisis came to save me. Breast cancer came to save me. I had to die and let go of my old self and my old reality in order to connect to a new life and a new reality.

Working with Jon helped me discover the message that cancer came to serve me, rather than harm or destroy me. Cancer came as a gift, two days after my 36th birthday. I was holding onto old psychological patterns and programs to which I was completely unconscious, but my Soul knew they needed to be healed. My body was sending me a message that I had to get real with life and begin to dismantle the Veil of Illusion I had created within my mind.

What we do not carry within our conscious awareness, our body is forced to carry for us. Our bodies do this as an act of love until we are ready to begin the healing process. What we are unable to process, the body will carry until we reach a point in our lives that we are able to heal. This unconscious material is stored as energetic patterns that block the flow of life through us. They get stuck in our body and that part of our life experience gets frozen in time, so to speak. Where there is a block in energy flow, it creates a disruption and distortion in the body's energy field. Where there is distorted information, physical illness and disease form as a symptom of the distorted information not flowing through us. Physical disease, illness, life crisis, and events in our life come as a message that something is misaligned and disconnected within.

Something within is calling to be healed. Your outer world will reflect the dysfunction and disconnection of your inner world.

This is exactly what happened for me with breast cancer. There were unconscious patterns my body was carrying. I wasn't able to resolve them because I consciously hid them years ago and became no longer aware of their existence. That part of my life was frozen in time and could no longer move through me. I needed to reconnect and thaw this past wounding, so energy and information could flow again. I needed to melt the ice with love and compassion to heal myself and my interior wounds. My inner world was reflecting in my outer reality in the form of breast cancer.

When working with Jon, we uncovered many past programs directly related to the breasts. There was a reason cancer formed in my breast tissue as opposed to some other area of the body. There is a reason the disease manifested as cancer, as opposed to some other chronic disease. Everything had a reason for forming and coming into my life, just as it does in your life.

Your body is a reflection of the unconscious mind and sends messages all the time, but most people ignore or don't know how to decipher them. Breast cancer showed up in my life to bring a very important message to me. So, what were some of these messages? Why did cancer show up in my breast rather than my liver or colon or some other part of my body? Why did I get cancer and not some other disease? Let's decode a few messages of my body in order to look for the deeper meaning behind the physical manifestation.

Let's start by looking at the function of the breasts and what they are physically designed to do. The physical function of the breasts provide nourishment for a new-born baby (a new life). A mother's breast provides whole and complete nourishment for this new life, for life itself. The breasts represent a mother's unconditional love and the ability to nourish, love and support new life.

Part of my healing journey was to let go of my old patterns and programs and birth a new life. I needed love and nourishment from myself, rather than seeking outside of myself for the love I so desperately needed. Cancer in my breast was representative of the lack of self-love and self-nourishment in my life. I was surviving instead of thriving. I craved love, nourishment, and support for myself, but I was not honoring and fulfilling my own needs. I was giving my own needs to everyone else and robbing myself of love and nourishment. I was literally dying from the inside out and giving away my life force. I was always giving, never receiving.

Does this sound familiar? How many women are giving themselves away, to everyone else, and not giving themselves the love and the nourishment they need in their own lives? Breast cancer is a self-love and self-nourishment deficiency. Every woman that I have talked to who had breast cancer can relate to this pattern in one way or another. It is not a surprise that breast cancer is most common in women.

Most women are trying to be everything to everyone at the exclusion of themselves. They want to be the perfect mother, perfect wife, and perfect provider all at the same time. The term "Super Mom" has been imbedded into our society's programming and we are all trying to live up to the world's standards at the expense of our own personal needs.

The more super we are or become, the more super we feel, right? Wrong. No, this never works. You will never find the inner love, nourishment, or acceptance you desire and deserve by becoming a super hero. Even if you make it to super-hero status, there will still be an emptiness inside. This emptiness can never be filled with external things or accomplishments. Super women get breast cancer all the time.

My cancer was in my left breast which is the side of the body tied to receiving. The right side of the body is tied to giving. My body developed cancer as a message that I needed to receive the love, nourishment, and support I desperately needed and wanted. I needed to receive this love from the inside out and stop trying to find it from the outside in. The outside world never had the capacity to love me or heal me.

LIVING PROOF

The world took, and I gave, until I had nothing left to give. All of my energy was going out and nothing was coming in. I was great at giving love, nourishment, and support. If fact, I was so good at it I gave it all away. Giving was not my problem. My problem was in receiving.

I needed to reconnect to myself and to the Divine love, wisdom, nourishment, and healing presence within me. I needed to stop giving me away and being a victim to life. I needed to stop giving so much and start living and loving life. I needed to love and nourish myself. My Soul knew I needed this, too, and sent cancer into my life as a wake-up call. I had to fill my inner emptiness by receiving my own source of love, nourishment, and support. I had to open and begin to receive love rather than giving it all away, so I learned to love and nourish myself through whole, healthy foods and creating a life that was full, rich, and rewarding. I took tender, loving care of me and attended to my internal needs, including the needs I didn't know I had.

The breasts also symbolize motherhood. They are a symbol and a physical tool for a mother to nourish and love her children. At the time of my diagnosis, I was terrified I would not be able to take care of my children because we were struggling financially. We were living off credit cards and had no steady income. I told myself it was okay if I was hungry or homeless, but I could not bear the thought of watching my children go hungry or become homeless. I was afraid I could not provide for my children.

I also hated motherhood itself. I hated it because I was giving all of my love, nourishment, and support to everyone else other than myself. I was literally giving away my life force and not nourishing, loving, and supporting myself in any way. I was simply surviving, rather than thriving.

I carried a lot of resentment toward motherhood. I resented being a mother because I viewed motherhood as a thankless, exhausting, lonely, and depleting job. I gave everything and received little in return. I never received a "thank you" or an

"I appreciate you, Mom." Being a mom, and all the duties it required turned into a thankless burden. The only thing I received for my efforts was an unending pile of dirty dishes, dingy clothes, and tedious household chores. Motherhood became a never-ending, thankless job and I couldn't see the beauty or blessing in it.

I also held an unconscious resentment that becoming a mother took my dream job and life away when I lost my athletic contract. I told myself it didn't bother me, but deep down, it did bother me. I carried a lot of resentment by losing my contract and everything I worked so hard for.

I also resented and blamed Ed for losing his business and making us move to Gillette, Wyoming. I resented that he spent more time at his job, fishing, hunting, and drinking than he spent with me and the kids. I felt like a single, married mom and I resented him for it. I resented all of my life, because it had taken everything from me. The resentment I carried within my body showed up in the form of cancer.

Cancer, when it shows up in the body, has a huge resentment piece attached to it. When cancer shows up in the body, no matter where the cancer is located, it is a sign of an unconscious or conscious wound around resentment. When cancer shows up, there is usually a feeling of deep resentment regarding something in your life you can no longer take or tolerate. I was carrying a lot of resentment and I hated my life until cancer snapped me out of it.

When I let my resentment go and began to love life and live life, cancer healed. When I reconnected to my Soul and starting fully living, loving, and appreciating life, cancer had done its job and went away. Listen to the messages from your body and Soul. They have so much to tell you. These messages have the power to save not only your health, but also your life.

When you proceed with deep healing work and decide to do the inner journey of your Soul, life becomes more than just a physical state of survival. Life becomes a synergistic symphony and has a language of its own. Once you begin to recognize, hear, see, feel, and understand the language, life completely changes and transforms. Life is here to help you, not hurt you. Life is trying to reach out to you in signs and symbols all the time, but are you listening and recognizing them? Once you begin to recognize and decipher the messages life sends you, life changes forever.

Answering the Call to Come Home ... Fully Healing my Body and Restoring my Life

While I didn't know or understand the unconscious messages of the body at the time of my cancer diagnosis, my Soul knew exactly what I needed and divinely guided me on the path to whole healing. My healing path was a process, not a 10-step program. All healing is a process, not a program. I was divinely guided on my perfect path not only to physically heal, but also to heal mentally, emotionally, and spiritually.

I had no idea what I was in for when I accepted this journey. All I really wanted to do was to physically heal from cancer, so that I could spend more time on this earth. I had no idea my life was going to completely transform and that I was going to birth a brand-new life through a full-blown spiritual awakening. I didn't even know what spiritual awakening was at the time, but apparently I was destined to find out. Cancer came into my life and invited me to participate in a complete and total life transformation process from the inside-out.

When I was diagnosed with cancer, I had no idea how far I had travelled down the pit of despair. I was so separated from my life, from God, and from my Soul, that I was physically sick, mentally broken, and barely surviving. Life was lifeless. I was dying from the inside out. Cancer came into my life as a wake-up call from my Soul. I was called to die, so I could finally live.

On December 16, 2008, I finally answered the call. I heard my phone ring, picked up the receiver and placed it to my ear.

The voice on the other line said, "Mary, it's me, Cancer, are you there?"

"Yes," I replied. "I'm here. What do you want? Why are you calling me?"

Cancer replied, "I'm here because your Soul has a very important message for you. Your Soul is calling you home."

"Home?" I questioned, "What does that mean? What does 'home' have to do with cancer?"

Cancer replied, "You are sick. Your Soul needs you to get well. You have separated yourself from God, from yourself, and from your life. You are not fully living. You are slowly dying, and I have come to heal you. I have come to heal your body and restore your life. I have come to bring you back home to the heart of who you are, so that you can fully live again. Are you ready to live again? Are you ready to heal your body and restore your life?"

"Wow," I replied. "I had no idea I was slowly dying. I thought I was just fine. I don't understand what's happening or what you are asking."

"That's alright," Cancer said, "you do not need to fully understand what is going on. You simply need to answer the call and say, 'Yes.' Yes, Cancer, I accept your call. I will then provide you everything you need to heal and restore your life. Are you ready?"

"OK," I said, "I'm ready. Show me the way. Show me another way to heal my body and restore my life. I will answer your call and I will trust you."

Thus began my journey of a life time. I answered the call and experienced another way to heal. I was able to let go of my own mind and reconnect to my Divine Mind. I was able to trust the inner guidance of my heart and open and allow its healing messages, which divinely and lovingly guided me down my path to healing.

I learned to reconnect to the Divine messages within my heart and within my life. I became "Living Proof" that there is another way to heal your body and restore your life.

I learned that life is so much more magical than I could have ever imagined because my human mind simply did not know. I was slowly dying and didn't even know it because I was living life from the illusion and deceptions of my own mind.

I now live my life in complete freedom, complete health, complete love and acceptance, complete peace and complete joy, because I am fully connected to the truth of my Divine Mind and my Soul. My life is now co-created and experienced with and through the Divine Itself. I am living my life with Divine purpose and passion. This is the way God intended me to live all along.

Love is the greatest healer of all. I experienced the power of love by first loving and accepting myself. By loving myself first, I am able to love and accept everyone and everything in my life with this same passion. I was able to let go of barely surviving and to start thriving in my life. I discovered that surviving sucks. I needed to do more than just survive cancer and survive my life. I needed to thrive. Thriving makes me feel alive.

I encourage you to embrace my life's example and my life's experience that I share in this book and relate them to your own life and your own experiences. Ask yourself if your life is calling you to wake up and experience more. Are you being called to a new way of being, living, healing, and restoring your life? Is something in your life calling you? Answer the call. This call is open and available to anyone who is ready and willing to answer the call.

You were never meant to barely survive. You are designed and meant to Thrive! There is a huge difference between these two ways of living. Thriving is living your life to the fullest expression of who you really are. You are a living embodiment of the Divine Source. You are part of God. Source God is in you and all around you. Live life from God's love within you. Express your life from your true essence and you will thrive beyond human potential. When you choose to thrive, you open yourself and your life to unlimited Divine possibilities.

Your Soul will be free to fully express itself as a divine being in human from. The two will become one and your life will flourish. You will be able to grow and evolve as the radiant being you were always meant to be.

This is why you came into this world. You came to grow and evolve as a Soul. You came to experience all that life has to offer you, so you can understand more of who and what you really are. Learning, growing, and evolving is a never-ending process. This journey never ends. Just like you, it has no beginning, no middle, or no end. This journey is eternal, as are you. Be and live life as your eternal Soul and you will come home and heal.

When you come home to the heart of who you are you are able to fill your internal love bucket with unlimited self-love and self-worth. You are free to be exactly who you are in any given moment because you love all of who you are. You are grounded and centered. There is nothing outside yourself that can throw you off course or damage your self-image because you know exactly who you are. You have nothing to prove because you are already precious and valuable. There is no pressure to be anything or anyone else because you know you are perfect and whole. This is life's ultimate freedom. The freedom to be, live, experience, and create from your divine expression.

FINAL REFLECTIONS -- A CALL TO COME HOME.

We will all receive the call -- or many calls -- to come home. The choice to answer the call is entirely up to you. Are you ready to answer the call and begin your own journey? It is not a question of *if* you will take this journey, it is a question of *when* you will take this journey. Why not start your journey today?

If not today, then when? What is stopping you? What is holding you back? Which day will be your day? Choose to take this journey today. You don't have to wait until you are so battered, beaten, and broken from life that you have no other choice but to take it or die. I've done that already, so you don't have to. Use my life, my crisis, my pain, so you don't have to. Choose to live now instead of later. You do not need to wait until cancer or some other crisis calls you. Answer the call today.

Now is the time to choose to fully Live your purpose, Love with passion and Thrive beyond your human potential. Now is the time to fully heal your body and restore your life. Be your own "Living Proof" and experience how your inner transformation has a powerful healing and restoration effect on your inner and outer world. You can heal your body and restore your life just like I did. I am "Living Proof" that there is another way to heal your body and restore your life. If I can do it, you can do it.

Answer the call and say "Yes" to yourself and your life today. Close your eyes, take a deep breath and feel the stillness, peace, and comfort of your being. From this space ask yourself, "Am I fully living my life from my greatest potential, or is there more?" Allow a message, a feeling, or an inner inspiration to answer. Whatever you hear, see, or experience is a call from your Soul. It is the true desire of your heart. Say "Yes" to that inner call. Investigate, explore, and be curious about it. Discover what it personally means to you. Why is it important to you? What visions do you see? What are you doing? Who are you with? How does it *feel* to be living from this new expression? Give yourself permission to own it, live it, and become it. Now ask, what steps will I need to take to become this living reality? Trust your internal guidance and bring it into your reality by taking action each day. By being a living expression of what you really what in your life, your new expression becomes your living reality.

My Final Reflection

Looking back on all the events that led me to where I am today, I wouldn't have changed a thing. It's funny how your perspective can radically change when you pause long enough to look back on your life and gain a broader perspective through an expanded level of conscious awareness. Through the eyes of Divine Wisdom, events in my life connect to one another and make sense. There was a purpose in everything that happened. It was just too hard for me to see or understand when I was fully engulfed in my own pain and misery.

My pain and misery served a valuable purpose. I had to go through the crisis in order to see, hear, learn, and grow into something more than I thought I was. I had to lose everything before I could recover, redeem myself, and find it all again. It was my personal fall, struggle, and "death" that paved the way to healing, repair, restoration, redemption and recovery.

LIVING PROOF

Without my fall, I would have never been able to live my life to my fullest potential. My pain and suffering were the beginning of the end of my pain, suffering, dissolution, discontentment, disease, worry, anxiety, betrayal, and fear. I had to go through all of these things before I could fully experience the beauty, magic, wonder, unconditional love, peace and joy that life can be. I had to go through all of the pain and misery and learn to love it all, before I could be all that I am in life. Before I could be all that I am, I had to become all that I am not. Only then could I become whole and complete and live life from a full and whole perspective.

That is what life is. Life is about embracing and learning to love and live it all. It is a journey of discovering and uncovering your whole self, all of yourself, your true self. It's a journey of the Soul. A journey to live life on purpose, love with passion and thrive. But before I learned to thrive, I had to barely survive.

Thank you for taking the time to witness the hills, valleys, potholes, detours, and winding road I followed from devastation to healing and restoration. I hope my story, victories, failures, inspirations, insights, and wisdom will be of value to you in your own journey of discovery and self-realization.

Most journeys of self-discovery and healing are not what you would have chosen, but they are invaluable tools to find the road that will lead you home. Discovering and finding your internal eternal home is the only way to find everlasting life, hope, love, peace, health and unlimited potential.

Home is the place where miracles happen. Home is the road to your Soul and new discoveries of what life is really about. Home will bring you answers of true health, true healing, and true happiness. Home is the restoration and redemption process of life itself. It's reconnecting to the original blueprint of our most genuine life and a return to living from center rather than being plugged into and dependent on external forces. It's a realization that our life comes from our selves and returns to ourselves – a continual cycle, a closed-circuit of reflections and cycles of growth.

This book is dedicated to each and every Soul going through their own journey and discovery of life. I pray my journey will touch you in a way that ignites your Soul. Allow your Soul to bring lessons into your life so that you can discover the deeper messages and meanings they have for you. Be brave and work through them, rather than get stuck in old patterns that no longer serve you. All of life is meant to serve you, not to harm you. When you are willing to look at life through an expanded level of consciousness, you will find the mysteries of life revealed to you in ways you never thought possible.

I didn't know this when my life began to unravel and self-destruct. I had no idea what was happening, but I know now. My tragedies were a gift from my Soul that knew exactly what I needed, when I needed it. I am grateful now that everything fell apart because it has led me right where I needed to be. I never would have personally chosen this life, but I'm so grateful that my life chose me.

I now love life, not because it provides everything I want, but because it provides everything I need. My life has purpose and I live it in the full potential that it can be. Every day is magical. I see, feel and experience miracles all the time. Every day is heaven on earth no matter what is happening around me. I know that if life can be magical for me, it can be magical to you.

There is no greater discovery or life mission grander than the pursuit of self-discovery and self-realization. When you find out who you really are, why you came to this world, and begin to fully live your life, life lives for you. You no longer need to suffer. You get to play in this world and live like children in the freedom and the full expression of who you are because you know yourself in a full and complete expression of God.

You are completely loved, whole, and complete. There is nothing you will ever want because you know you already have it. Your life provides all you will ever need. This is complete and total freedom. This is all you have ever wanted and have always been searching for. When you begin the journey within, you will find all you desire and deserve because it was within you all along.

Every time you have searched for love, peace, joy, and freedom from outside of yourself, you have or will come up short. You were never designed to find your heart's desires from outside yourself because you were always meant to find it within. That is why everything outside yourself eventually leaves you empty. It causes pain and suffering because that is what it is designed to do. It is designed to leave you empty, so that one day you will look within.

Life brings you pain, suffering, guilt, illness, stress, anxiety, and loneness not to hurt you, but to guide you to look within. It is within that you will find all your answers. It is within that you will connect to your Soul. It is within that you will find your home. It is from within that you will reconnect to the Divine, to God and to Life Itself.

You were never meant to be separated from your creator, but you needed to be separate for a while, so you could learn who you are not, then understand more of who you are. This was the plan of your life all along. Your purpose is to have a physical experience in this world, so you can experience all that you are. When you discover all that you are, you can fully be and live a whole expression of yourself. You needed to live separated from your Creator, so you can fully understand how to live connected with your Creator.

When you live as one with your Creator, you have the power of creation itself; you co-create life with your Creator and the Universe has your back. You can then begin to live and create together and express life from a fuller expression and broader comprehension of who you are and what you can become and create. You become a master of your life rather than a helpless victim. You begin to create heaven on earth and experience life in the Garden of Eden because you create with God in perfect expression rather than the imperfect, disconnected, limited, human expression that exists when you are disconnected from God and yourself.

Now is the time to look at your own life. Is life trying to get your attention? Is life trying to serve you through pain and suffering? If so, is it time for you to reconsider your life and ask, "What is my life trying to tell me? How are the events in my life trying to serve me?" Are you ready to begin you own journey within and transform your pain into powerful purpose, your suffering into serving, and your survival patterns into thriving patterns. Now is your time. Are you ready to fully heal your body and restore your life? Is life is calling you? If so, answer the call. I promise you will be glad you did.

Your Next Steps: A Call for Inspired Action

I hope the truths and concepts in this book have opened your mind to new and broader understanding of healing. There is more to healing than meets the eye and mind of the beholder. It is only when you open your heart and mind to new concepts that you can heal from a higher capacity than what our current system and physical world can offer you.

I have spent years researching how to heal and restore your life from this higher level of healing. While it is possible to connect to your inner healing capacities and begin your own healing journey by unraveling the Veil of Illusion in your human mind, it is not easy to do it on your own or follow through with the process. I know. It took me years of exploration, questioning, and understanding before I finally got it. Don't try to do this process alone. Work with me.

Allow me to be your guide and partner, your Soul Sister through your own healing journey and process. I know the way because I have found the way and already created a path for you to follow. I love you and there is nothing more that I want than for you to heal and restore your own life. There is another way to heal your body and restore your life … let me show you the way. We will walk your journey together, hand-in-hand, heart-to-heart, Soul-to-Soul.

If this book has touched you, and your heart is calling you to take the next step, reach out to me on my website at <u>www.MaryRust.com</u> and participate in my online programs and workshops. Share your personal pain, suffering, and struggle with me so we can work together and discover your next best step in your healing journey. I promise I will meet you where you are and gently lead you where you are called to go. I know how to find the answers within you that will lead you on your perfect path to health, life, and eternal happiness. There is another way to heal your body and restore your life. Let's find your way together.

EFT EXERCISE: USING EFT FOR YOUR OWN PERSONAL PRACTICE

Before you begin the EFT exercise, rate the intensity of your emotion, fear, or life circumstance from 1-10, 1 being a low charge and 10 being an extreme charge.

Use the tips of your fingers and tap on each point of the body (1-9) as you say your affirmation, "Even though I have/feel _____, I totally and completely love and accept myself." Continue to tap on the next body point and repeat your affirmation. Go through all the points of the body repeating your affirmation at each point. When you have tapped on all points on the body, repeat the entire cycle again, starting at the point on the top of your head. Repeat the full tapping cycle a minimum of three times or until you notice the charge in your body decreasing. Check into yourself and see how the emotional charge is shifting and changing. You will notice a decrease in the emotional charge the more you tap and repeat your affirmation.

You can do several different affirmations during your EFT session but do not move on to a different affirmation until the charge for the first affirmation has subsided. Allow your heart and mind to create new affirmations during the process. Your heart and mind already know what needs to be surfaced, acknowledged, loved, and accepted. This is part of your healing journey.

Open and allow this exercise to assist you in moving through your mind's fears, blocks, and emotional programming so that you can begin to integrate your human mind with your Divine Mind. If you are not able to acknowledge, accept, love, and move through your fears, they will hold you back from healing and living the life you desire and deserve.

Your mind is a powerful tool that will either assist you or resist you. You have the power within you to observe your mind and recognize when it is out of alignment with your inspired healing intention. You have the power to integrate your mind with your Divine Mind through acceptance and love. This is how you help yourself help your mind. EFT is a powerful tool to assist you.

EFT Tapping Points

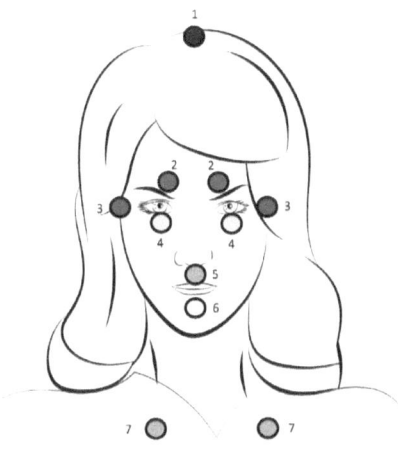

1. Top of Head
2. Top of Brow
3. Temples
4. Under Eyes
5. Under Nose
6. Under Mouth

7. Collar Bone

8. Side of Ribs (Bra Strap)

9. Both Wrists

DEFINITIONS

Source Energy (God): Energetic source of all there is, seen and unseen, physical and non-physical. Energetic source of all creation.

Spirit: Expression of Source Energy

Soul: Your individual expression of Source Energy

Mind: Awareness; consciousness.

Body: Physical energetic expression of conscious and unconscious thoughts and feelings. Your body is an energetic messenger and receiver of your inner and outer experience.

Thought: Idea, concept or mental image of life experience or creation.

Feeling: Energetic vibration of thought, experience or creation. Essential energy that gives power to thought and/or responds to thought.

Action: How you participate and move in life

Inspired Action: Participating and moving in life aligned with Source, Spirit and Soul.

Human mind: Awareness and consciousness that has been formed and accumulated through your human experience. Often based in survival and instinct.

Divine Mind: Awareness and consciousness that exist through Source, Spirit and Soul.

Divine Thoughts: Ideas aligned with your Soul.

Divine Feelings: Energetic vibrations aligned with your Soul.

Human Thoughts: Ideas not in alignment with your Soul.

Human Feelings: Energetic vibrations not in alignment with your Soul.

Thinking-Feeling Circuit: A vibrational energetic frequency created through thoughts and feelings.

Energetic Expression: The energetic signal or message you send out to the Universe. It is an energetic combination of your thoughts and feelings.

State of Being: The state of energetic expression you are sending or receiving at any given moment. It is a combination of your thoughts, feelings and actions.

Veil of Illusion: The Veil of Illusion is programmed information. It is mostly created by the human mind's thoughts, perceptions, beliefs, personalities, and truths. All information you send to your outer world and any information you receive from your outer world must pass through your Veil of Illusion. The Veil of Illusion acts as a filter and dictates how you create, perceive and experience your life.

Life: A unique opportunity to experience and experiment with all energies of duality to learn, grow, and evolve as a Soul. Life is a playground for your Soul.

AFTERWORD ... SO WHAT HAPPENED TO MY RELATIONSHIP WITH ED?

As I finished the first draft of *Living Proof*, I took a deep breath and felt a wave of completion rush over me. I wanted to complete this book for many years and now *Living Proof* was a living reality. I sat in humble gratitude.

Suddenly, a clash of thunder filled the air and broke my humbled silence. I glanced out the window and noticed a wall of dark thunderous clouds rolling toward me. "That's odd," I thought, "Storms normally don't roll in this time of day, especially ones like that. What's going on?" I knew in my heart there was massive change coming my way.

I knew Life was calling me, but I didn't know why or what was about to happen. All I knew was the storm was approaching and I was directly in its path. As with all personal transformation, when you change your inner world, your outer world must follow. This is a natural Law of the Universe.

My inner transformation had shifted so much that my outer world and relationship with Ed had to transform. Our relationship had to change because it no longer resonated with the interior vibration I had evolved into. I loved and honored myself enough that my life and outer world could no longer support a dysfunctional marriage. A transformational storm was coming to dismantle and transmute my love life. It was now Ed's turn to answer the call. Would he answer the call? Would he choose Love? Or would he reject Love and move out of my life?

The next six months were a living hell. This storm ripped and raged through my entire family. I was completely unprepared for what happened. Every member of my family was being called to go through our own version of the "Dark Night of the Soul." Pandora's Box had been opened and all hell broke loose. (Due to the sensitive and raw nature of the events that transpired, I will not go into details here and now. Simply know that it affected each member of my family on a deep mental and emotional level. One day I will write a book about alcoholism/co-dependency and its effects on the entire family as a way to shine healing light on this sensitive subject.) Now back to the storm…

The storm continued to tear my family apart. I was being called to let them go and allow them to move into and through their greatest pain, anxiety, fear and addiction so they could find their own way out. In the past, I tried to save them from their pain and rescue them, but this time Divine said, "No, Mary. This is not your fight. They must learn to connect to Me and themselves if they are ever going to be free. Let them go and trust Me. Hold them in a space of unconditional love and compassion as they move through their pain and process. They can heal just as you have done, but it is up to them, not you. Love them, but let them go."

Tears rolled down my face. How can I let the people I love the most go when I know they are going to be facing the greatest pain that they have ever gone through? I loved my family very much and I had always fought to keep us together. Now I was being asked to let go and allow my family to break apart. It didn't make sense from my human mind but in my heart I knew what I had to do. I had to let go of Ed by asking him to leave. I was being asked to send him into a pit of despair so he could reach his own breaking point and find his way out.

I screamed in anguish, "Why!!!? Why does it have to be this way? Why are you asking me to go through this? Please don't ask me to do this. Have I not been through enough? Why!!!?"

The only answer I received was, "It has to be this way, Mary. It's the only way. Trust Me. Trust Him. Trust Love."

The following day I asked Ed to leave. I felt like an empty corpse drained of all emotion. Numbing myself to all emotion was the only way I could ask him to leave. I still loved him but due to the events that transpired, he could no longer be in my life or in our family until he healed. When I asked Ed to leave, he was stunned. An icy glaze of bewilderment covered his eyes. I blindsided him. He never saw this coming. He complied, but deep down I could feel his buried anger, rage and resentment boil inside. I had just unleashed his beast.

By asking Ed to leave, I was forcing him to face his worst nightmare, deep seated fears of loneliness and abandonment. He was on his own. I could no longer help or support him. He had to face his own demons and addictions all by himself. He was either going to sink or swim. I thought I was saying goodbye to my life partner forever and it tore me apart. I never wanted to hurt him, yet I just stabbed him in the back.

"Ugh!" I belted, "What am I doing!? Did I just make the biggest mistake of my life!?" Only time would tell.

The first months of Ed's departure were brutal. He argued and fought with himself and with me. He suffered mentally and emotionally. He was plagued with daily panic attacks. He was angry, sad, resentful, confused, furious, bitter and … drunk.

Watching Ed suffer was torture. One part of me wanted to rush in and save him, the other part knew I had to let go. I had to stay strong in my commitment to let go and love him from a distance. This was his battle, not mine. I can no longer rescue him. He had to find a way to rescue himself.

Ed's fight continued to escalate with resentment and rage. I thought our relationship was over, past the point of return. Then, without warning or notice, Ed hit rock bottom and broke … and healing love seeped in.

Ed's Soul broke him to save him. His Soul finally brought him to his knees and Ed chose to reconnect and change. He opened the door to Love and Love opened up to him. Ed began the inner process of healing for himself. He let go of control, rage, resentment, alcohol and abandonment and he let Divine Love in.

By Ed opening up to Love, he began to restore the love and connection within himself and then restore the love and connection with me. After several months of inner work, Ed and I were able to start fresh again and rebuild our relationship and marriage on a new foundation of mutual partnership, love, compassion, respect and understanding. We were able to fall back in love again. Through this process, we were able to reconnect as best friends, lovers, and partners in life. We reconnected to Love and Love reconnected us, individually and together.

It's been over a year since Ed dropped the bottle and picked up Love. I was able to finish the final drafts of *Living Proof* with an expanded awareness of the healing potential within us all. Ed and I are living examples of the healing power of Love. We are "Living Proof" that Love has the power to heal your body and restore your entire life.

As each one of us makes the commitment to reconnect to ourselves and Divine Love within, healing simply happens. Love simply happens. Life simply happens and unfolds in mysterious and miraculous ways that we never expect.

Your inner world is the key to heal your body and restore your life. May you find your perfect reality in your inner world so that you can experience your perfect reality in your outer world. Accept this Truth as your reality and your reality will reflect the Truth.

ABOUT THE AUTHOR

Mary Rust is an inspired speaker and full-time health, healing and life transformation specialist. She is the owner of Mary Rust, Inc. and founder of the Live.Love.Thrive. Movement™. Mary's own healing journey began when she was diagnosed with breast cancer in 2008. Mary choose to treat her cancer through holistic methods which lead her on a journey to uncover the hidden healing potential that lies within us all. Mary not only restored her physical health, but more importantly, she reconnected and restored her Life through the process. Mary's passion is to share and mentor others to rediscover, illuminate and ignite the powerful potential and healing presence within. Mary (Yockey) Rust was declared the "Fittest Woman in the World" when she won the 1999 Fitness Olympia Championship. She has been featured in *Muscle & Fitness, Muscle & Fitness Hers, FLEX, Oxygen* and *Energy* magazines as a leading health and fitness expert.

www.ingramcontent.com/pod-product-compliance
Lightning Source LLC
Chambersburg PA
CBHW031101080526
44587CB00011B/779